Acclaim for

A HANDBOOK FOR
NEW STOICS

"In 52 pithy and practicable lessons, Pigliucci and Lopez explain how lessons plucked from an ancient Greco-Roman philosophy can reshape one's sense of self. . . . This successful blend of knowledge and action items will entice readers looking for thoughtful prompts for self-reflection."
—Publishers Weekly

"In an age that equates virtue with frenzies of outrage and denunciations of others' failings, *A Handbook for New Stoics* serves as an inspired self-help cure that, with insight and sympathy, will nudge you in the direction of the happiness and equanimity born of strength of character and wisdom."
—Rebecca Newberger Goldstein, author of *Plato at the Googleplex* and National Humanities Medal recipient

"A wonderfully simple approach to the core concepts and techniques of Stoicism, *A Handbook for New Stoics* gives readers an easy way to train themselves in Stoic practices, broken down into weekly exercises spanning a whole year. Through this book, Pigliucci and Lopez have managed to make Stoicism accessible to anyone."
—Donald Robertson, cognitive behavioral psychotherapist and author of *How to Think Like a Roman Emperor*

"A wonderful and potentially life-altering way to encounter the wisdom of the Stoics, *A Handbook for New Stoics* provides readers with structured lessons and exercises to explore Stoic philosophy alongside the lives they, themselves, are living."
—Professor William B. Irvine, author of *A Guide to the Good Life*

"In this book, Pigliucci and Lopez offer a great hands-on introduction to Stoic philosophy and practice while also providing valuable ideas for long-time students of Stoicism. Well-researched and carefully structured, with practical exercises that complement ancient texts, *A Handbook for New Stoics* will guide you through Stoic practice step-by-step throughout the year."
—Gregory Sadler, editor of *Stoicism Today*

A HANDBOOK FOR NEW STOICS

How to Thrive in a World Out of Your Control

52 WEEK-BY-WEEK LESSONS

MASSIMO PIGLIUCCI
and **GREGORY LOPEZ**

THE EXPERIMENT

NEW YORK

The Experiment, LLC
220 East 23rd Street, Suite 600, New York, NY 10010-4658
theexperimentpublishing.com

THE EXPERIMENT and its colophon are registered trademarks of The Experiment, LLC. Many of the designations used by manufacturers and sellers to distinguish their products are claimed as trademarks. Where those designations appear in this book and The Experiment was aware of a trademark claim, the designations have been capitalized.

The Experiment's books are available at special discounts when purchased in bulk for premiums and sales promotions as well as for fund-raising or educational use. For details, contact us at info@theexperimentpublishing.com.

Library of Congress Cataloging-in-Publication Data

Names: Pigliucci, Massimo, 1964- author. | Lopez, Gregory, author.
Title: A handbook for new Stoics : how to thrive in a world out of your
    control : 52 week-by-week lessons / Massimo Pigliucci, Gregory Lopez.
Description: New York : Experiment, 2019. | Includes bibliographical
    references.
Identifiers: LCCN 2018053814 (print) | LCCN 2019001296 (ebook) | ISBN
    9781615195343 (ebook) | ISBN 9781615195336 (flexibind)
Subjects: LCSH: Stoics.
Classification: LCC B528 (ebook) | LCC B528 .P529 2019 (print) | DDC 188--dc23 LC
record available at https://lccn.loc.gov/2018053814

ISBN 978-1-61519-533-6
Ebook ISBN 978-1-61519-534-3

Cover and text design by Beth Bugler
Author photographs by Simon Wardenier (Massimo Pigliucci) and T. Kogan (Gregory Lopez)

Manufactured in China

First printing May 2019
10 9 8 7 6 5

CONTENTS

INTRODUCTION

GETTING STARTED

Mike's twenty-five-year college reunion was supposed to be fun. Instead, it has turned into an exercise in inadequacy. His classmates Aziz and Saliah are still together, ever since their first date during sophomore year; Mike's marriage lasted less than five years, leading to financial trouble and an insecurity about romantic relationships that persists to this day. Steve, Mike's former roommate, has maintained his athletic physique while Mike's potbelly has only grown, a charming accompaniment to his thinning hair. And his roommate's business major propelled him to the C-suite, while Mike has stagnated in middle management of a company whose products he doesn't even believe in. Everywhere he looks, Mike sees success, but when he faces himself in the bathroom mirror after the cocktail hour, he can't help but feel like a failure. *No wonder I'm unhappy,* he thinks. *It's because my life is bad. Everything is awful.*

The Best Bet for Happiness

There are many things that we want and events we want to happen. We want to lose weight, get a raise, be liked by the people around us. Yet for many of us, including Mike, these desires never materialize, and we're left feeling inadequate, frustrated, and stuck. And it can get worse—for all of us. Things we specifically *don't* want actually *do* happen, ranging from trivialities (getting stuck in traffic) to more serious events (illness and aging). Getting what we don't want can be just as painful as not getting what we do want, and often more so. However painful this is, we keep on placing the same bad bets, staking our happiness and well-being on things outside our control through a cosmic roll of the dice.

What if we were able to train ourselves to desire only things that are firmly within our control? Then, in a very real sense, we'd always get what we want, and never get what we don't want. Our happiness would never spill, since the cup of our desires is reliable and holds firm.

The fundamental question, then, is: What is in our complete control? What's the sure bet?

Betting on Character: Why Stoicism?

The unreliability of obtaining certain goals—such as wealth, health, and other people's praise—is one of many common problems. Often, even when we're lucky and achieve these ends, we're still left wanting. Had Mike gone to his reunion a successful executive with a family and a still-boyish figure, he would likely still have found room for complaint.

Many of us can see this in our own life. We eat great food without even noticing the taste. When we do savor it, the pleasure quickly fades and is forgotten. We have to shift positions to remain comfortable on a nice, new sofa, which will become stained and worn with time. Status is nice when we get it, but we're often left wanting more. We get a new car that we love at first, but soon take for granted. We may succeed in starting a business, but protecting our assets and growing the company cause us to lose sleep. We can be head over heels for our romantic partner today, but may grow irritated by their habits with time. Many of the things we pursue don't satisfy—and can't provide lasting happiness.

Even if we achieve the objects of our transient desires, it doesn't guarantee we will use them well. What determines their good use is the character of who's using them. People with poor character put external advantages—money, fame, the U.S. presidency—to bad use. Those with good character will use what they have, no matter how limited, for the benefit of themselves and others. If they endure hardship, or if the cosmic dice roll snake eyes for them, a good character will help them persevere.

Here is the great insight of the ancient philosophy of Stoicism: Shaping your character is ultimately the only thing under your control. So in order to exploit your good luck and cope with the bad luck, it is necessary to be a good person. Through a combination of rational introspection and repeated practice, you can mold your character over the long term.

Betting on your own improvement is a guaranteed win with the biggest payoff. The goal of this book is to help you collect.

Meet the Stoics

Stoicism is a Greco-Roman philosophy that began around 300 BCE with Zeno of Citium (modern-day Cyprus). Zeno was a merchant who lost all of his goods in a shipwreck and arrived in Athens with a few drachmas in his pockets. He heard the keeper of a bookshop reading some philosophy and became intrigued by the subject, so he asked the shopkeeper where he could find a philosopher. He was told to follow a man who just happened to pass by, Crates of Thebes. Zeno listened and became Crates's student. Eventually, Zeno founded his own school, which came to be known as the *Stoa*, because its members discussed philosophy under a public colonnade called the *Stoa Poikile*, or painted porch.

During the last century BCE, Athens declined as a political power and cultural capital of the ancient world, and Rome took up both mantles. Shortly after, many of the prominent Stoic philosophers became active in the capital of the Roman Empire. The four major ones, whose writings survived to this day, are Seneca, a Roman senator and advisor to the emperor Nero; Musonius Rufus, a renowned teacher; Epictetus, a slave-turned-teacher who was Musonius's student; and Marcus Aurelius, one of the few philosopher-kings in history. It is from their writings that we will draw inspiration throughout this book.

Stoicism dwindled as a formal school of philosophy by the third century CE, but Stoic ideas continued to influence a number of important thinkers throughout the history of the Western world, from Paul of Tarsus to Augustine of Hippo, from Thomas Aquinas to Descartes, from Montaigne to Spinoza. In the twentieth century, Stoicism inspired a family of schools of effective psychotherapy called cognitive behavioral therapy (CBT), starting with Albert Ellis's rational emotive behavior therapy in the 1950s. The ideas of Zeno, Seneca, Epictetus, and others have also inspired a vibrant movement of new Stoicism in the modern day, attracting people from all over the world, such as the readers of this book, who want to find a better way to live their lives, and to become full members of the human community.

The Very Basics

While we will explore the philosophy of Stoicism through the fifty-two weekly exercises in this book, we present here a brief overview to get oriented. Stoicism's basic tenets can be distilled into three major topics: live according to nature, three-disciplined practice, and the dichotomy of control.

Live according to nature

> "What should we do then? Make the best use of what is in our power, and treat the rest in accordance with its nature."
>
> *Epictetus*, Discourses I, *1.17*

The Stoics thought that the best way to live our life, to make it count and derive meaning from it, is to live according to nature, particularly human nature. How do we determine what this means, in practice? By studying three interrelated topics: "physics," "logic," and "ethics." Each of these three terms had a much broader meaning in ancient times than it does today (hence the scare quotes).

By *physics*, the Stoics were referring to the study of all the natural sciences, as well as metaphysics—the understanding of how the world hangs together. *Logic* included what it does today, that is, the formal study of reasoning, as well as psychology and even rhetoric more broadly—everything you need to think and communicate well. *Ethics* was not limited to understanding right and wrong, as it largely is today, but was more broadly construed as the study of how to live with meaning.

To decide how best to live (ethics), one has to understand how the world works (physics) and reason appropriately about it (logic). Which brings us to the idea of living according to nature. The most important aspects of human nature, the Stoics thought, are twofold: that we are social animals (and are then deeply interdependent with other people) and that we are capable of reasoning-based problem solving. So to live according to nature means using reason to improve social living. Or as Seneca put it, "Bring the mind to bear upon your problems."[1] This aspect of Stoicism sets it somewhat apart from other forms of self-help, which focus more on making you *feel* better. Stoicism tackles this and goes beyond it by helping the practitioner, and the world around them, *be* better.

The three disciplines

How, then, do we live according to nature? The Stoics, and Epictetus in particular, translate this into living by practicing three disciplines: desire, action, and assent. This book is organized around these three disciplines, with weekly exercises that will help you master each.

The Discipline of Desire teaches us what is best to want (or to avoid): What should our goals be? Where do we channel our energy, time, and resources? The Discipline of Action shows us how to act in the social sphere: How should we behave toward others? And the Discipline of Assent helps us arrive at correct judgments about obstacles that life throws at us: Should we be angry at this person? Should we indulge in that pleasure?

Stoicism is roughly one part theory and nine parts practice. The Stoics were very clear that understanding the philosophy (not that difficult) without putting it to use is a waste of time and energy. Epictetus said, "If you didn't learn these things in order to demonstrate them in practice, what did you learn them for?"[2]

The dichotomy of control

The dichotomy of control is *the* central concept in Stoicism. Because of its importance, it's the very first exercise in this book. What is it? Put simply, it's the idea that certain things are under your control, while others are not. This may seem obvious—and it is—but from this observation stems the foundation of our practice: that we should focus our energy and resources on affecting what we *can* control, and turn away as much as possible from what we *can't*. This, as you may suspect, is much more easily said than done. There's a crucial difference between understanding something, which we can do by reading and reflecting on it, and internalizing that same thing, which can only be done with repeated practice. And that is precisely what this book is for.

How to Use This Book

The book you're holding is designed so that you can practice a modern Stoic exercise, pulled from an ancient source, every week for an entire year. We've divided it into fifty-two chapters, grouped into three parts. To help you track your progress, each part includes a questionnaire that you can fill out both before and after you finish the section, to keep track of the progress you've made in the three disciplines of Stoic training.

Each week starts with a lesson and continues with a practical exercise related to the lesson. At the beginning of each lesson you'll find a real-world scenario, followed by an ancient text relevant to the scenario, and an explanation. The exercise for each week is based on the lesson and is meant to be practiced throughout the week. We've also provided a reason for doing the exercise, and finally a space to reflect on your experience each week. At the beginning of each week, first read through the entire chapter to learn about the exercise; then start practicing the next day. At the beginning of the following week, take some time to reflect on your practice during the week before, completing a weekly review before moving on to the next chapter to prepare for the week ahead. We chose to start on Sunday, but you can choose any day that works for you. At the end of the year, you can proceed to the final section of the book, where you will put together your own set of Stoic exercises to continue using for as long as you'd like. This will provide you with a unique, personalized Stoic curriculum for a lifetime of practice.

The following is a diagram summarizing how to work through the book over the course of a year. For this example, we chose to start each chapter on a Sunday.

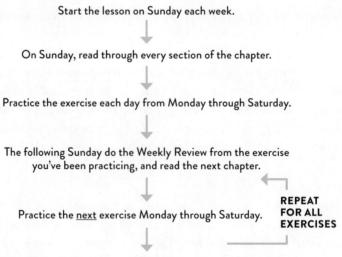

Start the lesson on Sunday each week.

On Sunday, read through every section of the chapter.

Practice the exercise each day from Monday through Saturday.

The following Sunday do the Weekly Review from the exercise you've been practicing, and read the next chapter.

Practice the next exercise Monday through Saturday.

REPEAT FOR ALL EXERCISES

When the final exercise is complete, move on to the last section to create a personalized Stoic practice curriculum for yourself.

We realize that not everyone is ready to commit to a year-long effort right away. If that's the case for you, we suggest you sample a few of the chapters and exercises from each of the three parts and see how it feels. If a deeper commitment to Stoicism intrigues you, go back to the beginning and follow the full series in the order presented. Here are some exercises you can try from each section if you are not quite ready to commit to a full year yet.

The Discipline of Desire

WEEK 1: Discover what's really in your control, and what's not (page 11)
WEEK 2: Focus on what's in your control (page 20)
WEEK 15: Remind yourself of impermanence (page 98)

The Discipline of Action

WEEK 18: Keep your peace of mind in mind (page 119)
WEEK 24: Premeditate on encountering difficult people (page 146)
WEEK 29: Review your actions nightly (page 172)

The Discipline of Assent

WEEK 36: Catch and apply the dichotomy of control to initial impressions (page 213)
WEEK 37: Catch and examine the judgements underlying your impressions and impulses (page 218)
WEEK 39: Keep basic Stoic concepts always at hand (page 230)

Hopefully this gives you a good idea of how to put this book to use. The next step is to jump right in! Choose a day when you'd like to start your year of Stoic practice (it can be today!), and write it down in the space below.

You may also want to set a reminder or put the date you chose on your calendar at this time. When the day arrives, proceed to the next chapter and get started.

Happy practicing! We hope this book guides you toward a more satisfying life for you and all those whose lives you touch.

PART I

THE
DISCIPLINE
OF DESIRE

THE GOAL

"There are three things in which a man ought to exercise himself who would be wise and good. The first concerns the desires and the aversions, that a man may not fail to get what he desires, and that he may not fall into that which he does not desire. The second concerns the movements (toward an object) and the movements from an object, and generally in doing what a man ought to do, that he may act according to order, to reason, and not carelessly. The third thing concerns freedom from deception and rashness in judgment, and generally it concerns the assents.

Of these topics the chief and the most urgent is that which relates to the affects [i.e., the Discipline of Desire]; for an affect is produced in no other way than by a failing to obtain that which a man desires or falling into that which a man would wish to avoid. This is that which brings in perturbations, disorders, bad fortune, misfortunes, sorrows, lamentations, and envy; that which makes men envious and jealous; and by these causes we are unable even to listen to the precepts of reason."

Epictetus, Discourses III, *2.1–3*

Quiz

Before you begin, take a moment to briefly rate yourself on the following items, which evaluate the main goals of the Discipline of Desire. After you complete Part I, you can answer these questions again to see if you've made progress.

Rate how much the following statements describe you as you currently are on a scale of 1 to 10, with 1 meaning it doesn't describe you at all and 10 meaning it describes you perfectly.

I get really upset when I don't get what I want or things don't go my way.

DOESN'T
DESCRIBE
ME AT ALL

DESCRIBES ME
PERFECTLY

I put a lot of effort into avoiding things I don't like or that I'm afraid of.

DOESN'T
DESCRIBE
ME AT ALL

DESCRIBES ME
PERFECTLY

I spend a lot of time pursuing comfort and pleasure.

DOESN'T
DESCRIBE
ME AT ALL

DESCRIBES ME
PERFECTLY

Discover what's really in your control, and what's not

It's easy to think that we have control over our lives when things are going the way we want. But what happens when we experience uncertainty? Consider our friend Alice who faces this question at her job. Her quarterly performance review is coming up, and though she's been doing well, a familiar anxiety floods her body as negative what-if scenarios cross her mind. Could learning more about what's really in her control help Alice? What effect would that have on her psyche?

> " Of all existing things some are in our power, and others are not in our power. In our power are thought, impulse, will to get and will to avoid, and, in a word, everything which is our own doing. Things not in our power include the body, property, reputation, office, and, in a word, everything which is not our own doing."
>
> *Epictetus*, Enchiridion, *1*

E pictetus's words may be more familiar to you in the form of the famous Serenity Prayer adopted by a number of twelve-step programs:

God, grant me the serenity to accept the things I cannot change,
Courage to change the things I can,
And wisdom to know the difference.

The prayer was written by theologian Reinhold Niebuhr in 1934, but it reflects wisdom that is common to Jewish, Christian, and Buddhist traditions, and of course to Stoicism. Indeed, the underlying concept is central to Stoic practice and is often referred to as the "dichotomy of control." Epictetus begins the *Enchiridion*—his manual on Stoicism—with it, and it is one of the most cited Stoic sayings, having countless applications in daily life. So, too, we begin our practice, and our study of the Discipline of Desire, with a study of control.

Let us first understand exactly what Epictetus means by his words. He is dividing the world into two big chunks: the set of things under our (complete) control and the set of things not (completely) under our control. If it occurred to you that there has to be a third set, that of things over which we have *partial* control, don't worry—we'll get to that concept next week.

The basic idea is that it is imperative to use our mental energy to focus on what is under our *complete* control, while regarding everything else as indifferent. For those things that are *not* under our complete control, it isn't that we stop caring about them, but rather that we come to a deep understanding that we cannot guarantee that these indifferent things will turn out the way we wish them to. The way we come to this understanding is through constant practice. This practice is the path toward *ataraxia*, the Greek word meaning serenity. We become serene by training ourselves to only want what is completely in our control—so in a very real sense, we'll be serene because we always get what we want! This is the promise of the Discipline of Desire.

Taking a closer look at Epictetus's categories, what does he say is in our control, and what is not? Under our control, according to him, are "thought, impulse, will to get and will to avoid, and, in a word, everything which is our own doing." We need to be careful here, because these

English words don't necessarily carry the same connotations as their original Greek counterparts. Moreover, modern Stoics (such as ourselves!) may want to take into account advances in the cognitive sciences that were not available to Epictetus, and so we may arrive at a somewhat modified list of what truly is under our control. To understand what Epictetus is getting at, let's break down the process further, starting with "thoughts" since it is listed first (for good reason, as we'll soon see).

"Thought" here is the English translation of *hypolepsis*, literally "grasping under" or "taking up." More figuratively, this means "judgment" or "opinion" (similar to scooping up an idea or viewpoint—you're grabbing under it to grasp or cradle it). These can be types of thoughts, and are not necessarily fully conscious ones. Epictetus may have listed "thought" first as it's the first step in how we upset ourselves: We judge things to be inherently good or bad. Sometimes these judgments are explicit (e.g., thinking to yourself *That guy's a moron!*). But they don't have to be. For example, if you get angry at a person, you are implicitly judging the person's actions as bad, even if the words "that person is doing a bad thing" never cross your mind.

Next comes "impulse" (*horme* in Greek). This is an impulse to act, but not necessarily in a base or automatic way (what we may think of as impulsive). Pulling your hand away from a hot stove and screaming is not an impulse in the way Epictetus uses the term. Instead, impulses come about from the first step of "thought" or "judgment." If you judge something to be good, you'll want it. If you judge it to be bad, you'll want to avoid it. Impulses are then urges to act based on value judgments.

From thought (the judgment) and impulse (the desire to act) comes the "will to get and to avoid." We decide if it is worth spending the energy, time, and money. For example, we consider these expenses when buying a brand-new car, reflecting the value judgment that possessing it is a good thing. Then we go about and make complex plans to acquire the new car. So our complex, conscious actions come about from value judgments and impulses to act.

Epictetus claims that all three of these things (thoughts, impulses, and the will to avoid and to get) are ultimately under our control. It is no accident that these three areas of complete control correspond to Epictetus's three disciplines: You work with thoughts in the Discipline of Assent, impulses in the Discipline of Action, and the will to avoid and to get in the Discipline of Desire. In this way, Stoic practice trains you to master all areas of what in theory you can control. That's Stoic training in a nutshell.

Just because these things are in your control doesn't mean that they aren't sometimes influenced by external factors (such as other people's opinions) or by internal ones (such as your physical sensations or more automatic urges, like a craving for a snack). But, ultimately, they are under your control because you can make a conscious decision to ignore your cravings or to override the opinions of others when it comes to your own choices.

What about the sort of things that Epictetus says are *not* under our control? They include "the body, property, reputation, office, and, in a word, everything which is not our own doing." This is a very large set that essentially comprises all things external to our conscious mind. Our body can get sick despite our best efforts at taking care of it; we may lose our property because of accident or theft; our reputation may be ruined due to circumstances we cannot influence; and we may lose our job through no fault of our own.

You may object that the sort of things we just mentioned are, however, under our partial control. They are not similar to, say, the weather, about which we can truly do nothing at all. Of course, Epictetus knew this! What he is saying here is akin to the "best bet argument" (see pages 1–2): If you bet your peace of mind on things not completely in your control, you're willingly forfeiting part of your happiness to random chance.

We'll explore this topic more next week. For now, let's move on to your first exercise.

What to Do

This week's exercise will help you explore the dichotomy of control. Take time now to choose when you'll do the exercise each day for the rest of the week. Try to place the exercise toward the end of the day. You can plan to do it at a specific time (e.g., at 9:00 PM) or after an activity you do every day (e.g., brushing your teeth at night). Write when you'll do this exercise below.

Sit down at this time Monday through Saturday of this week and choose something that happened that day to write about. It can be anything from seeing a friend for lunch to a meeting at work. We suggest that you choose an event that wasn't too emotionally upsetting, which could make the exercise more difficult, and you're just starting out! List what aspects of the event were *completely* in your control and which weren't. It may help to add some quick reasons *why* the thing was or wasn't in your complete control.

If you have trouble with the exercise, you can use Epictetus's suggestions of separating out value judgments, impulses, and what you wished to avoid or obtain, as things under your complete control. You can also try separating aspects of the event by "internal" factors (thoughts, desires, wishes) and "external" factors (results), since we can mostly control what goes on inside our heads, and much of what we can't control happens in the outside world. Don't feel shackled to these categories. Part of the goal of this exercise is to see whether Epictetus's suggestions hold true to your experience. Perhaps you'll find he was correct, and perhaps not.

Let's look at an example of how this would work. Suppose Alice chooses to do this exercise every day after her daily evening jog. After she runs, she sits down and chooses a meeting with her boss as the event she'll focus on. Here's what she writes.

Met with the boss at 2 PM to discuss latest sales numbers. I was a little nervous going in since I'm not quite at quota yet. We sat down and discussed what action steps I could take to reach quota by the end of the quarter. A lot of the suggestions were useful.

Notice that Alice chose an event that she was a little nervous about, but that wasn't extremely distressing for her. After Alice writes about the event, she rereads the narrative, looking for things that were completely within her control. She comes up with the following list.

COMPLETE CONTROL	INCOMPLETE CONTROL
The intent to show up on time to the meeting	Actually showing up on time (I could have been delayed by that business call that ran over before the meeting!)
Valuing my boss's opinion of me and my work	My boss's actual opinion of me and my work
The wish to meet my quota	Meeting my quota (I can't force people to buy from me)
The desire to get actionable tips from my boss (it'd help meet most of my goals above!)	Actually getting useful tips
Conscious nervous thoughts/what I tell myself	Automatic nervous thoughts and the physical feelings of nervousness

Alice repeats this exercise daily through Saturday after her run.

Notice that the left-hand column is mostly filled with internal things like wants, desires, wishes, and conscious intentional thoughts. The right-hand column is mostly filled with external results. The exception is the final row, which has automatic thoughts and physical sensations as not within complete control. This highlights the important point that not everything that goes on in our bodies and minds is willed. Alice didn't choose for her heart rate to rise, nor did she rationally decide to dwell on worst-case scenarios. However, once those have occurred, she can consciously choose what to tell herself and how to act in spite of those automatic responses.

Now it's your turn. Over the next week, use the following pages for this exercise.

COMPLETE CONTROL   *Monday*   INCOMPLETE CONTROL

Event:

Tuesday

Event:

Wednesday

Event:

COMPLETE CONTROL   Thursday   INCOMPLETE CONTROL

Event:

Friday

Event:

Saturday

Event:

Why Do It

By doing this exercise daily, looking at specific events in your life, you'll start to internalize what is really under your complete control and what isn't. As this principle sinks in, you will be equipped to practice the Discipline of Desire in future exercises. This exercise will also give you a clearer picture of what exactly you should focus your desires and aversions on to achieve peace of mind.

Weekly Review

On the seventh day of the week, after you've practiced exploring the dichotomy of control, set a timer for 5 to 10 minutes and write your impressions below. Was this week's exercise useful to you? How? Did you discover anything about yourself or your world? Did you find it useless? Is there any way you could tweak your approach to make it easier or more useful in the future? Write about your experiences here. If you need more space here or at any point in the book, you can use the notebook pages in the back.

_____

_____

_____

_____

_____

_____

Finally, if you think this exercise is useful, check this box: ☐

This will serve as a reminder at the end of the year that you found this exercise worth pursuing. You're now ready to read the next chapter and prepare for next week.

Focus on what is completely in your control

At some point in your life you've probably tried to prevent something from happening, but it happened anyway. Do you remember how upset you were by it? If you did everything within your power to prevent it, then *why* were you upset? This question haunted Suki after her annual physical. Although she's always been the paragon of health, her doctor has referred her to a cardiologist after a dizzy spell she experienced at the gym, and she's terrified. Let's explore why Suki is upset and, more importantly, what can be done about it.

> " Remember that following desire promises the attainment of that of which you are desirous; and aversion promises the avoiding that to which you are averse. However, he who fails to obtain the object of his desire is disappointed, and he who incurs the object of his aversion wretched. If, then, you confine your aversion to those objects only which are contrary to the natural use of your faculties, which you have in your own control, you will never incur anything to which you are averse. But if you are averse to sickness, or death, or poverty, you will be wretched. Remove aversion, then, from all things that are not in our control, and transfer it to things contrary to the nature of what is in our control."
>
> *Epictetus*, Enchiridion, 2.1–2

No matter how much we plan, worry, and attempt to prevent misfortunes from occurring, they sometimes do. People have very different reactions to similar misfortunes. Some shrug them off, some go numb, and some, like Suki, develop anxiety and fear. Why do we react in different ways? Epictetus suggests that those who fall into circumstances they wish to avoid are those who suffer misfortune, by which he means that much suffering comes from a disconnect between what you want to happen and what actually happens. Or, as the Stoics would say, what is in accordance to nature as opposed to contrary to nature.

Epictetus lists telling misfortunes: It is senseless to nurture aversion to poverty, illness, or death because these things are outside of our (complete) control. After all, illness and death are natural and unavoidable aspects of human existence, and while some people manage to avoid poverty, it, too, can strike at any moment independent of one's efforts to avoid it. Similarly with desires. If we desire great wealth, perfect health, or a lasting reputation, we are striving for things that we cannot control (though we may influence them), which will inevitably make us unhappy.

You may have noticed that we've been focusing on aversion in the Discipline of Desire. That's because aversion can be seen as a type of desire: the desire to avoid misfortune. We use the Discipline of Desire as shorthand for the Discipline of Desire and Aversion, the shortened name given to this discipline by French scholar Pierre Hadot.[1] The crucial idea here is to redirect our aversion away from things that we dislike but are not in our power, and to transfer it to things that we can completely control. You have a list of such things from last week (see pages 17–18). Similarly, we need to stop desiring things that we cannot control and instead develop a desire for what we can be guaranteed to achieve.

Let's look at an example: Suppose you are up for a possible promotion at your job. Your natural desire is to get the promotion, but this is not under your complete control. The promotion depends on possible competition from your colleagues, on the relationship you have developed with your boss, and even on random occurrences, such as your boss's mood or the weather. However, what *is* in your power, and what you then *should* desire, is putting forward the best possible case for a promotion, based on your best efforts in recent months to do your job well.

If you have a strong aversion to failure you might be unhappy if you don't get the promotion—as when trying to avoid poverty or sickness.

But if your desire is directed properly, toward doing the best job you are capable of doing, then you cannot possibly fail. In fact, if you do the best job you can at every moment, you've already succeeded! Moreover, since there is, presumably, a correlation between doing a good job and getting a promotion, you will increase the chance that you will, in fact, be promoted. When your desires and aversions are "aligned with nature" (i.e., with what is in your complete control), you are *guaranteed* to not be unhappy regardless of the outcome.

There are countless other examples of this principle. You should not desire to be loved by your partner, but only to be the most lovable person you can be. You should not indulge an aversion to losing a match when you play a game or sport, but instead focus on playing to the best of your ability. Once you internalize the distinction between proper and improper desires and aversions, the world will look very different to you. You will find serenity that springs from a magnanimous attitude toward whatever the universe happens to throw your way.

Finally, notice that this resolves a problem we encountered last week: the apparent neglect, by the Stoics, of the large category of things we can influence but not completely control. That third category, in Stoic philosophy, is itself split into two: the part you cannot control but can influence (e.g., your boss's decision, your partner's love, your chances of winning a match) and the part you can control (e.g., working hard and well, being lovable, playing your best game), which may influence the final outcome.

This week, we begin by building on last week's exercise. You'll do this in two broad steps.

1. Look for patterns from your lists from last week to see how aversions to things outside of your control may have been influenced by things within your complete control.

2. Explore how to transfer your aversions from those things that aren't under your complete control to those that are.

First, flip back to what you wrote for last week's exercise and write down things in your "Incomplete control" column that describe something you were averse to. In Suki's case, it's the results from the cardiologist's exam.

_____

_____

Next, look at your "Complete control" column for each of the items you listed above. What was in your complete control that preceded each aversion? Suki found that her thoughts about the test results bringing really bad news were in her complete control. Write your answers below.

_____

_____

Now set a timer for 3 minutes and brainstorm how the items that were under your control may have led to your aversion about those that weren't. Be sure to explicitly tell the story of how things in your control could have caused the aversion.

_____

_____

_____

_____

Finally, set another 3-minute timer and try to come up with ways you could transfer aversion from external things not in your control to things you can completely control. Suki found that the steps above helped her realize that her thoughts about the situation caused the aversion. So, she decided to explicitly remind herself that her thoughts were causing the upset, and to examine her thoughts more closely. What ways would work for you, in transferring aversion from things that you can't completely control to things that you can? Write them in the space below.

_____

_____

_____

By now, you should have a short list of things you can practice over the next week that are in your complete control. Each day, choose a specific time at which you'll set a 3-minute timer and review this list, and choose one to practice for that day. Write down when you'll do this exercise each day below.

The item you choose may vary day to day, as some techniques you came up with may be specific to certain days of the week. If Suki will be seeing her cardiologist on Tuesday, she may choose to visualize her visit Monday night to prepare, but she won't do that every day.

Why Do It

The Stoics have many exercises within the Discipline of Desire that can help work with transferring desire and aversion from external things to things within your control, which you'll learn throughout Part I. The purpose of this exercise is to generate some of your own that may work for you! By transferring your aversions from things that you can't completely control to things you can, you will ultimately "never incur anything to which you are adverse."

Weekly Review

On the Sunday after you've practiced transferring your aversions, set a timer for 5 to 10 minutes and write your impressions of this exercise below. Was it useful to you? How? Is there any way you could tweak this exercise to make it easier to do or more useful in the future? Write about your experiences with this exercise below.

Finally, if you think this exercise is useful, check this box: ☐

Take an outside view

You may excel at providing comfort to those in need, but are you equally good at comforting yourself? Robert just realized that he isn't. He has always been the person everyone turns to for comfort, and he rarely fails at helping others gain perspective on their situations. But as things have become stressful in his own life, it has been hard for him to gain a similar perspective. This Stoic exercise can help Robert—and the rest of us—gain equanimity through adopting a new perspective on our own troubles.

> " It is in our power to discover the will of nature from those matters on which we have no difference of opinion. For example, when another man's slave has broken the wine cup, we are very ready to say at once, 'Such things must happen.' Know then that when your own cup is broken, you ought to behave in the same way as when your neighbor's was broken. Apply the same principle to higher matters. Is another's child or wife dead? Not one of us but would say, 'Such is the lot of man'; but when one's own dies, straightaway one cries, 'Alas! miserable am I.' But we ought to remember what our feelings are when we hear it of another."
>
> *Epictetus*, Enchiridion, *26*

This is Epictetus at his most frank. It would appear that the Stoic philosopher is encouraging us to adopt a purposely callous attitude toward our own bad luck by viewing it as though it had happened to someone else. From a modern perspective, this isn't easy advice to swallow as we strive to cultivate empathy toward other people's situations. In fact, the Stoics, including Epictetus, aren't that callous—they were very clear that the goal of Stoic practice is not to turn us into lumbering robots incapable of emotional responses, because that would strip us of our humanity. As the Stoic philosopher Seneca writes to his friend Lucilius: "The first thing which philosophy undertakes to give is fellow-feeling with all men; in other words, sympathy and sociability."[1] If the Stoics promote this sense of shared feeling, what, then, is Epictetus trying to say?

To begin with, let's talk about the difference between sympathy and empathy. Both words entered our vocabulary much later than the times of Epictetus: in 1579 and 1850, respectively. Interestingly, they both carry the Greek root *pathos*, meaning "emotion," but they modify it in different directions. To have sympathy with another's distress, according to Merriam-Webster's Collegiate Dictionary, is to care for and feel sorry about another's grief or misfortune. To empathize, by contrast, means that—to the extent possible—you share another's experiences on an emotional level.

The Stoics suggest that we should cultivate sympathy more than empathy. Both modern psychology and philosophy provide some backing for this ancient insight. Yale University psychologist Paul Bloom[2] and City University of New York philosopher Jesse Prinz[3] have made compelling cases that empathy is ethically problematic because, as with all highly emotional responses, it is easy for others to manipulate. Empathy also tends to be disproportionate to the situation (we feel more empathy for people we know or see directly), and does not scale up (it is impossible to feel empathy for anonymous thousands or even millions of people, regardless of how deserving they are). By contrast, sympathy is informed by reason and is therefore more wide ranging. We can sympathize even with people we do not know, or whose specific situation we have never experienced, because we are able to recognize that similar situations would be distressing for us, and that it would be unjust both for us and for anyone else to have to suffer through them.

In a sense, then, what Epictetus is observing is that in the normal course of events we tend to self-empathize ("Alas! Miserable am I.") while we sympathize with others ("Such is the lot of man."). The difference stems from our capability for more balanced judgment when the event does not touch us directly. Attempting to rectify this imbalance does not make us callous; it simply makes us more reasonable.

Now let us turn this insight around to help ourselves and Robert, whom we met earlier. Once we recognize that helping our friends take a broader perspective on their troubles actually helps them cope with their situation, we can then accept and internalize the same insight and apply it to our own lives. Robert is able to aid his friends by helping them distance themselves from their natural and immediate emotional reactions. Reminding ourselves that difficult things happen—and not just to us—is comforting. We can start developing equanimity with respect to the things we don't fully control. Likewise, we can be grateful when things go our way but not become too attached to them, as they can just as easily be taken away. And when tough things happen, we are able to find the courage to face them in the best way possible, because such is the human condition.

What to Do

This week you have a short writing exercise in which you'll explore some struggles or worries, but with a twist. We suggest finding time to write at night, though feel free to choose a time that works best for you. In the space below, set a time each day when you'd like to perform the exercise.

_____

When you sit down each day this week, set a timer for 5 minutes and write about one of two topics: either a problem you encountered that day, or a worry you have about the next day. Choose whatever is most on your mind. If the day went well and you're not worried about tomorrow, choose a past issue to work with.

Each day, write in the space below and on the following pages about what you feel in response to the problem or worry and brainstorm possible ways to handle it, but from a different perspective. Instead of writing in the first person, use second-person pronouns or your name to give yourself advice. For example, instead of writing "I feel nervous about . . ." start by writing "You feel nervous about . . ." Write until the timer goes off.

When Robert did this exercise, he chose to do it each night at 9:00 PM, since he already sets aside alone time for himself every night. At that time, he sat down at his desk and thought about his day, which had been quite hectic. And the following day wasn't looking any better; dreadful, in fact. Robert caught that thought and decided to make it the focus of his writing exercise. Here's some of what he wrote.

I know you feel overwhelmed at work right now, Rob. You're juggling a lot of projects at once, and there are a bunch of things competing for your attention. It's no wonder you feel stressed. But it's not like this is anything new. You've felt this way in the past, and, yeah, it's unpleasant. But you're still at your job, and things are going well overall. This week will be unpleasant, but you get through it every time, and do your job well—or at least well enough! So, get some sleep now. It'll do you good!

Robert found that giving himself advice and words of comfort by using the second-person perspective worked well for him. See how well it works for you by writing about a problem or worry and then offering yourself some advice from the outside perspective each night this week.

Monday _____

_____

_____

_____

_____

Tuesday

Wednesday

Thursday

Friday

Saturday

Why Do It

By stepping back a little, you can take the emotional sting out of hurtful situations and will be able to see them more clearly. You are a better guide to yourself by offering self-sympathy than by magnifying internal turmoil through self-empathy. This type of exercise has modern scientific evidence behind it, too, but the Stoics were 2,000 years ahead of their time.[4] If you browse Marcus Aurelius's personal journal *Meditations*, you will notice that he almost always writes to himself in the second person.

Weekly Review

On the Sunday after you've practiced taking the outside view, set a timer for 5 to 10 minutes and write your impressions of this exercise below. Was it useful to you? Did writing in the second person help you gain perspective? Did the writing prompts spontaneously carry over to your thinking throughout the day?

Finally, if you think this exercise is useful, check this box: ☐

Take another's perspective

It's easy for us to justify our own feelings, yet not understand those of others. Take Felix, who has been waiting in line at the bank for what seems like forever. When he finally reaches the bank teller, the teller curtly informs him that the computer system is down and there's not much he can do about it. *Why the hell did he talk to me like that?! What nerve!* Felix thinks, feeling his anger rising. What Felix doesn't consider is that the teller has been dealing with frustrations of his own the entire morning and has reached his limit. Had Felix been practicing this week's exercise, he would have had a better chance of cutting off his anger at the pass.

> "Does a man do you a wrong? Go to and mark what notion of good and evil was his that did the wrong. Once [you] perceive that . . . you will feel compassion, not surprise or anger. For you have still yourself either the same notion of good and evil as he, or another not unlike it. You need to forgive him then. But if [your] notions of good and evil are no longer such, all the more easily shall you be gracious to him that sees awry."
>
> *Marcus Aurelius, Meditations, 7.26*

t's easy to feel righteous when we perceive that others are in the wrong. Our righteousness leads us to feel justified in retaliating, since we see ourselves as punishing them for their bad actions—which stem from their bad character. We are blind to the reality that the other person won't see it our way. They will likely see their actions as justified, given the circumstances, and our actions as stemming from *our* bad character!

This tendency to think that other people's actions reflect their character while our own actions depend on circumstance is called the *fundamental attribution error*, a term first coined by psychologist Lee Ross.[1] We favor our own skewed perceptions of things, mistaking them for objective truths, while at the same time downplaying how and why our fellow human beings may have a different perception. We easily convince ourselves that the asymmetry between how we behave and how we would want others to behave is, after all, perfectly justified.

Except that it isn't justified, as Marcus Aurelius reminds himself. It's likely that he, too, suffered the same error. The emperor-philosopher, unlike most of us, engages in a remarkable dissection of the problem, allowing him to see more clearly. We have a lot to learn from him.

When we perceive that another person has behaved wrongly toward us, the first step is to figure out what incorrect notion led them to act as they did. We can imagine ourselves in the other person's situation, and, by thinking about what they value, can make sense of their actions—even if we don't agree with them—immediately squashing the rising sense of righteous anger we might experience.

Which leads to the next step: Now that we know what they value, we should ask ourselves whether we sometimes have the same values. If we don't—and we are reasonably confident that our judgment is on the mark—then we know that they were acting on the basis of a wrong judgment, and we should pity them, just as we would be sorry for someone who made an elementary mistake in logic or math.

And if we do hold similarly mistaken ideas of what is good or bad, then we must consider why we are faulting the other person instead of working on ourselves. This can motivate us to forgive them, since we, too, have made mistakes in the past—and could make them in the future.

How may this have helped Felix? Felix knew he was grumpy and frustrated because he had to wait in a long line. Similarly, the teller responded in a curt manner because he was also frustrated that he had to deal with a long line of people, and that the system was down! We all become grumpy sometimes when things don't go our way. If Felix had realized this, it may have actually made him less angry at the teller's response.

Lastly, as Marcus suggests, our own views of what is good and bad may have changed, because we have learned from our mistakes and are a little less unwise than we used to be. We can then afford to be charitable toward someone who hasn't had the same breakthrough, just as we would toward someone who had not yet mastered logic or math as well as we have.

A similar technique appears in modern psychology, based on the empirically supported idea that people become more compassionate toward others when they take another person's perspective. As Sara Hodges of the University of Oregon and her colleagues put it:

> People behave better—more acceptably, more admirably, more prosocially—after perspective taking. First, perspective-taking has been consistently found to increase compassionate emotions . . . toward the person whose perspective has been taken. Second, perspective-taking leads people to view and treat other people more like the self, viewing them as possessing more traits in common with the self, and symbolically having 'merged,' at least partially, with the self in terms of cognitive representations and descriptions of personality and explanations of behavior.[2]

Just as the Stoics maintained, forcing ourselves to take seriously the point of view of another broadens our understanding. It reduces the likelihood that we will feel so emotionally attached to a particular perspective as to become angry when that view is challenged. Crucially, the Stoics are not suggesting that we necessarily agree with the other person; only that we give them a fair opportunity to make their case, in the spirit of human compassion and understanding.

A basic tenet of Stoicism is that nobody wants to do wrong on purpose, and everyone thinks they have good reasons for their actions. But it is up to us whether to indulge our anger, which the Stoics refer to as a "temporary madness," and likely make things even worse for both parties, or to be charitable and open-minded instead—ending up agreeing with our interlocutor if they are right, or just feeling sorry for them if it turns out that they are, after all, mistaken.

What to Do

For the next week, choose a time at the end of each day to think about someone you encountered who frustrated you or whom you perceived to do you wrong. What time each day works best for you? It might be the same time as last week's exercise or a different time. Write when you'll do this exercise each day below.

_____

Consider each of the following prompts each day. If you weren't frustrated with anyone, try to think of someone in your past who you feel did you wrong.

1. Who was it? What did they do? Why do you feel wronged? How do you feel about that person right now?

2. Why do you think they acted the way they did? What values might they hold that make sense of their actions? (Hint: From a Stoic viewpoint, these are usually values related to external things, beyond their complete control.)

3. Do you, or did you ever, hold any of those values, too? If yes, write about a time you acted on them, and perhaps frustrated or wronged another. If no, what internal character traits of yours do you value? List them, then write about how you could exercise those traits to lower your frustration with this person.

4. Take a final moment to express how you feel about this person now that you've gone through the exercise.

Monday _____

_____

_____

_____

_____

Tuesday
_____

Wednesday
_____

Thursday
_____

Friday
_____

Saturday _____

_____

_____

_____

Why Do It

Last week you practiced focusing on an outside view in order to quash your desires for things to go how you want them to. This week is similar. You're now countering desires about other people's behaviors. Instead of doing so by taking an *outside* view of your own struggles, you're taking an *inside* view of other people's actions. By performing this exercise, you'll gain perspective on why people's actions may seem reasonable to them, and, through that, develop sympathy.

Weekly Review

On the Sunday after you've practiced taking an inside view, set a timer for 5 to 10 minutes and write your impressions of this exercise below. How did it affect your understanding of other people's actions? Did it lead to more sympathy and less judgment? What similarities and differences did you discover with people who most frustrate you? Write about your experiences below.

_____

_____

_____

Finally, if you think this exercise is useful, check this box: ☐

Strengthen yourself through minor physical hardships

It's really hard to keep your composure when you feel physically uncomfortable, whether from pain, tiredness, or hunger. Hunger is the one Henry's been struggling with. Henry often works through lunch, thinking he would continue to be productive. All it winds up producing is grumpiness coupled with visions of pizza. No matter how hard he tries to focus, his mind just won't settle down and spoils his mood for the rest of the day. The Stoics understood that physical discomfort can sometimes lead to emotional upset. This week's exercise offers a simple technique: intentional, repeated practice.

> Now there are two kinds of [Stoic] training, one which is appropriate for the soul alone, and the other which is common to both soul and body. We use the training common to both when we discipline ourselves to cold, heat, thirst, hunger, meager rations, hard beds, avoidance of pleasures, and patience under suffering. For by these things and others like them the body is strengthened and becomes capable of enduring hardship, sturdy and ready for any task; the soul too is strengthened since it is trained for courage by patience under hardship and for self-control by abstinence from pleasures."
>
> *Musonius Rufus*, Lectures, *6*

Even though the Stoics thought the mind was our most valuable asset—it's the most sophisticated and important tool we have at our disposal—they did not neglect the body. In fact, as Epictetus's teacher Musonius Rufus suggests, the mind (or "soul") and body work together, each influencing the other, for good or for bad.

We can and should train our mind, which is why we study philosophy to begin with. This book is, after all, a series of exercises to train your mind by thinking more precisely about what is worth pursuing, what you should avoid, and what it means to have a life worth living. But philosophy, the Stoics rightly insisted, cannot be solely a matter of theory. Just as we can't learn to ride a bicycle simply by listening to someone's instructions on how to do it, so, too, we don't become virtuous just by reading Epictetus or Seneca. We need to practice.

You may practice relatively mild exercises of self-imposed discomfort, following the examples listed by Musonius: Try going out in the cold without a coat, or in the heat while being overdressed; abstain from drinking water when thirsty (within reason); fast for a day or two (unless you have a medical condition—check with your doctor); sleep in a sleeping bag instead of your bed for a night or two; skip that yummy dessert after dinner, or decline the taste of that wonderful red wine you so enjoy; or choose the longest line at a checkout aisle to test your patience.

Why would anyone want to self-inflict any of these discomforts? The point isn't to indulge in self-flagellation for the sake of making yourself miserable. These are all instances of *mild* self-deprivation. The Stoics did this in order to strengthen their character and resolve, and their ability to deal with hard times in a virtuous manner. The core idea is that the mind allows us to get through these situations unscathed. Here it is our own choice to go through the exercises; then when imposed on us by circumstance, we are already used to the idea that discomfort is no big deal. If others get through similar situations just fine, why complain and become frustrated when it's our turn?

Henry's problem is not that he is incapable of skipping lunch to focus on work, but rather that he has not trained himself to do it. Part of his mind actively resists the idea, making him feel resentful toward himself, frustrated both by the sensation of hunger and by the fact that he isn't getting done what he wanted to do anyway.

We learn from Stoic philosophy, as well as modern empirical research in cognitive science, that unless we are well trained we should avoid difficult tasks or situations that are hard to handle when we are tired, hungry, sick, or otherwise physically distracted.[1] When our body is strained, so is our mind, preventing us from being able to handle, say, a delicate discussion with our boss at work or our partner at home. In such a case, know thyself, gently ask for a postponement, and practice!

What to Do

This week's exercise is to expose yourself to minor physical hardships. You'll be guided in how to choose the hardship safely, and in a way that expands your comfort zone, while also setting you up to succeed.

For your first step, let's brainstorm: Think about areas in your life where physical discomfort tends to trigger emotional distress. It may be helpful to recall areas that Musonius lists. Do you tend to get upset when hungry? When uncomfortable? If so, under what specific circumstances? When cold? When not able to get certain pleasures? Take one to two minutes and list the kinds of discomforts that upset you.

_____

_____

_____

Now that you've listed some possibilities, choose a type of discomfort you'd like to focus on for the week. Here are some tips: Concentrate on something that happens often. Ask yourself: If you were able to wave a magic wand to make yourself completely resilient to this discomfort, would your life improve dramatically? If yes, you've likely picked a good discomfort to work on.

Before you settle on your choice, you should also be sure that the exposure is doable for you. Ask yourself: How hard will the exercise be for you on a scale of 1 to 10, with 1 being super easy and 10 being next to impossible? If your answer was 3 to 5, then great! This seems like an exercise you're likely to accomplish while still pushing your boundaries. If your answer was 1 or 2, it may be too easy. And if it was 6 to 10, it's probably too hard. If your chosen exercise seems too easy or too hard for you, go back to your earlier answers and choose an entry that you estimate to be of a difficulty between 3 and 5.

Once you've chosen something specific, the next step is to devise an action plan for consistent exposure over the next week. For example, in order to tackle his grumpiness when hungry, Henry would plan to expose himself to hunger over time, so as to have a decent chance of succeeding while still pushing his boundaries. After thinking about it, Henry may realize that skipping lunch entirely for a whole week will be too much for him—it would just increase the chances that he'd snap at his coworkers. Instead, he may decide to eat smaller lunches over the next several days. That way, he'd still be a little hungry, but it wouldn't be unmanageable. Now it's your turn: Pick a discomfort from your list that you'd like to practice over the next week, and write it down in the space below.

_____

_____

_____

Now make sure your plan is safe. There are many conditions that may make exposure to discomforts unsafe. If you have *any* concerns, now is the time to raise them with your doctor or healthcare professional. Contact your physician with the plan you laid out above, and ensure that it is safe for you. If it is not, return to the first step and repeat the process.

The final step is to create some "at-hand" phrases you can tell yourself when intentionally practicing discomfort. At-hand phrases are an important part of Stoic practice; we'll encounter them more throughout this book. They're generally used as reminders of basic Stoic principles. Here, the purpose of these phrases is to remind yourself why you're doing what you're doing, which will motivate you to continue—for example, "I'm doing this to become more resilient," or "This is so I can become a better person." Take some time to write one to three at-hand phrases in the space at the top of the next page that you can tell yourself before starting your exercise.

1. _____

2. _____

3. _____

With your at-hand phrases in hand (we call them that for a reason!), you're ready to start practicing tomorrow.

Why Do It

Our aversion to physical discomfort often leads us to lose control of our mood and thoughts, Henry's hangriness being just one of many examples. The purpose of physical training is not to prove how tough you are, nor to be a punishment, but rather, as Musonius says, to train your mind to deal with hardships. By voluntarily exposing yourself to physical hardships you will build resilience and strength of character, if you can act virtuously while enduring them. As a result, you will be prepared with a steady mind should these hardships arise by chance at other times in your life.

Weekly Review

Now that you've been practicing the endurance of a minor physical hardship for a week, set a timer for 5 to 10 minutes and write about your experience. Were you able to practice every day? If not, what obstacles did you face and how could you have overcome them? Did the hardship ease over time? How useful were the at-hand phrases you used, and could they have been improved? And, most importantly, how useful did you find this exercise in building strength of character? Write about your experience.

_____

_____

_____

_____

Finally, if you think this exercise is useful, check this box: ☐

Premeditation of future adversity

When you've experienced an inconvenience or misfortune, have you ever thought to yourself, *I can't believe it!*? James has exactly this thought as he sits in his motionless car, late for a promising job interview, having been unemployed much longer than is ideal. It crosses James's mind to call the interviewer to let him know that he's running late, but he's just too upset. The Stoics would say that much of James's distress is caused by his failure to anticipate how things might go wrong. This week's exercise is to soften the blow of misfortunes by anticipating them in advance.

> **"** If an evil has been pondered beforehand, the blow is gentle when it comes. To the fool, however, and to him who trusts in fortune, each event as it arrives 'comes in a new and sudden form,' and a large part of evil, to the inexperienced, consists in its novelty. This is proved by the fact that men endure with greater courage, when they have once become accustomed to them, the things which they had at first regarded as hardships. Hence, the wise man accustoms himself to coming trouble, lightening by long reflection the evils which others lighten by long endurance. We sometimes hear the inexperienced say: 'I knew that this was in store for me.' But the wise man knows that all things are in store for him. Whatever happens, he says: 'I knew it.'"
>
> *Seneca*, Letters to Lucilius, *76.34–35*

ome modern Stoics refer to this exercise by the Latin term *premeditatio malorum*, the premeditation of bad stuff happening. It's not that Stoics are pessimists; on the contrary, they are among the most realistic of people—they know that sometimes things won't go their way, and are always mentally prepared for that occurrence.

Of course, having a prepared mind is not like having a magic wand; no matter how prepared James is, there will still be traffic, and he will likely miss the interview. But there are two additional aspects of his unpreparedness that make a difference. First, once it's inevitable that James will be late and miss the interview, thereby forfeiting the job, it becomes what the Stoics would call *dispreferred*, or something we'd rather not do or happen. Getting upset at this point won't solve anything, but it is guaranteed to make you more miserable by adding a self-inflicted injury to one imposed from the outside. Second, James decided not to call the interviewer to alert him of the problem, because he was just too upset about his circumstance. This is a hallmark of what Stoics call a *passion*—it clouds your mind, stopping you from doing or thinking what is reasonable. (Not all emotions are passions, only the ones that take over your mind.) Had he been able to embrace the situation with equanimity, he may have realized that he had nothing to lose by calling the interviewer. The decision to call ahead or not was under his control; however, because of his distress, James could not bring himself to act in his own best interest.

The Stoic philosopher Chrysippus of Soli, the third head of the ancient *Stoa* (as the Stoic school was called) came up with a good metaphor for dispreferred situations, and, really, for life in general. Imagine a dog that is tied to a cart by way of a leash. The dog is minding his own business, maybe playfully barking at another dog nearby, just for fun. All of a sudden, the cart starts moving. The dog would rather stay a bit longer and keep barking at the other guy, but he has no choice. The leash makes sure that he will have to follow the cart. At this point, the dog could do one of two things: He could take note of the situation, accept what he cannot control, and gingerly start to follow the cart, maybe even hoping that he will meet other dogs down the road. Or, he could get upset, drag himself on the pavement, and try to resist the cart. Which do you think would be the wiser course of action?

As the dog and the cart, so we and the universe. Things will happen that will make it impossible for us to do what we intend to do. We can either approach the unwanted situation with equanimity and do the best we can given the circumstances, or we can drag ourselves kicking and screaming. The end result will be the same, but we can spare ourselves a hell of a lot of suffering.

What to Do

Last week we practiced coping with present-moment difficulties; this week we're focusing on possible *future* adversity. While *premeditatio malorum* is a fundamental Stoic exercise, there's one problem: no Stoic philosopher described how to do it. In true Stoic fashion, we're turning this lack of detail to our advantage. Instead of giving you one technique, we will offer three approaches. By completing this week's prompts, you'll gain experience premeditating on both shorter- and longer-term future adversity.

We suggest you do this exercise each morning, in order to help prepare for your day. Write the time you'll do the exercise in the space below.

Method 1: Plan for things to go wrong.

We'll start this exercise by writing out a few plans for the day. Then we'll assume that what could go wrong *will*. Next, recalling what we learned from Week 1 (page 19) and Week 2 (pages 23–24) about what's under our complete control, we'll write out how we could respond to the situation. If you need a refresher, flip back and review those chapters now.

This exercise, like many future exercises in this book, is bolstered by a technique called *implementation intentions*, which are a well-studied, effective way to increase the chances that you will remember to do something in a specific situation.[1] Instead of intending to do something, tell yourself under what circumstances you will do it. For example, rather than saying, "I'll remember what's under my complete control," you can say, "If my plan goes wrong, I'll tell myself that my thoughts, not the outcome, are under my control."

Monday

Use this table to strategize how you can respond Stoically if things go wrong. Try this for up to three of your plans for the day.

Goal you have for today	How could it go wrong?	If it does go wrong, what would be under your complete control?	What could you do or say to yourself if this plan goes wrong?	Write an implementation intention to remember if the plan goes wrong.
Example: Do taxes (way too close to the filing deadline!)	May find I don't have all the forms I need.	My thoughts about the outcome and planning next steps.	I could tell myself that the worst that might happen is a financial penalty.	When I start getting upset, I'll tell myself that a financial penalty isn't the end of the world
1.				
2.				
3.				

Good work! You are now ready to go about your day. Come back tonight to write in the space below about how the exercise went for you. Were you better able to handle adversities during the day? Did you remember how you wanted to act when your plans were derailed?

You're all done for today!

Tuesday

Goal you have for today	How could it go wrong?	If it does go wrong, what would be under your complete control?	What could you do or say to yourself if this plan goes wrong?	Write an implementation intention to remember if the plan goes wrong.
1.				
2.				
3.				

Come back tonight and write about your experiences below. Do you think this exercise may be useful to you in the future?

_____

_____

_____

_____

Finally, check the box if you found the exercise useful: ☐

Method 2: Premeditate on others' adversity.

Wednesday and Thursday

Now we're shifting gears. So far this week you have focused on your own experiences. Today we're expanding the power of *premeditatio malorum* to internalize the reality that you may be subject to unexpected misfortunes that happen to others. Today's exercise is simple: Whenever you encounter something unfortunate happening to someone else, whether it be in person, on the news, or on social media, take a moment to remind yourself that it could happen to you as well.

Below, set an implementation intention to remind yourself to do this throughout your day.

_____

_____

_____

_____

That's all for now. Come back at the end of the day to write about your experience in the space below. How did you feel as you repeatedly reminded yourself that you could be susceptible to these misfortunes? Did your reaction change over the course of the day? What use, if any, did you find in the exercise?

_____

_____

_____

_____

_____

_____

Tomorrow, you'll practice this exercise again. In the morning, review the implementation intentions you set for yourself, and revise them if they didn't work for you. Then come back here at the end of the day to write in the space below about how this exercise went for you.

_____

_____

_____

_____

_____

To wrap up, check this box if you found the exercise useful: ☐

Method 3: Practice imaginative premeditation

The final take on *premeditatio malorum* is to imagine a situation you wouldn't want to happen as if it's actually happening. This approach is similar to imaginal exposure, a type of exposure therapy used to help people overcome their anxieties.[2] However, while imaginal exposure is used to treat clinical conditions, the Stoic *premeditatio*'s goal is to loosen our attachment to external events in general, from something as simple as breaking your favorite cup (to use Epictetus's example from Week 3) to the death of a loved one. Since you're only doing this for a day, we do *not* recommend starting with a serious situation.

To get started, list five situations that are not under your complete control. On a scale of 1 to 10, with 1 being very easy and 10 being very hard, rate how difficult each would be for you to manage if it happened to you. Be sure to include at least one easy and one hard situation, though most should fall in the 2 to 5 range.

External situation	How hard would this be to cope with, on a scale of 1 to 10?

Now choose the easiest item from the list to work with today. Grab a timer and set aside 10 minutes to complete the exercise. At least 10 minutes are necessary to train your mind to become familiar with the event—perhaps even bored—as Seneca suggests at the beginning of this chapter.

NOTE: You may feel emotional discomfort during this exercise. That's okay! Do your best to continue with the exercise and to feel the discomfort. It may help to have an at-hand phrase to remind you why you are engaging in the *premediatio*, or simply to describe the discomfort objectively. Some possible at-hand phrases are "I'm doing this to build courage," "This is to overcome anxiety," or "This is for my benefit." Take a moment to generate your own at-hand phrase.

Now read and internalize these steps, set the timer for 10 minutes, and start imagining!

1. Close your eyes and picture the event from your point of view, as if it's happening in real time. Go through it step by step, thinking about what you hear, smell, and feel. If you use words to assist you, be sure to use the present tense and first-person descriptions.

2. Play the scene out until it's complete. Once done, make a quick mental note of how intense your negative emotions are on a scale of 1 to 10.

3. Repeat the same visualization of the situation as if it's actually happening to you in the present moment, and again rate the intensity of your emotions at the end of the visualization.

4. Repeat until the timer goes off.

Congratulations—you have completed your first imaginative premeditation! Now let's see how you did. Did you find your emotional discomfort drop over time? If not, don't worry—this process takes time. You may have encountered some common problems that can get in the way of this exercise working well. Common obstacles include not enough time for the premeditation, trouble imagining the situation, and lack of focus on the image. Describe how the emotional discomfort changed for you over time, or what problems you may have had.

_____

_____

_____

_____

_____

_____

That's all for today!

Saturday

Today, you'll again try your hand at imaginative premeditation. Take a few moments to review your experiences from yesterday before you begin. Were there any problems that you think you can fix? If so, write in the space below about how you can tackle things differently today.

_____

_____

_____

_____

Now choose another situation from yesterday's list to practice with today. If yesterday's practice was too easy for you, choose the next hardest item on your list. However, if you found it challenging yesterday, we suggest meditating on the same subject.

Once you've chosen a topic, reread the imaginative premeditation steps one more time, then set a timer for 10 minutes, and practice the meditation.

When you're done, write in the space below about how it worked for you this time around. Was it easier with time? Did you find any specific techniques that worked well for you?

_____

_____

_____

_____

If you keep working on this every day, you will eventually find yourself bored at the *start* of your premeditation—and then you are ready to move on to a harder entry in your list.

If you found this exercise useful, check this box: ☐

Why Do It

There are three different methods of *premeditatio malorum* presented in this chapter, but they all aim at one objective: to train yourself to cope when things outside of your complete control don't go how you want them to.

Weekly Review

Now that you have gone through three types of *premeditatio*, take some time today to review your experiences over the past week. Write in the space below about which methods worked for you, which didn't, and what you liked better about some over others.

_____

_____

_____

_____

There are no boxes to check today, since you have already marked which methods worked for you. That leaves some extra time to prepare for the next exercise! Turn the page to read more about what you'll be doing next week.

Take a (much) broader perspective

According to the Stoics, negative emotions—or "passions"—are unhealthy because they grab hold of your attention and ability to reason, practically forcing you to focus on the perceived problem. With this narrowed view, the problem will seem much larger than it actually is. Isabella experiences this firsthand—she's still fuming over how the mechanic cheated her, even a week later. Whether sitting down to work or to dinner, she stews over it. All she can think about is how he charged her way above the estimate, and how she now has new problems with the transmission that didn't exist before she took the car in. This week's exercise is to widen that narrow, unhealthy focus, putting things into perspective to help anyone who stews over problems.

> " The agitations that beset you are superfluous, and depend wholly upon judgments of your own. You can get rid of them, and in so doing will indeed live at large, by embracing the whole universe in your view and comprehending all eternity and imagining the swiftness of change in each particular, seeing how brief is the passage from birth to dissolution, birth with its unfathomable before, dissolution with its infinite hereafter."
>
> *Marcus Aurelius, Meditations, 9.32*

Marcus Aurelius had bigger fish to fry than Isabella did. Much bigger. He had to deal with two frontier wars, against the Parthians on the east and the Marcomanni and other German tribes on the north; he had to face the worst plague to strike the ancient world, possibly causing as many as five million deaths; and he had to put down a rebellion initiated by one of his trusted governors. All the while, he was of fragile health and had no previous experience as a military commander. No wonder he so often resorted to what modern Stoics refer to as the "view from above" meditation in order to put his troubles into a broader, cosmic perspective.

Don't be fooled into thinking that contemplating the vast expanse of time and space will simply solve your problems. At the end of the day, Marcus still had to wage war and take concrete actions against the plague and his governor. Similarly, Isabella's bank balance is objectively lower than it would have been had her mechanic been honest, and her car still needs work, which would not have been the case had her mechanic done his job properly. Stoicism does not magically make these problems disappear—but it does invite you to think about them in a different, hopefully more helpful way.

When Marcus tells himself in his *Meditations* that the agitations of his mind are superfluous, he is saying that nurturing one's anger at an injustice ("I've been overcharged by the mechanic!") is not going to redress the injustice itself, and moreover that these agitations will keep you miserable for days, weeks, or months. Your misery is *self-inflicted* and doesn't help you remedy the initial offense. In this sense, it is completely under your control whether to keep harping on what was done to you, or to stop and shift your attention toward something more constructive. Perhaps Isabella may file a complaint against her mechanic with the Better Business Bureau, while at the same time checking online reviews of other local mechanics to find a better one.

Marcus takes us one step further and teaches us how to halt an unproductive train of thought: He compares his admittedly big problems (millions of lives at stake) with the grand expanse of time and space. This reminds him that no matter what he thought was so important, it will soon be forgotten and will become but a footnote in history. Again, the idea is not to cultivate callousness—the war still needs to be waged, the car still needs to be repaired. Rather, we should calm down about it! This equanimity will allow us to better tackle whatever problem we face.

If considering your problems in the context of the entirety of the universe is *too* broad a perspective, try one of the following variations. The first is to consider the problems that feel most significant to you in comparison to another (much more serious) class of situations, putting your own into perspective. Take the sort of issues that people like Marcus had to deal with regularly. Surely the fact that Isabella's mechanic overcharged her by a few bucks isn't even remotely in the same ballpark as having to deal with war, betrayal, and pestilence, is it? The second variation—again in order to gain a healthful perspective—is to remind yourself that your experiences are not unique. Plenty of other people have been swindled by unethical business owners, and plenty of other people have had to look for another professional once they realized that the first one was not reliable. You decide which version of the view from above is most useful to you. Just remember that keeping things in perspective is both emotionally helpful and practically beneficial.

What to Do

This week, we'll practice taking the view from above in two ways: in daily living and at night as a more formal meditation. There are a few vantage points from which you can practice this technique:[1]

1. The vastness of time: Visualize aspects of history and prehistory backwards in time. Consider, too, as Marcus does, the expansion and ultimate dissolution of the universe.

2. The vastness of space: Starting by visualizing yourself where you are right now, imagine your vantage point floating up, seeing in succession your building, your neighborhood, your town, your country, and ultimately the earth. From there, you can continue, if you want, visualizing our solar system, galaxy, and the whole universe.

3. The relative size of your problem: Think about what is bothering you, then compare your situation to other problems that people experience now, and have experienced throughout history, from getting a bad haircut to plague or war.

Take a few moments to close your eyes and try each visualization to figure out which works best for you. First, bring a minor problem you have to mind. Next, try visualizing it by zooming out temporally (number 1), spatially (number 2), or by comparing it to problems large and small that others have experienced throughout history (number 3). Then write in the space below which ones you were able to visualize with more ease, and which ones gave you a useful perspective.

Now that you have a sense of what works best for you, let's move on to this week's exercise.

Daily living practice

To start, use an implementation intention (as we learned last week) to try to remember to do the view from above when convenient. Write down an implementation intention for using the view from above during your day.

The first way you'll practice the view from above is during your day. Practice the visualization technique that works best for you when something upsetting pops into your mind or something stressful happens. Needless to say, this should only be done if there's an appropriate opportunity—don't do it on the freeway, or in the middle of a conversation!

Nightly practice

This week you will also practice the view from above more formally, at night. What time would work best for you? Write it in the space below.

Now, let's review the steps of our evening meditation.

1. Find a quiet place, set a timer for 5 to 10 minutes, and close your eyes.

2. Remind yourself of a mildly upsetting event that occurred earlier in the day, or, something that frequently concerns you.

3. Mentally note how distressed you are, on a scale of 1 to 10.

4. Practice your preferred technique of the view from above until the timer goes off.

As you practice taking the view from above, you'll gain perspective and live a more stress-free life. Happy practicing!

Why Do It

Just like taking the outside view in Week 3, this exercise is meant to help you get perspective on your problems. While you were encouraged to take another person's perspective in Week 3, this week you gain a wider, more objective view of your own situation, in light of the entirety of space, time, and history. As the Stoics teach, passions such as anxiety and anger tend to narrow our focus to the perceived problem at the expense of everything else. This exercise helps you broaden that view.

Weekly Review

Now that you've practiced gaining perspective on your concerns, consider how this exercise worked for you. Since you've been practicing for a few weeks, we'll stop suggesting an amount of time to journal—take as much or as little time as you'd like to write about your experiences below.

_____

_____

_____

_____

Finally, if you think this exercise is useful, check this box: ☐

Meditate on nature and the cosmos

Sometimes, it can seem that the universe itself is out to get us. When delayed at the airport, it sure seems that way to Albert. He had really been looking forward to being with his wife and children for Christmas, after being deployed overseas for ten months. Now all he can do is sit at the airport, staring out the window as yet another inch of snow falls on the tarmac. Instead of cursing nature, this week we'll explore how to pay attention to it more carefully, as the ancient Stoics recommended.

> " The Pythagoreans bid us every morning lift our eyes to heaven, to meditate upon the heavenly bodies pursuing their everlasting round—their order, their purity, their nakedness. For no star wears a veil."
>
> *Marcus Aurelius, Meditations, 11.27*

Contemplating the universe as Marcus describes helps us view ourselves as part of the cosmos. This approach actually predates the Stoics, as it goes back to the Pythagoreans of a few centuries earlier. Marcus uses the Pythagoreans' meditation to observe the order of nature and to remind himself of the "purity" of the cosmos—the sun and stars go about their rounds, doing what they do. The sun doesn't shirk its duty to rise and set due to worries or concerns. Nor does it hide what it is by wearing a veil, but rather blazes brightly in the sky and does what it is fated to do.

Which brings us to the question: Do these things happen for a reason? Well, it depends on what you mean by "reason." Ancient and modern Stoic views differ somewhat, and it's important to understand to what extent, and how it matters. The ancient Stoics were pantheists—that is, they thought that God was the same thing as the universe. The God/universe was made of matter and regulated by cause and effect. In a sense, the cosmos itself was a living organism, and whatever it was doing was for its own benefit. However, since we are literally bits and pieces of the God/universe, we also play a role in what happens.

So, is the universe out to get us? No, not *us* specifically. A famous metaphor to explain this, used both by Marcus and Epictetus, is that we are like a foot attached to a body. If we have to step in mud because the body has to cross a sodden field to get where it's going, we still don't like it—and we may not understand why we have to do it. But there *is* a reason why we find ourselves splattered with mud, as unpleasant as this may feel. That is, it is ultimately in the universe's best interests.

Most modern Stoics are not pantheists, but accept the contemporary scientific account of the world: The cosmos is not a living organism—it's a wonderfully dynamic, complex system of interchangeable matter and energy. Just as the ancient Stoics thought, it is regulated by a web of cause and effect, but there does not appear to be any rhyme or reason for what happens to us individually. The foot-in-the-mud metaphor doesn't hold up to modern physics and biology.

Does it matter? Even the ancient Stoics entertained the possibility that the cosmos is not living. Marcus gives the same answer several times in his *Meditations*, including:

Either there is a fatal necessity and invincible order, or a kind Providence, or a confusion without a purpose and without a director. If then there is an invincible necessity, why do you resist? But if there is a Providence that allows itself to be propitiated, make yourself worthy of the help of the divinity. But if there is a confusion without a governor, be content that in such a tempest you have yourself a certain ruling intelligence.[1]

In other words, if we are indeed the parts of a cosmic organism, all is well. But if we are not, we still need to get up in the morning and do our job as human beings, which is to be helpful and kind to other such beings.

How might this help Albert, stuck in an airport at Christmas, with dimming hopes of being reunited with his family? Well, if Albert is a pantheistic Stoic, he will recognize that the cosmic being is doing its thing, and that he is playing a part in it. It's a tiny part, given the smallness of an individual as compared with the cosmos, but he can be consoled by the fact that there is a reason for his current predicament. If, however, Albert is a modern Stoic who thinks the universe is just what it is, and that, although he is a part of it, there is no particular reason (outside of the law of universal causality) for what's happening to him, then what? He can remind himself of Marcus's reflection: "Be content that in such a tempest you have yourself a certain ruling intelligence." This intelligence allows him to understand that sometimes planes are delayed.

Observing the order and churnings of nature fills us with awe for the very fact that we are alive, and that we have a family, or friends, to go back to for the holidays in the first place. There are billions of other beings just like us out there, experiencing the same emotions, subject to the same cosmic laws. Too often we become so wrapped up in what is happening to us right now that we forget we are all literally made of stardust.

What to Do

What can you learn about yourself and the world by observation? This week, you're going to find out by practicing your own version of Marcus's Pythagorean meditation on nature. There are many ways to take in the world around you, so let's start off by brainstorming. Set a timer for 3 to 5 minutes and write some ideas. We included a few to get you started.

- Watch the sun rise or set, contemplating your place in the cosmos while doing so.
- Go for a walk or hike in nature, taking in the life around you.
- Watch a nature documentary, noting the patterns and order of the natural world and your relationship to it.

- _____

- _____

- _____

Now that you have some ideas, use the space below and on the next page to plan an activity each day that will help you study and take in the world around you. While doing these activities, be sure to contemplate how nature behaves and your place in the universe. Feel free to repeat activities or to choose different ones each day.

	WHAT WILL YOU DO?	AT WHAT TIME?
Monday		

	WHAT WILL YOU DO?	AT WHAT TIME?
Tuesday		
Wednesday		
Thursday		
Friday		
Saturday		

Why Do It

As we mentioned in the Introduction (page 4), many ancient Stoics thought that knowing physics is essential to developing ethics; they believed that understanding how the world works is important to learning how to live. After all, if you don't know the basics of how the world behaves, how can you find your place in it? Seneca took this quite seriously, writing an entire book on the matter, called *Natural Questions*, most of which still survives today. However, you don't need a PhD in physics to be a Stoic! Instead, by situating yourself in the world and improving your understanding of the world's patterns, you can maintain perspective and internalize that, no matter what problems arise in life, the world keeps on moving on. Ideally, as we gain more perspective on ourselves and the world around us, we will, too.

Weekly Review

How did your week of contemplating nature go? Did you learn something about the world you occupy? Did it help clear your mind and keep things in perspective? Maybe you didn't find it useful. If not, why not? Take some time to write your thoughts about this exercise below.

_____

_____

_____

_____

If you think this exercise is useful, check this box to remind yourself that you might like to try it again in the future: ☐

So far, we've been working on exercises that focus mostly on dealing with aversions. Starting next week, we'll learn about practices that help with both aversions and desires.

Be careful about what you call "good" and "bad"

The words we use to describe something affect how we feel about it. Leela is fond of "horrible" to describe when something goes wrong, but "great," "amazing," or "awesome" when she enjoys it. She's had a "horrible" month, but recently things have been looking "great"! These words are accompanied by big emotions, both positive and negative. The Stoics claim that this isn't a coincidence. This week, you'll see for yourself if they're right.

> " True happiness, therefore, consists in virtue: and what will this virtue bid you do? Not to think anything bad or good which is connected neither with virtue nor with wickedness."
>
> *Seneca*, On the Happy Life, 16

E valuating circumstances that happen using strong value judgments can lead to strong emotions, as in Leela's case. When Leela uses value-laden words such as "great" and "horrible" in describing her experiences, she's not just reporting on facts. It isn't a simple fact that her last month is "horrible"—horribleness is not out there in the world—it's a value judgment that exists in her mind. On top of that, using strong words when we evaluate things can fire up our emotions in a vicious cycle; the words we use to describe them can make us feel more strongly about the thing we are describing. This is one reason why Seneca advises us to call only virtue "good" and vice "bad." Virtue and vice are the main things we should feel strongly about, as they're the most valuable things in life. Everything else should come after.

The type of preference ordering in which one set of things ranks more highly than others is known to modern economists as *lexicographic preferences*.[1] This is much like sorting things in alphabetical order. We start with all words that begin with A first, then sort again within that class, then proceed to the letter B, and so on. Our preferences can behave in the same way; we group items in an A class, then move on to the B class, and so on. Things in our A set are always more important to us than things in our B set, which in turn outrank all things in our C set. Crucially, we are not willing to trade members of the A set for members of the B set.

Here's an example: Massimo loves his daughter, who is in his A set. He also happens to love Lamborghini cars, which are in his B set. If Massimo had a lot of money (also in the B set), he would gladly trade $150,000 of it for a Lamborghini, particularly an orange one. Since he'd be willing to trade at least some amount of money for a Lamborghini, it suggests that they belong in the same set. And the fact that he'd pay up to $150,000 for a Lamborghini suggests he values the Lamborghini more than that amount of money (but only if it's orange!). But no way on earth would Massimo ever trade his daughter for a Lamborghini. That's not because it would be illegal (although it is), but because these rankings truly reflect his values, and those values are lexicographic to an extent. Studies have found that people sometimes order issues on the environment lexicographically,[2] especially if they view environmentalism using a deontological (duty-based) ethical viewpoint.[3] Other research suggests that lexicographic ordering extends beyond environmentalism, into other areas of preference.[4]

If all this seems confusing, take a look at the following diagram.

Massimo's preferences according to a utility function

Daughter > Lamborghini > $150,000

Massimo's preference according to a lexicographic ordering

Now, the ancient Stoics thought that virtue (or to be more precise, the four virtues: practical wisdom, justice, courage, and temperance, which we'll explain further in Week 11, page 78) ought to be in our A set. Everything else is in the B set. The things that Leela feels she should be happy about, therefore, are in the B set: her relationship, good times she has with friends, and her job. Could it be that she does not feel satisfied because she hasn't taken good care of the A set—that is, she has not been virtuous?

The Stoics went one step further than modern behavioral economists, arguing that things in the B set are not really good, they are just preferred (other things being equal). Likewise, if we do not have those things, it isn't really bad, it is just dispreferred. Since these are outside of our control and not necessary for our happiness, they are known as *preferred* and *dispreferred indifferents*. Virtue is the only thing in the A set, because it is the only true good. It follows that acting unvirtuously is the only true bad.

The Stoics inherited this essential idea from Socrates, who defends it in the Platonic dialogue *Euthydemus* (from the name of a Sophist with whom Socrates is talking). Socrates argues that the only thing that can always benefit us is virtue, and the only thing that can truly hurt us is the lack of virtue. *But wait a minute*, you might say. *Surely wealth, power, or fame is also good, no?* Not really. They may be used for good or for bad. Being wealthy may be a conduit for doing good for humanity, but it may also be what enables you to do harm. The same goes for all the other preferred or dispreferred things. As Epictetus puts it: "What decides whether a sum of money is good? The money is not going to tell you; it must be the faculty that makes use of such impressions."[5] That faculty is reason, which tells us that virtue is the only true good.

There's one more step to understand why Leela experiences big variations in her emotions due to changing external circumstances. Seneca suggested that true happiness consists in virtue (see page 64). That's because external circumstances, such as a job, friends, and even relationships come and go in life, so if we let our happiness depend on these circumstances, we risk being constantly at the mercy of luck or of other people's decisions, which we cannot control. Note that all the things that Leela values are external; they are subject to the whims of fate. Virtue, however, will always repay us. It is always firmly within our control. If Leela aimed to call only virtue "good" and vice "bad," and remove value judgments involving external things outside of her control, she would have a much more peaceful mind, the Stoics would claim. This week, you'll test this hypothesis for yourself.

What to Do

The Stoics offer a few ways to internalize the notion that virtue is the only good and vice is the only bad. This week, you'll be practicing with the one Seneca recommended, which is simple, but also difficult to do consistently, as you'll soon see!

The practice for the week is to only call things related to your character "good" and "bad," and to rephrase your thoughts and speech throughout the week to not call anything else by those terms.

The words "good" and "bad" have a lot of synonyms, so let's warm up with a brainstorm. Set a timer for 2 minutes and write as many synonyms as you can think of for "good" and "bad."

SYNONYMS FOR "GOOD"	SYNONYMS FOR "BAD"

Good . . . er, we mean, nice job! Feel free to come back to this list either to review it each morning before you start your day, or to add to it, if more synonyms come to mind during the week.

The final step is to actually replace your use of "good," "bad," and their synonyms whenever you say them to yourself in your head, or to someone else while speaking, throughout the rest of the week. Do use these terms when referring to your own character, though. Before you start this on your own thoughts and speech, take a look at the sentences below, mark which ones Seneca would think are valid uses of the terms "good" and "bad," and then attempt to come up with a replacement.

	STOIC USE OF "GOOD" OR "BAD"?	IF NOT, HOW CAN YOU REPHRASE IT?
Example: This cheesecake is awful.	No	I really don't like this cheesecake
Example: I have a bad temper.	Yes	N/A
1. I treated him badly.		
2. You're a great driver!		
3. He treated her horribly.		
4. That was an excellent movie.		
5. It's a good idea for me to help her out here.		

How'd you do? Hopefully not good or bad, as the results of your performance are beyond your complete control and not directly connected to your character! But some of these are quite difficult. Out of these sentences, we would say that numbers 1 and 5 are Stoic uses of "good" and "bad," and the rest aren't. Number 3 is a borderline case—while the way someone else treats a person is connected to *their* character, it is not directly connected to *yours*; it would be what the Stoics call a *dispreferred indifferent* to you, but a bad for that person. For this week, try your best to change your vocabulary only for things directly related to *your own* character.

Now that you're all warmed up, you can start your practice right away! To help yourself remember to replace your words, let's set some implementation intentions. If you need a refresher on implementation intentions, go back and skim over Week 6 (pages 44–52) now, and then set an implementation intention or two of your own below.

_____

_____

_____

_____

Feel free to come back and review your implementation intentions daily, or change them during the week if you feel you're having trouble remembering to change the words you use.

Finally, one optional piece of advice: Some people find it useful to tally whenever they successfully catch themselves using a non-Stoic use of "good" and "bad" and replace it. Doing this also allows you to see if you're improving during the week; if your tally goes up each day, then you're getting better at catching yourself. You could use an app to do this, a physical counter, or just a sheet of paper. Remember, though, you'll be bound to forget to do this a lot of the time, and that's okay. The goal here is progress, not perfection!

Why Do It

Modern psychology has found that the words we encounter carry an emotional valence with them, and whether those words are positive or negative can affect our behavior.[6] Stoic psychological theory suggests that we either subconsciously or explicitly judge every single thing we pursue in life to be good. Similarly, we presume that if a thing is bad, we'll try to avoid it. The goal of this exercise is to start prying those labels off of externals that are not completely within our control, and to put them only on what's in our control—namely, our moment-to-moment character. The Stoic sage always does this. By attempting to emulate a sage, we put ourselves on the path to the same "true happiness" that the sage has achieved, to use Seneca's words.

Weekly Review

Now that you've spent a week attempting to change your value judgments through changing your words, it's time for some reflection. Was it hard? Did you see improvement? Did you find yourself desiring and being averse to externals a little less? Take some time to write about your experience below.

_____

_____

_____

_____

_____

Finally, if you think this exercise is useful, check this box: ☐

Over the past week, you focused on changing desires and aversions by changing your words. Next week, you'll work on changing your actions to make progress toward the same goal.

Act the opposite

Have you ever found that giving in to your cravings makes them come back stronger? Asha knows the feeling. Just the other day she returned from a successful trip to Prada with all the latest designs. While Asha can easily afford it, the Stoics would suggest that mindlessly pursuing one's desires or avoiding what you don't like isn't the best way to live a good, or even pleasant, life. This week's exercise will help you put that hypothesis to the test.

> " How much better to follow a straight course and attain a goal where the words 'pleasant' and 'honorable' have the same meaning! This end will be possible for us if we understand that there are two classes of objects that either attract us or repel us. We are attracted by such things as riches, pleasures, beauty, ambition, and other such coaxing and pleasing objects; we are repelled by toil, death, pain, disgrace, or lives of greater frugality. We ought therefore to train ourselves so that we may avoid a fear of the one or a desire for the other. Let us fight in the opposite fashion: Let us retreat from the objects that allure, and rouse ourselves to meet the objects that attack."
>
> *Seneca,* Letters to Lucilius, *123.12–13*

In an exquisite military metaphor, Seneca tells his friend Lucilius that he should adopt a strategy that is the opposite of what most people are inclined to do. Like Asha, we are attracted by material objects, or perhaps fame, or money; consequently, we decide that we need to do what we can to obtain them. Similarly, we do whatever we can to avoid things we truly dislike, such as hard work, pain, and of course death. Seneca's advice is strange: We should train ourselves to not pursue the things we enjoy, and moreover, we should actively prepare to face the things we avoid. The latter is sometimes referred to as *winter training*—that is, what ancient soldiers used to do to keep themselves ready for battle. Even though they could not engage the enemy during the cold season, they would proactively exercise their skills during that time to prepare for the following fighting season. The same goes for us: Stoic training is not just a matter of withstanding adversity when it actually comes, but also of preparing ourselves ahead of it, during the good times.

Now why would anyone want to follow this recipe for what surely isn't going to be a pleasant life? Keep in mind, as Seneca implies, that "pleasant" is a value judgment, not an objective fact of the world. And we are in charge of our judgments, which means that we can change them through consistent practice if reason tells us they are off track. Recall from last week our lexicographic ordering of things we value. Virtue is in the A set, not to be traded with anything else; other things—including riches, pleasures, beauty, and so on—are in the B set, to be preferred, but not at the cost of virtue, because they are not truly good and do not really make us happy. Turns out that this notion has some backing from modern psychology, in what is called the *hedonic treadmill*.[1]

We have all experienced it: We salivate over a shiny new iPhone, we really want it, and we finally get it. For a few days we're proud of our new possession; we admire it in our hands, we use it a lot. But a few weeks later it is just a phone, a utilitarian object (admittedly with some aesthetic appeal!), which can be replaced if lost or damaged, and which is certainly not going to change our life. And what do we do? Do we acknowledge that Seneca was right after all, that it is fruitless to spend so much time and energy desiring and pursuing external things? Of course not. We just shift our attention to the next shiny object. (*Hey! That bag really looks nice. And I definitely need a new bag.*) This will keep us "happy" for a few more days or weeks, and then the process will start over. Psychologists refer to this as the hedonic treadmill: Just like the treadmill at the gym, you keep running on it and don't get anywhere. Unlike the one at the gym, this isn't even good for your health!

Seneca, then, is telling us how to get off the hedonic treadmill. It's a two-step process: First is the philosophical step of realizing that what is superficially pleasant may not make us happy—and conversely, that what appears to be unpleasant may not make us unhappy. Second, to act on our realization and little by little to internalize what we cognitively recognize to be the case: Every time you successfully retreat from the objects that allure you, and every time you successfully rouse yourself to meet the objects that attack you, you are taking a step toward wisdom and happiness.

Last week you changed the way you think about what's good and what's bad. This week, the focus will be on behaviors.

To start, brainstorm a list of your desires and aversions to which you can safely act the opposite. This isn't the time to tackle fear of death (we'll get to that in a few weeks). Instead, stick to mild-to-moderate pleasures or aversions.

DESIRES (THINGS YOU ENJOY AND PURSUE)	AVERSIONS (THINGS YOU DISLIKE OR AVOID)

Now let's plan for the week ahead by listing an exercise each day where you'll intentionally act the opposite of your desire or aversion.

Desire or aversion	When? Write a time of day or the beginning of an implementation intention	Instead of ... Write what you'd normally do in this situation	I will ... Describe the opposite action you'll do	Is this action: a) safe, and b) challenging, but not too hard?
Example: Window shopping	I leave work at 6	Walking down Madison Avenue	Say to myself "I'm acting the opposite today," and walk down a residential street instead	Yes and yes
Example: Saying "yes" to please people	Someone asks me to take on more work	Agreeing	Say "No, there's too much on my plate right now"	Yes as long as it's a side project and not my main job, and yes
Monday				
Tuesday				

Desire or aversion	When? Write a time of day or the beginning of an implementation intention	Instead of . . . Write what you'd normally do in this situation	I will . . . Describe the opposite action you'll do	Is this action: a) safe, and b) challenging, but not too hard?
Wednesday				
Thursday				
Friday				
Saturday				

As you pay more attention to your desires and aversions this week, you may discover more about them and want to switch up your plan above. Feel free to do so. Alternatively, you can come back to this chart at the end of each day and plan just for the next one.

You may want to take a few moments to congratulate yourself every time you act the opposite. You can use whatever words or imagery works and gives you a warm glow afterward. This step is an important part in turning the "honorable" into the "pleasurable." You may also say, *Good job!* since acting the opposite is directly related to your character, and is, indeed, a good, according to the Stoics. In fact, the joy that the Stoic sages feel comes directly from their own goodness of character. Consistently acting the opposite puts you, too, on that path.

Why Do It

Acting the opposite is a key way the ancient Stoics trained their brains to understand that their desires and aversions don't necessarily have to be obeyed unquestioningly. Modern research in cognitive behavioral therapy (CBT) suggests that changing our behavior can impact our emotions. This theory is used to treat both anxiety[2] and depression.[3] While useful for clinical conditions, the basic premise is also helpful to train ourselves about the nature of what's good or bad. By acting the opposite, as the Stoics did, we grow to realize over time that it isn't necessary to pursue many of our desires and that we can face many of our aversions.

Weekly Review

How did your week of acting the opposite go? Were the desires or aversions you chose too easy? Too hard? Did it help weaken your attachment to the external world? Write about this week in the space below.

_____

_____

_____

_____

_____

If you think this exercise is useful, check this box: ☐

The past two weeks have focused on both desires and aversions. For the rest of our time with Epictetus's first discipline, we will turn our attention exclusively to desire.

Moderate at mealtime

For many, food isn't just a source of sustenance, it's also a source of pleasure. Take Thomas, for example, who is a philosophy major. He's heard of Stoicism before, but he strongly prefers the epicurean lifestyle—not like the ancient Epicureans practiced it, mind you, but in the modern sense. When he's not out hitting the latest restaurant, Thomas can be found in his state-of-the-art kitchen cooking up *Ragù alla Bolognese* in his Dutch oven. Food is one of the pleasures of life, but the Stoics thought there were many pitfalls surrounding it, too, as we'll soon see.

> " Thus the oftener we are tempted by pleasure in eating, the more dangers there are involved. And indeed at each meal there is not one hazard for going wrong, but many. First of all, the man who eats more than he ought does wrong, and the man who eats in undue haste no less, and also the man who wallows in the pickles and sauces, and the man who prefers the sweeter foods to the more healthful ones, and the man who does not serve food of the same kind or amount to his guests as to himself. There is still another wrong in connection with eating, when we indulge in it at an unseasonable time, and although there is something else we ought to do, we put it aside in order to eat."
>
> *Musonius Rufus, Lectures, 18.B4*

O ne of the four cardinal Stoic virtues is temperance, the ability to do things in just measure—not too much and not too little. There are many opportunities to practice temperance, but one of the most frequent is when eating. Two or three times a day, depending on your habits, you will be sitting at a table to eat, and you will be tempted to go wrong by eating too much, too quickly, too slowly, or by choosing unhealthy options, as Musonius lists. The Stoics aren't trying to kill the joy of eating a good meal. That, for them, is a preferred indifferent. Rather, the idea is to stay on guard, since eating can lead us onto the unvirtuous path. Precisely because it is such a frequent and mundane activity, we tend not to pay attention to it. But we should be alert, both because of the intrinsic value we get from exercising moderation at lunch or dinner, and because paying attention helps strengthen our temperance muscle.

Let's consider each item on Musonius's list in turn: (1) Eating too much is bad for our health, as the ongoing obesity epidemic in wealthy nations demonstrates.[1] (2) Eating in a hurry has also been shown by medical research to be bad for us, both in terms of our digestion[2] and waistline.[3] (3) Wallowing in "pickles and sauces" is a reference to indulging in eating habits that are not healthy, pursuing pleasure over nutrition (although the two, by the way, are not at all incompatible), which is the same problem presented by (4) eating foodstuff that is sweet rather than salutary. (5) Helping ourselves to better or larger portions than our guests is clearly rude, showing little concern for others and too much preoccupation with satisfying our own appetites. Finally, (6) eating at the wrong time, when we should be doing something else instead, gets in the way of our duties as members of the human polis. To Musonius's list we could add also the twenty-first-century problem (7) of not being sufficiently concerned with our food's provenance, in terms of three criteria: environmental impact, fair treatment of labor, and, if we are not vegetarian or vegan, suffering imposed on animals.

Isn't this a bit too much, though? Why risk spoiling a perfectly ordinary and often enjoyable activity of everyday life by overcomplicating it? And yet, if we do not pay attention *hic et nunc* (to the here and now), when, exactly, are we going to start working on our virtue? As Epictetus, Musonius's famous student, says: "When faced with anything painful or pleasurable, anything bringing glory or disrepute, realize that the crisis is now, that the Olympics have started, and waiting is no longer an option; that the chance for progress, to keep or lose, turns on the events of a single day."[4]

The goal is not to become obsessed with every detail of every meal, but rather to more carefully consider what you are doing, and whether you could be doing it better. Call it the Stoic version of mindfulness, as in being mindful of your decisions and actions, which are, after all, the only things you can truly control.

What to Do

This week, you'll continue last week's theme of acting the opposite, but focus on your desires around food. For each hazard of eating that Musonius lays out, you can act in the opposite way. In the table below, you'll find a nice spread of Stoic delicacies to choose from. Since meals are sometimes spontaneous, we suggest that for the coming week you revisit this table each morning and choose an exercise that's appropriate to practice for the day, rather than plan the entire week in advance. For example, if you're having guests over or going out to eat with others, then it's a good time to practice number 4. Feel free to repeat the same exercise if you think it would be useful, or try different ones each day.

In the third column, write down the day of the week, and a quick implementation intention to help you remember to do the practice during the course of your day. Finally, go out and practice!

Musonius's "hazard"	Suggested exercise	Write the day of the week and an implementation intention to help you remember when and what to practice
1. Eating too much	Intentionally limit your portions for the day.	
2. Eating quickly	Slow down the pace of your eating over the course of each meal.	

Musonius's "hazard"	Suggested exercise	Write the day of the week and an implementation intention to help you remember when and what to practice
3. Eating for pleasure	Aim to eat the less popular option, and less of it, when eating with company.	
4. Taking more or better food than others at the table	Avoid treats for the day.	
5. Putting off duties to eat	Postpone a meal until you come to a natural stopping point in your work.	

Why Do It

To quote the Roman politician and orator Marcus Tullius Cicero: "You must eat to live, not live to eat."[5] For those of us who are lucky to have enough to eat, we are often confronted with easy access to a wide variety of scrumptious options to choose from. We're constantly bombarded with temptations. This can be a bane for many, but a boon for Stoic practice. It provides us with many natural opportunities throughout the day to practice the Stoic virtue of temperance.

Weekly Review

How did your week go? Did the exercise change your relationship with food at all? Were some of the exercises more useful than others? Write your thoughts about your practice for the past week in the space below.

_____

_____

_____

_____

_____

_____

Then, if you found practicing with your desires around food to be useful, check this box: ☐

This week's exercises gave you some practice working with desires when the temptation (namely food) is present. Next week's practice will turn the table and explore putting temptations out of sight.

Put temptations out of sight

Temptations are, well, tempting! They can be especially hard to resist when they're easily accessible. Romain knows this all too well. For convenience, he keeps some snacks at work in case he gets hungry. Plus, it gives him some semblance of pleasure during the work day. He always keeps his home pantry well stocked with snacks, too, so he doesn't have to run out when he has a craving. While keeping snacks around makes things easier for Romain in some ways, his doctor demurs after seeing his creeping weight and poor lipid panel results. The Stoics understood that sometimes the best way to deal with temptations is to put them out of sight. You'll test this idea yourself over the next week.

> " Just as he who tries to be rid of an old love must avoid every reminder of the person once held dear (for nothing grows again so easily as love), similarly, he who would lay aside his desire for all the things which he used to crave so passionately, must turn away both eyes and ears from the objects which he has abandoned. The emotions soon return to the attack; at every turn they will notice before their eyes an object worth their attention."
>
> *Seneca, Letters to Lucilius, 69.3–4*

P eople often ask why on earth we, sophisticated denizens of the twenty-first century, should pay attention to what some long-dead folks wrote two millennia ago. This quote from Seneca is a splendid answer to that question: The ancient Greco-Roman philosophers, and the Stoics in particular, had a very sophisticated, intuitive grasp of human psychology. And living a good life has a lot to do with human psychology, obviously.

Seneca states what has become a truism in modern psychological research: The best way to avoid temptation is to minimize exposure to the source of the temptation. In a study published in *Psychology of Addictive Behaviors*, social drinkers of alcohol were exposed to two experimental conditions: sniffing water (control) and sniffing alcohol (temptation).[1] The researchers then measured people's ability to exercise self-control. The results were clear, as people were significantly less able to resist a drink after sniffing alcohol than after sniffing water. Just as Seneca said, exposure to what we crave is a sure way to lose control and yield to our emotional responses. It goes further, again as predicted by Seneca, as the researchers found that the intensity of the urge to drink also negatively affected the ability to exercise self-control. The more we want something, the less able we are to resist it if we are exposed to the thing we desire.[2]

It's fascinating that Seneca compares unhealthy cravings with falling in love again. Modern research shows that the neural correlates of romantic feelings are similar to feelings of craving and even addiction. A study conducted by cognitive social scientist Helen Fisher, an expert on the biology of love, and her collaborators investigated how the brain responds to images of people who have rejected us romantically.[3] The researchers found that the parts of the brain that became active in response to romantic rejection were those normally involved in evaluating gains and losses, motivational relevance, craving, addiction (including specifically cocaine addiction), and emotion regulation. Seneca was no neuroscientist, but he had a keen sense of the inner workings of human beings, a sense that was just as useful in ancient imperial Rome as it is in the modern day.

What is Romain to do, then? Simple: Avoid the stimulus. This is easier than relying on brute willpower for two reasons. First, a healthier lifestyle is a preferred indifferent, and second, by removing temptations that may compromise his self-control, he can improve his character. Self-control is most effective when exercised preemptively by removing the temptation altogether. Should his character improve enough down the road, he may not have to put temptations out of sight. While putting them out of sight may be seen as a crutch, crutches are necessary for healing.

Your goal for this week is to identify behaviors that are triggered by cues in your environment, and then to either remove those triggers or intentionally put barriers in the way to prevent you from acting upon them. Let's jump right in by brainstorming some common desires and identifying possible triggers in the table below and on the next page.

Behavior: What desire do you indulge in that you'd like to reduce?	Possible triggers: What do you see, hear, taste, or feel that leads you to engage in the behavior?	What can you do to remove or obstruct the trigger? Write a specific action to make it harder to act upon your urge.	When will you act on removing the trigger or adding the barrier? Do it as soon as possible.
Example: Snacking	Feeling hungry, time of day, seeing the snack	I can't do much about the first two, but I can throw out all snacks I have at home and in my desk. That'd make it harder to indulge.	Right now!
Example: Constantly checking social media and news on my phone during work	Whenever I reach for my phone for other reasons, such as getting a notification	Turn off all notifications and put on do not disturb mode during work. Keep my phone in a drawer, not on my desk	Right now. I also set the implementation intention that whenever I sit down at my desk I'll put my phone in my drawer.

Behavior: What desire do you indulge in that you'd like to reduce?	Possible triggers: What do you see, hear, taste, or feel that leads you to engage in the behavior?	What can you do to remove or obstruct the trigger? Write a specific action to make it harder to act upon your urge.	When will you act on removing the trigger or adding the barrier? Do it as soon as possible.

How did it go? You may have encountered some trouble identifying triggers. That could be because we're often not aware of the external triggers. Try setting an implementation intention to pay attention to what precedes your behavior the next time you engage in it. It may also be that there are no external triggers you can influence. Perhaps they are internal triggers such as an automatic thought, in which case go back and try to identify temptations with external triggers. In this exercise we're focused on changing your environment. As long as you have at least one behavior to work on for the week, you're all set.

Once you have your plan in place, be sure to remember to act on it at the appropriate time listed in the fourth column using your strategies in the third column. You may find it helpful to keep a tally of when you encounter a trigger over the course of the week. This will help you be more aware of the cues that influence you. When you notice a trigger, pause to think about whether engaging in the behavior is a good idea.

Why Do It

The Stoic sages would never mindlessly give in to temptation when triggered (although they may still experience the trigger!). But we ain't sages. This practice helps us recognize our limitations by using our environment to our advantage; we improve our temperance not by struggling with temptation, but by making temperance easier to practice in our environment. Researchers at Duke University found that useful strategies for breaking bad habits include disrupting cues and making certain unwanted behaviors harder, backing up the efficacy of Seneca's approach.[4] Interestingly, the researchers also offered evidence that vigilant monitoring is an effective way to break automatic habits, so tallying exposure to your triggers may be more helpful than you would think.

Weekly Review

Reflect on how this practice went for you. Did you engage in your target behaviors less? Did this help improve your temperance? What were some struggles you had, and what are some possible ways you may overcome them should you choose to continue this practice in the future?

_____

_____

_____

_____

If you found practicing with this to be useful, check the box: ☐

Next week we will focus not just on putting things out of sight, but also on getting rid of them altogether. Turn to the next chapter to dip your toe into the waters of minimalism.

Start practicing minimalism

While people find joy in collecting items of meaning and beauty, having many possessions comes with plenty of strings attached. Nice cars need maintenance, and big homes need more cleaning. More stuff needs more space. Takashi enjoys being handy, so he doesn't mind that he has to build another display case for the latest collectibles he purchased. But he *is* having trouble figuring out where to put it. This week, we'll explore taking steps to minimize the possessions we have.

> **"** How far happier is he who is indebted to no man for anything except for what he can deprive himself of with the greatest ease! Since we, however, have not such strength of mind as this, we ought at any rate to diminish the extent of our property, in order to be less exposed to the assaults of fortune. Those men whose bodies can be within the shelter of their armor are more fitted for war than those whose huge size everywhere extends beyond it, and exposes them to wounds; the best amount of property to have is that which is enough to keep us from poverty, and which yet is not far removed from it."
>
> *Seneca,* On Tranquility of Mind, 8

As we know by now, Stoicism hangs our happiness only on the things we control—that is, our judgments, values, and intentions. Our happiness does not include any "externals"—no objects, possessions, or money. Here Seneca is arguing that the more we own, materially or financially, the more we expose ourselves to the vagaries of Fortuna, the Roman goddess of luck. True, people like Takashi get pleasure from owning things, but the tradeoff is stress; we have to worry about maintaining our possessions, not breaking or losing them, and shielding them from the envy of other people who may steal them from us. All of this distracts us from the main goals: to work on our character in order to become better people, and to approximate *ataraxia*, or mental tranquility.

Seneca recognizes that to do away with possessions entirely—that is, to adopt the lifestyle of the ancient Cynic philosophers—is not for everyone. The Cynics (a word that means "dog like," because their critics thought they lived like dogs rather than as human beings) sought an existence with no material possessions and no affective bonds. They lived in the streets, surviving on the charity of others, and did not marry or have children.[1] The Cynics spent their whole lives practicing virtue and telling others how bad they were at it. Needless to say, they weren't extremely popular at parties.

But that is not the Stoic way. For Stoics, you may recall, externals are preferred or dispreferred indifferents, meaning that you may or may not pursue them, so long as they don't get in the way of working on your character. And that is exactly Seneca's point: Too many possessions, and likely also too much money, *do* get in your way if your chief project is to become a better person. That said, Seneca didn't exactly practice what he was preaching here, as he was one of the richest men in the empire, with excess properties and possessions. Accordingly, he was often criticized for it. Then again, he also never claimed to be a wise person; quite the opposite. He often wrote to his friend Lucilius about just how much he failed his own expectations:

> Pray, pray, do not commend me, do not say: "What a great man! He has learned to despise all things; condemning the madnesses of man's life, he has made his escape!" I have condemned nothing except myself. There is no reason why you should desire to come to me for the sake of making

progress. You are mistaken if you think that you will get any assistance from this quarter; it is not a physician that dwells here, but a sick man.[2]

As we learn from Seneca, if we are to make progress in improving our character, we should embrace minimalism.

This week you will dip your toes into minimalism by not buying anything extraneous and by getting rid of items you no longer use.

Step 1: First start by brainstorming up to five possessions you may be able to toss, by filling out the table below.

Possible item to get rid of	Have you used or appreciated the item in the past six months?	On a scale of 1 to 10, how much use or joy does the item bring?	On a scale of 1 to 10, how difficult would it be to part with the item?
1.			
2.			
3.			
4.			
5.			

Step 2. Decide to part with any item in the first column if:

- You answered "no" in the second column.
- The item is rated between 1 and 5 in both the third and fourth columns.

If you don't have any items that meet these criteria, go back to the first step and list items that do.

Step 3. Circle the items you'll part with, and in the space provided below, come up with a plan to donate, recycle, or dispose of them. Be sure to write specific times when you'll research your options if needed, and, most importantly, to get rid of the items.

What?	Research when?	Donate, recycle, or dispose?	When to get rid of?

Step 4. Now that you have a plan, set an implementation intention to remind yourself not to purchase anything unnecessary over the course of the week. This doesn't mean you should avoid grocery shopping, or not get new clothes for an important interview, if needed. Rather, remind yourself not to buy things that are just for pleasure, and resist the desire you have for impulse purchases.

Step 5. Act on your plan from Step 3. You may find it useful to write your action plan in your to-do list or calendar, and to review your implementation intention daily.

Why Do It

As Seneca mentions, a sage would be unaffected by maintaining or losing possessions. However, since we're not sages, the goal of this practice is to minimize the amount of external things we own that are subject to the winds of chance. By starting with a few small items and a week of buying only what's necessary, you will prove to yourself that you don't need to own things to be happy. If Seneca's advice works for you this week, then it may be worth it for you to pursue even more minimalism in the future.

Weekly Review

How did your week of minimalism go? Did you remember to minimize your purchases? Did you miss the items you disposed of as much as you thought? Write your thoughts about this exercise, and whether you think minimalism is for you in the space below.

_____

_____

_____

_____

Finally, check this box if minimalism worked for you: ☐

Minimalism helps you realize that you can be satisfied with little, and helps you focus on what's important in life. This is a theme we'll also be exploring in the coming week.

Evaluate your goals

There are two types of goals that the Stoics believed to be harmful to pursue: those where you aren't likely to succeed, and those you will likely regret if you do succeed. As he slips off his wedding ring and approaches the attractive woman at the bar, Troy's current goal checks both of these boxes, although checking only one would have been more than enough for the Stoics to consider it harmful. But Stoicism isn't about judging Troy's desires; it's about judging your own. This week, you'll examine your own desires to see how fruitful they really are.

> **"** Take care that we do not labor for what is vain, or labor in vain; that is to say, neither to desire what we are not able to obtain, nor yet, having obtained our desire too late, and after much toil, to discover the folly of our wishes. In other words, that our labor may not be without result, and that the result may not be unworthy of our labor, for as a rule sadness arises from one of these two things, either from want of success or from being ashamed of having succeeded."
>
> *Seneca*, On Tranquility of Mind, *12*

T he Stoics may come across to some as the killjoys of ancient philosophers. Far better to be an Epicurean and go for sex, drugs,
and rock 'n' roll, right? Except that the Epicureans never actually
pursued hedonism of that sort, quite apart from the fact that rock 'n' roll
had yet to be invented when they roamed the agora. Although Stoicism is
often perceived as a demanding moral philosophy, you'll be hard pressed
to find a philosophy (or religion) that isn't ethically demanding. That's a
big part of their job, and if you think it is more difficult to be a Stoic than
a Christian, or a Buddhist, you have not entirely understood what the
latter two are all about.

Troy should not take his ring off, or chat up the attractive woman,
regardless of whether he is trying to pursue Stoic virtue, achieve Epicurean *ataraxia* (tranquility of mind), or be a good Christian. Why not?
Because he is being disloyal to his wife, and lying to the woman, too, by
hiding his marital status. All in the pursuit of lust. That is what Seneca
means when he says that we should not labor for what is vain. And lust
is a vain pursuit, because it does not improve you as a person even under
the best of circumstances (i.e., when you are not married and not lying
in order to get in bed with someone). Suppose Troy does succeed: he
will feel good in the moment, and perhaps somewhat smug about his
accomplishment for a little bit afterward. But if he is a decent person at
all, eventually his conscience will begin to speak up, demanding to know
why he betrayed the trust of his wife, possibly the mother of his children.
Even if his conscience should stay silent, he may face consequences if his
wife finds out: his marriage will be in ruins, and everything he has built
up to that moment, including his relationship with his children, if he has
any, will crumble or be radically altered, and not for the better. As Seneca puts it, Troy will discover the folly of his wishes, and be ashamed of
having succeeded.

But there is a second side to this coin: Seneca says we should not labor
to achieve things that we are not able to obtain. This is often interpreted
by critics of Stoicism to mean that we should not dare to achieve new
heights—and without that sort of spirit, where would the human race be?
But that's not at all what is meant here. The Stoics are simply advising
us to calibrate our efforts to the likelihood of the results we may obtain,
based on our best judgment of that likelihood. To attempt the impossible,
or what is clearly not achievable for us, is to waste a lot of time and energy.

If there is something we have in short supply, it is time. Incidentally, if you've heard of someone achieving the impossible, by definition whatever was achieved was not impossible. Modern Stoic Larry Becker writes about the "axiom of futility" in his book *A New Stoicism*: Do not feel compelled to do things that are not possible for you to do. It seems to be eminently reasonable advice, and Stoicism is all about being reasonable.

What to Do

Since you've spent the past few weeks working on your aversions and desires through actions, you deserve a break! Instead of daily action, this week's exercise will involve taking time to reflect on what you're pursuing in life, to see if it's both attainable and worth attaining.

We suggest reflecting at night, so you can review your day and take a close look at what you've spent time, energy, or attention pursuing. We'll provide a step-by-step guide with questions to reflect on.

You'll begin your reflections starting tomorrow night. Consider the following questions, and write your reflections each night.

1. What did I spend significant time or energy pursuing? Note that "pursuing" doesn't necessarily mean material acquisition—it could be anything that grabs your attention (as the woman at the bar did for Troy at the beginning of this chapter), or anything that you obsess over. If nothing jumps out at you from today, then choose something you often pursue.

2. Why are you pursuing this? Consider the reward or benefit you may get if you succeed. Or what benefit do you receive from engaging in the activity in the moment?

3. On a scale of 0 to 100 percent, what are the chances that, if you continue putting energy into the pursuit, you will a) succeed consistently, and b) live a happy, satisfied life?

4. What are some ways in which you *won't* succeed consistently, or in which your pursuit may *not* satiate your desires? Spell out in detail how one or both of these aspects could go wrong.

5. On a scale of 0 to 100 percent, are you still as confident that you'll succeed consistently and be satisfied if you keep pursuing this endeavor? Again, rate your chances at success and satisfaction. Are you still as confident as you were in Step 3 that you aren't laboring in vain?

Answer these questions once a day through Saturday. On Sunday, take a look at your pursuits from the week, and seriously consider if you're laboring in vain. If you need more space, use the notebook pages at the back of the book.

Monday

Tuesday

Wednesday

Thursday

_____

_____

_____

Friday

_____

_____

_____

Saturday

_____

_____

_____

_____

Why Do It

Remember from Week 2 (pages 20–21), the goal of Epictetus's Discipline of Desire (which also includes aversion, that is, a desire to avoid things) is to ensure you always achieve what you want and avoid what you don't want. The only reliable way to do this is to desire and avoid things that are in your complete control. The first aspect of Step 3 helps identify those things. The second part of it serves as a check to make sure your pursuits aren't likely to lead to unintended consequences, as Troy's may.

The next step, number 4, helps verify your ratings; research in psychology has shown that people who generate alternatives tend to become less confident in their initial assessments.[1] By thinking about how your pursuits may not go as you'd like, you are confirming that your confidence ratings in Step 3 are accurate, while also brushing up on your *premeditatio malorum* from Week 6 (pages 45–52) in the process. A double win!

After completing this exercise, you'll likely find that at least some of your labors are in vain. The goal is to help you figure this out for yourself by taking a closer look at how you spend your time and energy.

Weekly Review

For this review, take some additional time for reflection on your goals and pursuits, rather than spending time evaluating the exercise. First, look back over the six pursuits you wrote about over the course of the week. Then write about which pursuits you are confident continuing, and which ones you may like to stop.

_____

_____

_____

_____

_____

_____

If you think this exercise about your pursuits was useful, check this box: ☐

Remind yourself of impermanence

At some level, we know that nothing lasts forever, but the fact that we haven't fully accepted that truism becomes apparent when we get upset at losing something we cherish. For some, breaking a favorite possession stings. The most painful types of losses, however, are of the people we love, especially if the loss is unexpected. This helps explain why Yu Yan couldn't cope while attending her son's funeral after an unfortunate motorbike accident. The death of a son or daughter is the biggest tragedy a parent can endure, even a practicing Stoic parent. However, the Stoics did suggest exercises that take the bite out of losses. This week, you will practice working with one such exercise, starting with small mishaps and moving up to larger calamities.

> " When anything, from the meanest thing upwards, is attractive or serviceable or an object of affection, remember always to say to yourself, 'What is its nature?' If you are fond of a jug, say you are fond of a jug; then you will not be disturbed if it be broken. If you kiss your child or your wife, say to yourself that you are kissing a human being, for then if death strikes it you will not be disturbed."
>
> *Epictetus*, Enchiridion, *3*

This is arguably the toughest passage to absorb in all extant Stoic literature, and it sometimes turns people off Stoicism entirely. One of us (Massimo) is a parent, and when he read this passage in the *Enchiridion* he could not refrain from cringing inwardly. Does Epictetus really expect Massimo to kiss his daughter while telling himself that she is a mortal and may not wake up tomorrow? Yet what Epictetus says makes sense, both in terms of the particular historical moment he was living and, more generally, for us today. Let us start with the historical context.

Epictetus lived in the Roman Empire during the late part of the first century CE and the early part of the second. Even though the reign of the so-called five good emperors was about to begin[1]—representing the pinnacle of Roman civilization—life was not easy or devoid of tragedy for anyone from the lowest slave to the emperor himself (though, of course, all else being equal you'd be far better off in the second role than the first one). Just to give you two relevant statistics: Under the emperor Marcus Aurelius, who lived shortly after Epictetus, the empire was struck by a plague that killed five million people including Lucius Verus, who was co-emperor with Marcus for eight years. Marcus himself had thirteen children, only four of whom survived to adulthood—despite the fact that he was the most powerful man in the Western world, and that his personal physician was Galen, the most famous doctor of Roman antiquity. When Epictetus talks about the possibility of kissing your wife and child goodnight and not seeing them the day after, he is not speaking hypothetically.

Right, you might say, but we don't live in ancient Rome. We have good healthcare (if we can afford it), child mortality is way down, and life expectancy way up. This is all true, but it is *also* true that catastrophe may strike at any moment. Part of Stoic training is to prepare for catastrophes. Hopefully you will not have to experience the loss of a child (if you have any), but you will certainly experience the loss of your parents, and likely of a good number of friends, eventually. How are you going to cope? These losses amount to a tough test of your character.

While Epictetus speaks of not being "disturbed" by these seemingly catastrophic events, the more relatable Seneca says it is natural and unavoidable for human beings to suffer and experience grief. In a letter to his friend Lucilius about consoling the bereaved, he writes: "Am I advising you to be hard-hearted, desiring you to keep your countenance unmoved at the very funeral ceremony, and not allowing your soul even to feel the pinch of pain? By no means. That would mean lack of feeling rather than virtue."[2]

Think for a minute about how we react when someone else experiences a loss, even someone we care about or love, as you did in Week 4 (pages 34–36). As the Stoics advise, we try to console them by putting things in perspective. We remind others that life isn't always fair, that loss is natural, that they should think about the happy times they shared with the person who died, and that they should focus on the future—on the many things they can still do and the people still here to care for. This is sound advice, and it works. The losses we suffer don't become trivial or unimportant, and we don't become uncaring or unfeeling. Putting things in perspective makes us more attentive to what we have and often don't appreciate, and more resilient in the face of tragedy.

Epictetus counsels his students to work their way up to the big stuff by paying attention to the little things first. Suppose your favorite mug breaks. Instead of getting angry or upset, pause, look at it, and tell yourself: *Well, it was a mug, I knew it could be broken, but I enjoyed many wonderful cups of coffee thanks to it!* Then, slowly, tackle more difficult things. Perhaps your car has been damaged in an accident. That's unfortunate, but cars do get into accidents, it is in the nature of cars; be grateful for the many nice rides you had while the car was working. Or maybe some of your savings evaporated because of the latest downturn of the market. Well, that is what markets do, after all, and you did take advantage of the good moments to enjoy your vacations or buy a new house. Again, the point is not to become callous or indifferent in the modern sense of the word, but to become indifferent in the Stoic sense—you still have your virtue and your character, and they allow you to handle anything that the universe throws your way. The word to describe this attitude is *equanimity.* Equanimity gives you serenity in the face of both the good times (when you may otherwise get carried away) and the bad ones. It's how Stoics strive to navigate the entirety of their lives.

What to Do

Let's start our preparation for this week by taking a few minutes to brainstorm some things that are impermanent and subject to loss. Try to include a broad range of difficulty, as Epictetus recommends.

_____

_____

_____

_____

Now rate each item you listed above on a scale of 1 to 10 in terms of difficulty, with 1 being easy to deal with if lost, and 10 being difficult.

Finally, in the table below, lay out a new item to work with each day of the week. Start with the easiest item on your list on Monday, and gradually increase in difficulty throughout the week. For each item, write an implementation intention to help remind yourself of the impermanence of the item whenever you encounter it.

Day of the week	Item of impermanence and its rating	Implementation intention
Example	My television (2)	Whenever I sit down to watch TV, I'll say to myself, "This will break one day."
Monday		
Tuesday		
Wednesday		

Day of the week	Item of impermanence and its rating	Implementation intention
Thursday		
Friday		
Saturday		

Each morning, come back to this table. Whenever you encounter what you're working with for the day, remind yourself of its impermanence as you laid out in your implementation intention.

Why Do It

This exercise is a kind of *premeditatio malorum*, which you practiced in Week 6 (pages 45–52). By constantly reminding yourself of the impermanent nature of externals, the sting of surprise will slowly diminish over time should the unfortunate event happen. Think of this exercise as a vaccine against impermanence and loss—it inoculates and strengthens your psychological immune system to change. It isn't just about preventing negative passions from occurring; many who practice this exercise find that it also instills a sense of gratitude, allowing you to appreciate what you have while you have it.

Weekly Review

How did this week's exercise go? Did you experience gratitude while practicing? Were you less distressed as the week went on?

Finally, check this box if you found this exercise useful: ☐

This week's theme was about the impermanence of the things *in* your life. Next week, we'll continue by working with the impermanence *of* life.

Contemplate death, and how to live

We know at some level that we're going to die. How deep does that knowledge go? We sometimes obsessively pursue health or beauty in an attempt to delay the inevitable. Even though we can take precautions, we still don't have complete control. Katie found this out the hard way, seeing both of her parents die of cancer at a young age. Since then, she's been focused on health, carefully monitoring her food intake and exercising daily. A long, prosperous life is a preferred indifferent according to the Stoics; they were more focused on quality of life over quantity. They didn't think one's quality of life depended on health or traditional notions of success. Instead, they thought it consisted of quality of thought and character. This week you will focus on ingraining this concept ever more deeply into your psyche.

> " No man can have a peaceful life who thinks too much about lengthening it, or believes that living through many consulships is a great blessing. Rehearse this thought every day, that you may be able to depart from life contentedly; for many men clutch and cling to life, even as those who are carried down a rushing stream clutch and cling to briars and sharp rocks."
>
> *Seneca,* Letters to Lucilius, 4.4–5

Seneca's advice to not unnecessarily delay death is sharply at odds with much of the current zeitgeist. We don't want to talk about death, we don't want to see dying people, and we engage in fantasies of immortality by way of uploading our minds to computers.[1] We do all this while ignoring mounting problems that we could actually tackle, from the poverty of hundreds of millions of people to looming environmental disaster fueled by our greed and obsession with consumption. And yet it is precisely because Stoicism strikes such a different chord that it has become popular again. We intuitively grasp that there is something not quite right in the way we are conducting our lives, and the Stoic diagnosis of what is wrong is clear: We put too much value on the wrong things (externals), while at the same time not valuing enough what we should (our character and integrity).

Seneca is not saying that a long life is not preferable, other things being equal. He is attempting to recalibrate our system of values: it is not length that is important, but what we do with the time we actually have. Anglo-American writer Susan Ertz famously quipped that "Millions long for immortality who don't know what to do with themselves on a rainy Sunday afternoon,"[2] reiterating Seneca's point. You should worry about whether you are living a good life in the Stoic sense (something you can control), and not about how long your life will be (something you can't control). Elsewhere in his letters, Seneca observes that it is odd that people talk about young people dying "prematurely," as Katie says about her parents. In a universe governed by a web of cause and effect, there is no such thing as early or late—everything happens when it happens, as a result of things that happened before. We do not have knowledge of much of the universal web of causation, so we cannot tell what will happen and when. It makes sense, then, to not lose our tranquility of mind over what we don't know and to focus our energy instead on the here and now, where we can act in order to make this a better world. One way to remind us of that is, as Seneca suggests, to think about death every day—not to be morbid, but to internalize the idea that death is a natural and inevitable process. What counts is what we do before that moment arrives.

Seneca's advice has implications for contemporary conversations about how we should handle the end of life, as individuals and as a society. Notice his comment on people who desperately cling to life even when they are about to die. As animals, we are endowed by natural selection with an instinct for survival at all costs. But as thinking beings we are unique in the biological world. We are the only species (so far as we know) whose members are capable of reflecting on their own demise, preparing for it, and acting accordingly. Seneca says that we "die every day," meaning that we inch in that direction from the moment we are born. Death, then, truly is the ultimate test of our character.

What to Do

This week, you'll take Seneca's advice literally by rehearsing Stoic thinking around death every day. We suggest that you do this through free-form writing.

To start off, think about when you'll have time to do this week's exercise, and write it in the space below.

Starting tomorrow you'll write about the topic of death from a Stoic perspective. Each day, reread Seneca's advice, which we've rewritten below in a modern form:

> No one can have a peaceful life who thinks too much about lengthening it, or believes that a long life is a great blessing. Rehearse this thought every day, that you may be able to depart from life contentedly.

Then write for however long you'd like. Use the notebook pages in the back if you need more space. Below are some statements and questions that can serve as prompts. Feel free to try a new one each day, and use only the one that resonates with you most, or ignore the prompts entirely.

- Why do you *not* have complete control over the length of your life?
- How does the knowledge that you don't have complete control over how long you live affect how you should live your life *now*?
- Why does Seneca claim that thinking too much about longevity leads to an unpeaceful life?

- How is not fearing death related to the four cardinal virtues of Stoicism?

    Practical wisdom: the ability to differentiate between what's truly good and bad

    Justice: the capacity to treat people fairly and kindly

    Courage: proficiency in acting well despite fear or aversion to externals

    Temperance: skill in reducing desire for external things that aren't in your complete control

- How does a fear of death and a strong desire for longevity cause you to act unvirtuously in your life? How does it affect your peace of mind?

- What would be some benefits of not fearing death and not obsessing over longevity? How might you live your life differently?

Monday

_____

_____

_____

_____

Tuesday

_____

_____

_____

_____

Wednesday

_____

_____

_____

_____

Thursday
_____
_____
_____
_____

Friday
_____
_____
_____
_____

Saturday
_____
_____
_____
_____

Why Do It

Many of the Stoics, especially Seneca, believed that fear of death is the root of many of our other fears. Most of the absolute worst-case scenarios we envision ultimately end there, from losing a job (since it could lead to poverty, in turn leading to death) to illness (for more obvious reasons). When Seneca's friend Lucilius was suffering from a disease, Seneca wrote him a letter calling the lack of fear of death a cure for all ills: "[M]y counsel to you is this—and it is a cure, not merely of this disease of yours, but of your whole life—'Despise death.' There is no sorrow in the world, when we have escaped from the fear of death."[3] Further to achieving peace of mind, Seneca claims that a benefit of this thinking is a clear path for virtue: "For the mind will never rise to virtue if it believes that death is an evil; but it will so rise if it holds that death is a matter of indifference."[4]

The goal of this week's exercise is to see if Seneca's claims hold true for you. A week likely won't be enough to completely eliminate your fear of death and desire for longevity, but you will be able to put Seneca's claims to the test.

Weekly Review

Now that you've had some practice exploring Stoic thoughts about death, take a bit of time to reflect. Did Seneca's claims hold up in your own experience? Did you find this exercise useful? If it was difficult, do you think that it would become easier with practice? Write your thoughts about this exercise and what you learned over the course of the week in the space below.

_____

_____

_____

_____

Finally, check the box if you think you'd like to use this exercise in your future Stoic practice: ☐

Next up is our final, and more cheerful, exercise in the Discipline of Desire.

Meditate on others' virtues

That's amazing, thinks Yael as she watches her friend Abigail hand the homeless man a $100 bill. Yael was more concerned with avoiding the stench coming from the man, but not Abigail—she can't help but give to those in need. Abigail is the kindest person Yael knows. *I want to be more like that*, Yael thinks to herself, and smiles.

> **"** When you want to cheer your spirits, consider the excellences of those about you—one so effective, another so unassuming, another so open-handed, and so on and so on. Nothing is more cheering than exemplifications of virtue in the characters of those about us, suggesting themselves as copiously as possible. We should keep them always ready to hand."
>
> *Marcus Aurelius, Meditations, 6.48*

Your work for the past several weeks has been focused on one main aspect of Stoic practice: reducing the desire for externals. We've addressed what Stoics think you *shouldn't* desire, but what do they say you *should*? We'll begin answering this question this week, but it will also be the focus of the Discipline of Action, which we'll explore next.

The Stoics encourage us to seek virtuous friends. Yael is inspired by Abigail's actions, which she believes reflect her friend's virtuous character. This is the sort of friend that the ancient Greco-Romans, from Aristotle to the Stoics to Cicero, would have approved of. Aristotle even called it a *friendship of virtue*, and considered it the highest kind of friendship. The Stoics thought of it as the only one deserving that name. To appreciate the contrast, think of how we accumulate more and more "friends" on social media, made up mostly of people we haven't even met.

Becoming a good person is not just a matter of avoiding desire of the wrong things; it is also a matter of desiring the right ones. Training ourselves not to covet another person's sexual partner, for example, is most certainly a good thing. But it is even better to train ourselves to be just, kind, temperate, and courageous. It's admittedly hard to improve on our own; we need help, and we need yardsticks against which to measure our own progress. That is why positive friendships are so crucial in Stoicism: A friend like Abigail is, in a strong sense, a guiding light for the aspirations of Yael. If you think this is putting too much burden on your friends, recall that sages are very rare, and that people who inspire us don't have to be perfect. Surely Abigail has her own limitations and faults, and perhaps it is Yael who can help her with those in turn. They pull each other up, encouraging one another to become better and better.

Notice that Marcus mentions the character of "those about us," which is a broader category than just friends. While friendship is the obvious place to look, we can also learn how to be virtuous from colleagues, relatives, and even perfect strangers. Had Yael witnessed the same scene where the homeless man was instead helped by a stranger, she would likely have learned the same lesson in practical virtue. And one more thing: Marcus says that "nothing is more cheering" than witnessing people engage in virtuous acts. This is an interesting point, because joy at the sight of virtue is one of the positive emotions that the Stoics thought we should nurture, and that would be present in a sage. So we know that Stoicism is *not* about suppressing emotions, only about escaping from the destructive ones.

What to Do

This week's exercise is simple: Take a few minutes each day to write about the admirable character traits of your friends and acquaintances. Choose a time of day when you'd like to do this exercise, and write it in the space below.

Then, every day, use the space on the next two pages to write a few sentences concerning the person whom you admire, as well as to rate your mood before and after the exercise. If you find you have a lot to write, you may want to use a separate sheet of paper, or write out what you admire about the person on your computer or tablet instead of just writing a paragraph. You can still use the space to plan out what you'd like to write about and rate your cheerfulness.

Answer the following questions each day. Be sure to rate your mood at the beginning and end of each writing session.

1. Rate your level of cheerfulness from 1 to 10, with 1 being the lowest.

2. Whom will you be writing about?

3. What character trait of this person do you admire?

4. What do you find admirable about this person and why?

5. Rate your cheerfulness again on a scale of 1 to 10.

Be sure to keep these points in mind when writing:

- The focus should be on what character traits you admire about the person, not material or superficial aspects that are not in that person's complete control.

- The person does not have to be a saint. Just focus on one thing you admire about that person, even if they have flaws. If flaws do come to mind while writing, try to stay focused on what you admire, and don't write about what's not admirable.

- These can be friends, family, or acquaintances. You don't have to know the people well in order to find something admirable about them.

Monday

Tuesday

Wednesday

Thursday

Friday

Saturday

Why Do It

One of the main reasons for doing this exercise that Marcus suggests is that it's a wholesome way to lift our spirits. We can take an educated guess as to why he thinks this is the case. First, it focuses on the positive. Marcus implies throughout his *Meditations* that he may have been surrounded by people who were difficult to work with or be around. Focusing on the positive aspects of both friends and difficult people may have lifted his mood. Second, recollecting how others have positively influenced him may have instilled a sense of cheerful gratitude. Book I of the *Meditations* is almost exclusively devoted to this exercise. Marcus reminds himself of the virtues he learned from others throughout his life, which also serves as a reminder to work on exemplifying those character traits as much as possible. Finally, focusing on what's in a person's control (i.e., their character) may have helped Marcus practice the dichotomy of control, taking his mind off of dispreferred indifferents whose outcome he could not completely control. But this is mostly speculation!

Your goal this week is to find out if and how this exercise may help you.

Weekly Review

Did you find that Marcus's experience was true for you? Did focusing on the virtues of others around you raise your spirits? Were there other positive, unexpected side effects? Take a few minutes to write about your experience.

_____

_____

_____

_____

Finally, check the box if you think you think this exercise would be useful in your future Stoic practice: ☐

That's it for the Discipline of Desire! You've spent the past seventeen weeks focusing on reducing your desires and aversions to external things. Now it's time to retake the brief quiz that started off this section to see how much progress you've made in the discipline. Take the quiz on the next page now.

Quiz

Now that you've spent seventeen weeks on the Discipline of Desire, it's time to retake the quiz that started this section. Rate how much the following statements describe you as you currently are on a scale of 1 to 10, with 1 meaning it doesn't describe you at all and 10 meaning it describes you perfectly.

I get really upset when I don't get what I want or things don't go my way.

I put a lot of effort into avoiding things I don't like or that I'm afraid of.

I spend a lot of time pursuing comfort and pleasure.

Once you've completed this quiz, flip back to page 10 to see your progress. Stoic practice takes a lifetime of work, so while hopefully you will see some improvement, don't fret if you didn't. By completing the exercises, you have taken a big step in testing out which exercises in the Discipline of Desire may work for you in your future practice. You'll be able to create a personalized Stoic curriculum at the end of this book, using only those exercises that worked best for you.

PART II

THE
DISCIPLINE
OF ACTION

THE GOAL

"There are three things in which a man ought to exercise himself who would be wise and good. . . . The second [the Discipline of Action] concerns the movements toward an object and the movements from an object, and generally in doing what a man ought to do, that he may act according to order, to reason, and not carelessly. . . . The second topic concerns the duties of a man; for I ought not to be free from affects like a statue, but I ought to maintain the relations natural and acquired, as a pious man, as a son, as a father, as a citizen."

Epictetus, Discourses III, *2.1–4*

Quiz

Before you begin your journey in the Discipline of Action, take a moment to briefly rate yourself on a scale of 1 to 10 on the following items. One means it doesn't describe you at all, and 10 means it describes you perfectly. After you complete the exercises in Part II, you will answer these questions again to see if you've made progress.

I tend to act impulsively, on the basis of my initial urges without questioning them.

| 1 | 2 | 3 | 4 | 5 | 6 | 7 | 8 | 9 | 10 |

DOESN'T
DESCRIBE
ME AT ALL

DESCRIBES ME
PERFECTLY

I shy away from my responsibilities in life.

| 1 | 2 | 3 | 4 | 5 | 6 | 7 | 8 | 9 | 10 |

DOESN'T
DESCRIBE
ME AT ALL

DESCRIBES ME
PERFECTLY

I can be selfish, and don't care much about other people's well-being.

| 1 | 2 | 3 | 4 | 5 | 6 | 7 | 8 | 9 | 10 |

DOESN'T
DESCRIBE
ME AT ALL

DESCRIBES ME
PERFECTLY

Keep your peace of mind in mind

As we go about our day, our minds naturally turn toward accomplishing our goals. This can be useful in achieving those goals, but can also come at a cost. If all we think about is accomplishing the goal, we put our mental well-being in the hands of chance. This is what happened to Ameerah as she felt her anger rising as she considered the guy using the squat rack for biceps curls. Her main goal was to get her squats in, and by chance someone was using the equipment for something he didn't need it for. While curling in the squat rack is definitely bad gym etiquette, the Stoics would caution that anger isn't useful in this situation. How can we maintain our composure when coping with the frustrations we encounter while going about our day?

> " When you are about to take something in hand, remind yourself what manner of thing it is. If you are going to bathe, put before your mind what happens in the bath—water pouring over some, others being jostled, some reviling, others stealing; and you will set to work more securely if you say to yourself at once: 'I want to bathe, and I want to keep my will in harmony with nature,' and so in each thing you do. For in this way, if anything turns up to hinder you in your bathing, you will be ready to say: 'I did not want only to bathe, but to keep my will in harmony with nature, and I shall not so keep it, if I lose my temper at what happens.'"
>
> *Epictetus*, Enchiridion, 4

T his is the first exercise of the second discipline: action. In this section we are going to focus on how Stoics behave in response to external situations, particularly when it comes to dealing with other people. But as you just read from Epictetus, responding to external situations still places heavy emphasis on our internal state. Here we find Epictetus at his best: clear, insightful, and even a bit poetic. We love the image of someone going out to do something, such as visiting the thermal baths or the gym, keeping in mind that we always have two objectives: to do what we set out to do, but also to keep our inner calm, or what Epictetus refers to as "harmony with the universe." We may or may not succeed at the first task since that is not (entirely) up to us, but we will definitely succeed at the second one so long as we don't let ourselves lose our temper at the first inconvenience. Another translation, by Robert Dobbin, of this piece from Epictetus is more funny than poetic, ending instead with "I cannot keep harmony with nature if I go to pieces every time someone splashes some water on me."[1]

The point is to reflect on what is likely to happen before it happens. We know, as a matter of experience with fellow human beings, that people will splash each other at the baths or violate gym etiquette. It is precisely this experiential knowledge of how people behave that we now turn to our advantage and use to mentally prepare for what might happen. As we discovered in Week 6 (pages 45–52) when practicing *premeditatio malorum*, mental preparation is crucial to maintaining our calm and not allowing predictable annoyances to disturb our serenity and inner equilibrium. It's also significant in Stoic physics (which admittedly sounds abstract): By knowing and accepting how the world is ahead of time, the world becomes less surprising and frustrating when we actually face it.

There are countless occasions on which this exercise is useful, because we can rely on some person or other to behave improperly in pretty much every situation. Perhaps you are out in your car enjoying a nice drive with your family when someone cuts you off because that's the sort of thing he does. Or you take the subway and the person next to you, mistaking the train car for her bathroom, gingerly cuts her nails. Or . . . you get the point, right?

What to Do

This week's exercise consists of three steps, one of which you are already familiar with, but there's a twist. In Week 6, you learned to premeditate on adversity. Now, in addition to reminding yourself of things that can go wrong, you'll set an intention to accept the things that go wrong. These intentions will help you cope with possible adversities and keep your calm.

Step 1. Visualize a task you are likely to encounter today that you sometimes find frustrating.

Step 2. Mentally rehearse "I want to do this activity, but also want to keep my cool by accepting what happens" or something similar.

Step 3. Finally, imagine yourself behaving calmly in the situation.

Before going to the gym, Ameerah might briefly envision a common annoyance she has previously encountered, such as the guy doing biceps curls in the squat rack. She can practice some at-hand phrases to help her gain control, like "I'm here to work out and, just as importantly, keep my cool," and then mentally rehearse calmly asking the guy to do his curls elsewhere. Note that accepting something doesn't mean being a pushover. Ameerah can take the same action as she otherwise would have, but without being upset in the process.

We suggest doing this exercise in the morning. Look at your day ahead, think about what parts of the day may be frustrating, and then try the exercise. Alternatively, you can practice this immediately before entering a possibly stressful situation. Use the space on the next two pages to write the task you are likely to encounter.

Monday

Tuesday

Wednesday

Thursday

Friday

_____

Saturday

_____

Why Do It

Research has shown that mental rehearsal can activate pathways in the brain that are similar to actually performing the task.[2] This mental exercise can both help manage stress and improve performance for a wide range of people, from health care trainees[3] to athletes.[4] By rehearsing adversities and your serene reaction to them, over time you will increase your likelihood of acting and behaving calmly.

Weekly Review

How did your first week practicing the Discipline of Action go? Did you find yourself acting and feeling more calm in response to adversity? Take some time to write about what worked and what didn't, in the space below.

_____

_____

Check this box if you think this exercise is one you'd like to add to your personal toolkit: ☐

Cut out busyness

Many of us live in a culture where being busy is a badge of pride. Having full days means you get things done. This signals that you're a productive member of society and value hard work. However, being busy has its downsides. Liam lives a productive professional and family life, and his days are always packed. He often has to turn down spending quality time with friends, and also loses out on time for himself. While the Stoics valued making the most of your time, can taking things on be taken too far?

> " You will hear many of those who are burdened by great prosperity cry out at times in the midst of their throngs of clients, or their pleadings in court, or their other glorious miseries: 'I have no chance to live.' Of course you have no chance! All those who summon you to themselves, turn you away from your own self. . . . Check off, I say, and review the days of your life; you will see that very few, and those [that are] the refuse . . . have been left for you. . . . Everyone hurries his life on and suffers from a yearning for the future and a weariness of the present. But he who bestows all of his time on his own needs, who plans out every day as if it were his last, neither longs for nor fears the morrow."
>
> *Seneca,* On the Shortness of Life, 7

Time is the only thing that, once loaned, can never be paid back, and therefore the one resource we really need to be careful to apportion wisely. Seneca was writing two millennia ago, but he may as well have been speaking in the twenty-first century: Our lives are becoming ever busier, but not necessarily more meaningful. The first question a Stoic would ask of someone who is too busy is whether they have their priorities straight. Are we paying sufficient attention to what is most important in our lives, or are we being distracted by inconsequential or downright destructive pursuits? The second issue is one of quality versus quantity, as we moderns would put it. While the phrase "quality time" is more than a bit overused, it gets to the idea that we cram too much into our days, which is not a good recipe for life, or even to get those things done. There is empirical evidence[1] that beyond a certain threshold, more hours spent on a task can actually be deleterious. The reason is simple: Human beings need rest and variety of stimuli in order to keep their minds focused.

There are two other aspects of busyness that Seneca focuses on and that are worth mentioning. The first is that there are few days left, and those are the "refuse," that is, the lowest quality ones. Seneca is referring to people who have lived long enough that they begin to sense the final stretch. Looking back at their lives, they realize that their time had not been used well. We certainly don't want to get to that stage only to find that we're out of time, do we?

Second, we should plan each one of our days as if it were our last. This is another example of Stoic motivation: Awareness of death gives value to life. Imagine for a moment if today really were your last day. We bet you would spend it very differently, focusing on things that are important to you, not on trivialities. Of course, you don't know which day will be your last, or how much time you may have ahead of you, so you should feel the same sense of urgency every day.

Don't fret about the future, and don't regret the past. The future hasn't come yet, and the past is outside of your control. It is the present that demands your attention—a demand that requires you to make important decisions about how you are going to spend this day, and every day, in the moment.

What to Do

The Discipline of Action can be as much about culling useless actions as it is about cultivating virtuous ones. This week, we encourage you to "check off your days" in order to see if there are any actions that should be cut.

Take some time each night to review how you spent your day, and whether your activities satisfied two factors: They served "your own needs," that is, helped build character, and they were truly important. Use the table below for guidance. At the end of each day, write up to three activities you did and ask yourself if doing them helped preserve or build your character and whether they were important. Would you still do them, or something like them, if you knew your life were to end soon? The things you list can be short and trivial (e.g., browsing social media, having a beer, or texting a family member) or long and significant (e.g., working on a major project or running a marathon). A mix of both types of activities will be useful, since those that only take a few minutes can add up to huge chunks of time over a lifetime!

List up to three activities you did today, large or small	Did this activity help build character, or fulfill an important role?	Would you have done this activity if today was your last day?
Monday		
Tuesday		

List up to three activities you did today, large or small	Did this activity help build character, or fulfill an important role?	Would you have done this activity if today was your last day?
Wednesday		
Thursday		
Friday		
Saturday		

Why Do It

The Discipline of Action is ultimately about one goal: to act intentionally to become a better person. This exercise allows you to see how many of your current actions help you in this pursuit. With this in mind, you can make more informed, deliberate decisions about how to act, in order to improve as a person. You'll see this theme recurring in many of the weeks to come.

Weekly Review

Now that you've spent a week cataloguing your actions throughout the day, take some time to reflect on them. Review your notes from the past week, then write about any trends you've noticed. Did you discover any recurring activities that aren't fulfilling, and don't improve your character, or help you carry out your responsibilities? Did you discover some actions that you'd like to keep, or do more frequently?

_____

_____

_____

_____

_____

Finally, check this box if taking an occasional Stoic inventory of your actions was useful: ☐

Now that you've taken an inventory and thought about culling some of your current actions, let's move on to the next chapter, where we'll explore Epictetus's advice about acting intentionally and minimally in one specific action: speaking.

Speak little but well

Social media has allowed unprecedented connection between people throughout the world. But are these connections always worthwhile? Jamal's newsfeed is abuzz with people sharing their opinions on everything from politics to the latest superhero movie— that is, when it's not filled with chatter about a photogenic meal, or a friend's vacation. What would the ancient Stoics have to say about the quality of our social media feeds and social interactions today?

> " Be silent for the most part, or, if you speak, say only what is necessary and in a few words. Talk, but rarely, if occasion calls you, but do not talk of ordinary things, of gladiators, or horseraces, or athletes, or of meats or drinks— these are topics that arise everywhere—but above all do not talk about men in blame or compliment or comparison."
>
> *Epictetus*, Enchiridion, *33.2*

We may not have much occasion to talk about gladiators these days, but we sure are obsessed with athletes nonetheless . . . and with actors, and singers, and royal weddings. It's more evidence that people haven't changed much in two millennia! And of course we talk about the latest trendy restaurant we visited with its stupefying cocktail menu, as if these were really consequential matters.

We don't have to take Epictetus's list of "ordinary things" as a literal prohibition. Social interactions are also made of small talk. Though perhaps we should take seriously the suggestion to ratchet up the level of our conversation, both for ourselves and for our friends. There are so many important issues to talk about, so much conversation that would improve us as people, increasing our awareness of what's going on in the world and what we can do about it. It's a shame that we, instead, indulge in trivialities for so much of our social life.

Similarly, we don't need to interpret literally the injunction to be mostly silent. We have a duty to do our part in social discourse. At the least, some of us could use the advice of speaking less and listening more. It will help improve ourselves—hey, we might learn something, if we just stopped pontificating all the time—and others as conversations become more lively and interesting when different voices participate, particularly when there are people of different genders, ethnicities, or cultures in our company.

Notice especially the last bit of Epictetus's advice: to avoid what we would call gossip—blaming, comparing, or even praising people. Most of the time we simply don't know enough about others to arrive at judgments about their character or actions. And even if we did, what others do is their business, not ours. We should be focused on improving ourselves, because that's the locus of our control.

All of the above is just as valid for online interactions as for in-person ones, and perhaps even more so. When interacting online, we not only replicate all the questionable behaviors that Epictetus criticizes, but we do so while our presence is amplified to what we think is a much larger audience. Our conversations could be far more interesting and edifying if we paid more attention to what we say. If we don't pay more attention, the internet—with its potential to become a global village in which everyone has a voice—risks descending into a cacophony of irrelevancies.

What to Do

The exercise this week is straightforward: speak little and well—though it isn't as simple as it sounds. The following two steps will help you work through with speech over the course of the week.

First, define for yourself what "well" means to you. Epictetus mentions a few instances of what he thinks isn't speaking well—"ordinary things," such as food or gossip. By reducing the amount of time spent discussing these topics, you would naturally speak less while also speaking well. That kills two birds with one stone. But as we mentioned earlier, you don't have to take Epictetus's list literally. Instead, generate your own list of topics that it would serve you well to speak about less over the coming week.

_____

_____

_____

_____

Second, browse your list of topics to create a few implementation intentions to help remind yourself to reduce the amount of time you spend talking about these topics. One tip: If you tend to talk about one of your topics when in a certain situation, then you can use that trigger for the first part of your implementation intention. For example, if you tend to gossip with your father, your intention can be: "Whenever I talk with my father, I'll tell myself silently, *Don't gossip.*" Or if you post a lot of political opinions on social media, a useful intention might be: "Whenever I scroll through my social media feed, I'll keep my hands off the keyboard," which will definitely make it harder to type out your opinions. Write your implementation intentions below.

_____

_____

_____

Review your implementation intentions each morning to remind yourself of what areas of speech you are trying to limit for the week.

Why Do It

Speech is one of the most important actions we engage in during our day. We use it to communicate with others and with ourselves. We tell ourselves both helpful things (such as Stoic precepts you say to yourself, which we've been encouraging throughout the book) and unhelpful things (including putting yourself down or dwelling on things you can't change). By limiting frivolous conversation, you will be able to interact more meaningfully with those around you and build stronger social bonds in the process. And cutting down on shallow internal chatter clears the way for more significant internal conversations about what really matters in life.

Weekly Review

How did your practice go this week? If it was hard to remember when and how to limit your speech, take some time now to think about why. Did you see any expected or unexpected benefits in limiting your speech? Write some (nonfrivolous!) thoughts about how this exercise worked for you in the space below.

_____

_____

_____

_____

If this is an exercise you'd like to come back to in the future, check the box: ☐

Choose your company well

It can be hard to resist going along with the crowd. Sometimes following the crowd can be fun, as when joining in on the excitement of cheering for the home team in sporting events. Sometimes it can be useful, as you might push yourself harder in an exercise class. But it's often problematic. Alex considers himself relatively introverted and reserved, but when he hangs out with some of his old friends, he finds himself acting much more aggressively and boisterously than usual. He often insults people, once even narrowly avoiding a fistfight. As you'll see this week, the Stoics were well aware of others' ability to influence our own thoughts and behaviors and held fast to the old saying: "You are the company you keep."

> " Refuse the entertainments of strangers and the vulgar. But if occasion arise to accept them, then strain every nerve to avoid lapsing into the state of the vulgar. For know that, if your comrade have a stain on him, he that associates with him must needs share the stain, even though he be clean in himself."
>
> *Epictetus*, Enchiridion, *33.6*

E pictetus may sound insufferably snobbish and elitist, but he is essentially giving you the same advice that your mom likely did when you were growing up: Be careful who you associate with. Seek people who are better than you, so you can learn from them; avoid those whose character and habits will drag you down. It's important to note that you should not feel superior to others because you are a Stoic. On the contrary, precisely because you are a Stoic you recognize that you are flawed and that you need to avoid temptations and seek help to improve.

Friendship and companionship are serious business for the Stoics. The whole idea of "friends" on social networks, especially those you don't know personally, or don't know well, is an oxymoron from a Stoic perspective. That said, you may wonder about a potential paradox lurking in Epictetus's advice: If we all put this into practice, wouldn't our "better" friends also avoid our company? But we don't need to go that far. It isn't as though we should (or even could) rank everyone on a simple scale of virtue, then pick those who score higher and hang out with them exclusively. What Epictetus is getting at here is the far more commonsensical idea that some companionships are mutually rewarding, others are mutually destructive, and some don't go anywhere (these are also to be avoided).

Once you start internalizing Epictetus's perspective on friendships, you will begin to see consequences in your social life and on your broader outlook in general. Just as you began to wonder during last week's exercise whether particular conversations were really worth having, you will now begin to ponder your choice of friends and acquaintances. Which ones are mutually beneficial, and which might you want to reconsider? Your time is limited; you'd better make the best of it.

What to Do

Dive right in by taking a few minutes to think about two or three people of the mutually destructive variety whom you see often. Think about those who may reinforce your negative habits or moods, or situations in which you're bound to encounter these people. What negative thoughts and behaviors do they promote? Write them down.

_____

_____

_____

_____

_____

_____

_____

_____

Now that you've identified possible negative influences, your goal for this week is to come up with an action plan, based on Epictetus's advice, to reduce the impact of those influences. As Epictetus mentions, there are two ways to go about this: either by avoiding "the vulgar" or by trying extra hard to not indulge in these behaviors, moods, or ways of thinking if you do encounter these people. After all, not all poor company in your life can—or should—be avoided. They may be family or colleagues, and it would be irresponsible to simply drop them. This exercise is not teaching you to run away from all possible bad influences; instead, the goal is to "not share the stain" of their influence on you.

Use the table on the next page to plan how you will reduce the impact of your circle of negative influences, whether by reducing contact with them or preparing beforehand. Put your plan in action every time you encounter the person over the course of this week.

Who is the negative influence?	What specific behavior, mood, or thought pattern would you like to avoid when with them?	Is it possible to limit exposure to this person over the next week without shirking responsibilities?	If yes, write out a plan for how you will reduce contact with this person. If no, write out an implementation intention to remind yourself to avoid the behavior, mood, or thoughts you mentioned in the second column
Alex's example: Bob	Drinking too much while we watch the game together	Yes, we sometimes watch the game on Saturdays, but it's no big deal if I skip it	I won't mention getting together for the game this Saturday, and if he mentions it, I'll say that I'm not up for it.

One final note: This exercise, like all of Stoicism, is about focusing on yourself. Do not use it as an excuse to judge or berate others; that itself is a negative thought pattern that the Stoics would suggest you avoid.

Studies in behavioral science suggest that the old adage "you are the company you keep" has something to it: People tend to reinforce the behaviors[1] and emotions[2] of those around them. This week you will test this theory for yourself.

Weekly Review

Did you succeed in reducing your exposure to or indulgence in some of the negative influences in your life? If not, what might you have done to be more successful? If yes, how did it impact your mood, behaviors, and thinking patterns? Take a few moments to reflect on your week, and then write about it below.

_____

_____

_____

_____

_____

_____

Check the box if you'd like to work on choosing the company you keep in the future: ☐

Next week we'll continue the theme of working on how other people affect you.

Roll with insults

How much do you care about what other people think of you?
Taking people's opinions of you into account is an important part of
the Discipline of Action. However, we must care in the right way. Emil
takes it personally when people criticize him to his face or when he
hears through the rumor mill that somebody thinks badly of him. It
stings, and it provokes Emil to use a great deal of time and emotional
energy to defend himself. This week, you'll practice a simple technique
to better respond to criticism and rumors.

> " If some one tells you that so and so speaks ill of
> you, do not defend yourself against what he says, but answer,
> 'He did not know my other faults, or he would not have
> mentioned these alone.'"
>
> *Epictetus*, Enchiridion, *33.9*

We're easily offended these days—and our society takes insults seriously, going so far as to enforce strict rules of conduct within organizations and governments, and on university campuses. This would have been rather puzzling to the Stoics, because insults are a perfect example of the dichotomy of control, and provide us with a very good chance to exercise it.

An insult is, in effect, a three-step process: First, someone has to say something to you that is meant to be offensive. Second, you have to take whatever has been said as offensive. Last, you have to react to the insult, since without a reaction the insult falls flat. Eliciting your reaction is precisely what the other person wants; it is the very point of the insult. Let's take the three steps in turn and analyze them from a Stoic perspective.

The first step is clearly not in your control. It is entirely up to the one who insults to decide to say those words. Which brings us to the second step: internalizing what is said to you, which is entirely under your control. There are two possible ways to understand the insult: either your interlocutor *did* mean to insult you, or they meant to convey a criticism but *not* an insult. Which brings us to step three: how you respond. In the scenario of conveying criticism, the reasonable response would be to thank the person for alerting you to a possible mistake—that is, to take what they are saying as constructive criticism. But what about the first case? If what they are saying is in fact incorrect, or obviously not meant constructively, the joke is on them: It's no skin off my nose if you say something about me that does not correspond to the truth; it is you who will look like a fool. Epictetus uses the analogy of a syllogism, a basic type of deductive logical inference: If someone gets a syllogism wrong, it isn't the syllogism that is going to suffer, it's the one who made the reasoning mistake.

So, then, how do we respond, as Stoics, to an insult? Here, too, there are two options. One, which is mentioned by Epictetus elsewhere, is to behave like a rock—that is, do nothing.[1] Try this one out on your own. Pick up an actual rock, and hurl some good and satisfying insults at it. Done? Good. Do you feel like an idiot? Of course you do, because the rock did not react, thus entirely nullifying the very reason for the insult. The second, more sophisticated option, is to do what Epictetus says and engage in good old-fashioned self-deprecating humor: "Oh, you think that's the worst you can say about me? Then you obviously don't know me well." This completely disarms your opponent, and makes them feel like a fool. But you need to be mentally prepared for this sort of reaction; it isn't always easy to pull off in the middle of a heated situation.

What to Do

The exercise for this week may already be clear: Whenever someone tries to insult or offend you, either act as if it didn't happen, or add some self-deprecating humor to the mix! The trick is to remember to do it in the moment. You'll practice using implementation intentions and mental rehearsal.

Use one or both of these techniques every morning for the next week. Before you begin your day, look ahead and see if there may be situations in which you will be insulted. If there are, mentally rehearse not responding, or responding with self-deprecating humor. Run through the scenario a few times. Try to visualize the entire experience as if it were actually happening. If you can't think of any situations in which you are likely to be insulted, take a few moments to generate an implementation intention or two to remember how to respond if someone does insult you. Repeat them to yourself a few times to let them sink in. Write down the scenario(s) in which you may be insulted or the implementation intention to help remember how to respond.

Why Do It

Self-deprecating humor allows you to take yourself less seriously while also acknowledging your faults. Scientific evidence even suggests that self-deprecating humor is correlated with increased well-being and happiness.[2] In addition, by stepping back from the insult you may be able to extract constructive criticism and use the occasion to learn and grow. And not reacting can help you act calmly and rationally, helping further your practice of the Discipline of Action.

Weekly Review

How did your week of rolling with insults go? Did mental rehearsal and setting implementation intentions help you remember how to respond to insults? You may not have found that you've been insulted this week; in that case, do you think this exercise would have been useful if you had been? Write your thoughts about this exercise in the space below.

_____

_____

_____

_____

_____

_____

Check this box if you think this would be a useful exercise to add to your Stoic regimen: ☐

Don't speak about yourself

It's natural to discuss what's going on in your life with people who care about you. Opening up to others not only keeps them informed, but it can also create closeness. However, not all forms and quantities of sharing are created equally. That's what Valerie's friends think, anyway. While they care about what's going on in her life, they find she tends to overshare in person and especially on social media. It's not just the quantity that bothers them, but the fact that Valerie often redirects her online comments back to herself. Many in-person conversations with Valerie also wind up being about her. How much sharing is too much for you? You'll find out for yourself this week with an experiment on cutting down on talking about yourself.

> " In your conversation avoid frequent and disproportionate mention of your own doings or adventures; for other people do not take the same pleasure in hearing what has happened to you as you take in recounting your adventures."
>
> *Epictetus*, Enchiridion, *33.14*

You know the stereotype of the couple who go on vacation and then invite their friends over in order to subject them to an excruciatingly long slideshow featuring every moment of said vacation? Well, that's when there were slides. Now there is social media, and our audience is made of hundreds of "friends," potentially—depending on your privacy settings—the entire world. Oversharing hasn't gotten any less annoying as we've become more efficient by electronic means.

Now ask yourself: Why do you overshare in the first place? Granted we're all excited about updates that we want to share with friends and family, but what causes us to overdo it? Are we engaging in some sort of virtuous activity, perhaps sharing so that people will develop a better understanding of the world? That seems unlikely. More probably we're simply indulging in a bit of narcissism—and narcissism has little, if any, redeeming value.

This narcissism can come at the expense of paying attention to what's going on in other people's lives, as it did in Valerie's case. By focusing on our own lives, we leave little mental energy to concern ourselves about the lives of people we care about. That's a problem according to the commonsense notion of what friendship should be, as well as in terms of the Stoic virtues.

In deciding what and how much to share, which virtues are we calling on? Temperance comes to mind, the notion that we should do things in the right measure—neither too much nor too little—as we previously explored with Musonius Rufus in the context of eating (see Week 11, pages 77–79). But speaking less about yourself also exercises the virtue of justice: By using less mental energy to focus on our own exploits, we free up space to care more about other people. When thinking about our public persona, then, we can act in a similar manner and exercise moderation.

You're likely already thinking about ways in which you overshare—whether updates about your family or relationships, photos from your recent vacation, or details about your day at work. Take some time to explore if and how you overshare in the space below.

_____

_____

_____

_____

_____

Looking at what you wrote, identify any areas, large or small, that you talk about often. If you haven't identified any areas, take a few more minutes to think about it.

Next, come up with your own plan to reduce the amount you talk about yourself and your accomplishments over the next week, and write it in the space below. How you do this depends on when and where you tend to overshare. If you find you post a lot about yourself on social media, perhaps you can spend the week only posting positive feedback on others' posts, or refrain from social media entirely. Or if you find yourself immediately telling your significant other about your day as soon as you come home from work, you can resolve to ask them about their day first, and only tell them about yours if they ask. Implementation intentions can be useful here by helping you come up with an alternative behavior to talking about yourself. For example, "If I feel the urge to share my vacation pictures on social media, I'll navigate to a friend's feed and read their posts instead."

_____

_____

_____

_____

To remember your plan, revisit the intentions you wrote on the previous page each morning. Alternatively, set a reminder to refresh your memory during the day. If that sounds useful, set the reminder right now.

At the beginning of this chapter, Epictetus directly mentions one reason for speaking less about yourself and your activities: to not bore others. Remember, the Discipline of Action is ultimately about acting well, and pushing details of your life on people who may not be interested is a prime case of acting poorly. Speaking less about yourself has another important upside that is a major theme in the Disciple of Action: You clear the way for focusing more on others. This goal will come up again later on.

Weekly Review

Now that you have spent a week speaking less about yourself, how did it go? Was it difficult or easy? Did you notice any benefits from it? Take some time to write out your thoughts about this exercise below.

_____

_____

_____

_____

_____

Finally, check the box if you think this exercise was useful: ☐

Premeditate on encountering difficult people

We occasionally encounter people who are frustrating and difficult to deal with. This gets in the way of not only our own peace of mind, but also our ability to work well with and be kind to others. Mia has experienced this firsthand. Her sales job means she constantly has to communicate with current and potential clients, as well as collaborate with coworkers. She gets along with some of them fine, but many of them can be . . . difficult, to put it mildly. When someone raises her hackles, it can cost Mia both social capital and commissions. The Stoics used *premeditatio malorum* (premeditation of adversity), which you practiced in Week 6 (pages 45–52), to help work through dealing with others. Their view of the world helped them act with a sense of kindness and justice as well. But how did they put their theory into practice?

> " When you wake, say to yourself: 'Today I shall encounter meddling, ingratitude, violence, cunning, jealousy, self-seeking; all of them the results of men not knowing what is good and what is evil. But seeing that I have beheld the nature and nobility of good, and the nature and meanness of evil, and the nature of the sinner, who is my brother, participating not indeed in the same flesh and blood, but in the same mind and partnership with the divine, I cannot be injured by any of them; for no man can involve me in what demeans. Neither can I be angry with my brother, or quarrel with him; for we are made for cooperation, like the feet,

> the hands, the eyelids, the upper and the lower rows of teeth. To thwart one another is contrary to nature; and one form of thwarting is resentment and estrangement.'"
>
> *Marcus Aurelius, Meditations, 2.1*

This is one of our favorite pieces of advice from Marcus, and there is much to unpack. To begin with, notice that the emperor-philosopher is simply reminding himself of a fact of life: Some people are meddlers, ingrates, violent, cunning, jealous, and selfish. This is just the way things are, and to wish otherwise is to yearn for a fig in wintertime (to use one of Epictetus's metaphors).[1] Facing the facts instead of indulging in wishful thinking better prepares us for what is to come and how to handle it.

Marcus then reflects that he has developed a better understanding of the nature of good and evil, and in particular that he knows he cannot be injured by someone else's words or behaviors. This will sound strange to a non-Stoic, but by now it should be a familiar concept, as it is also the focus of the Discipline of Desire: The only things that are truly good and evil are the ones we control, that is, our own judgments, values, and decisions. Other people's judgments, values, and decisions are not under our control, so they are preferred (when they favor us) or dispreferred (when they disfavor us) indifferents. By truly internalizing this concept we cannot be hurt by what others say or do, because it is our decision to become involved or not in "what demeans."

Likewise, it is unnatural to fight with others. This concept is also rooted in the Stoic ideas of cosmopolitanism and living according to (human) nature. What sort of beings are we? Highly social, and capable of reason. It follows that we are made (by natural selection, we would say today) to cooperate, because that's the only way we survive and thrive. It also follows that our ability to reason reveals this truth and suggests that the best course of action is to help our brothers and sisters instead of quarreling with them.

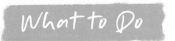

This week, you'll practice doing exactly what Marcus was doing when he wrote the advice that started this chapter. Each morning, take a few moments to remind yourself that you may meet difficult people, but that you will do your best not to be angry or frustrated with them, and instead work with them.

Every morning, before you start your day, write out your own premeditation on encountering difficult people in the space below and on the next page. Reading Marcus's words for the first few mornings may be a useful way to start. Writing out these concepts in your own words will help further ingrain them. If you get stuck, try incorporating in your own writing these three ingredients that Marcus used to remind himself of how to work with difficult people:

- A premeditation to remind you that you will likely encounter frustrating people—this helps take the sting of surprise out of such occurrence.

- A reminder that they are doing what they think is right and that you are trying to improve yourself by focusing only on what's in your control.

- Some reasons you'll be better off if you try to work with other people—this part of the recipe provides motivation to work with difficult people, that is, in order to cultivate your own prosocial tendencies.

If you choose to read Marcus's passage instead of writing for the first couple of days, make a brief note that you did so.

Monday

Tuesday

Wednesday

Thursday

Friday

Saturday

Why Do It

This exercise marks a turning point in your practice of the Discipline of Action. The exercises for the past several weeks have primarily focused on the first part of the discipline according to Epictetus: to "act according to order, to reason, and not carelessly." Starting with this exercise, we've shifted the focus to becoming a better, more prosocial person or, in Epictetus's words, "not to be free from affects like a statue, but . . . to maintain the relations natural and acquired."[2] So far, we've worked on controlling our actions as a result of strong emotions with the Discipline of Desire, and we've practiced acting more thoughtfully and less out of habit with the first part of the Discipline of Action. These two phases have set the stage for this next step: to become a better person.

Weekly Review

How did your premeditation on other people go this week? Did you find that it helped you act and feel calmer around people who would have frustrated you in the past? If not, is there anything you could have done to make your practice more effective? Take some time to reflect on your experience over the past week, and write in the space below.

_____

_____

_____

_____

_____

If you found this exercise useful, and would like to add it to your Stoic toolbox, check the box: ☐

Deal virtuously with frustrating people

The way we view other people's actions can affect how we feel and act toward them. Linh found this out when she learned why her usually reliable coworker Seth kept dropping the ball on a shared project, leaving Linh with most of the work. When Linh angrily confronted her colleague about slacking off, she learned that Seth was dealing with his mother's Alzheimer's disease, which had progressed to a point where his mother could no longer care for herself, and Seth was left as the main caregiver. This piece of information instantly transformed Linh's anger to compassion. What kind of Stoic practice could help this paradigm shift happen more frequently, especially those who we initially find frustrating?

> " First. My relation towards men. We are made for one another. . . .
>
> Second. What are men like in board, in bed, and so on? Above all, what principles do they hold binding? And how far does pride enter into their actual conduct?
>
> Third. If others are doing right, you have no call to feel sore; if wrong, it is not willful, but comes of ignorance.
>
> Fourth. You are like others, and often do wrong yourself. Even if you abstain from some forms of wrong, all the same you have the bent for wrongdoing, though cowardice, or desire for popularity, or some other low motive keeps you from wrong of the same kind.

Fifth. You cannot even be sure if they are doing wrong; for many actions depend upon some secondary end. In short, one has much to learn, before one can make sure and certain about another's action.

Sixth. When sorely provoked and out of patience, remember that man's life is but for a moment; a little while, and we all lie stretched in death.

Seventh. Men's actions—resting with them and their Inner Selves—cannot agitate us, but our own views regarding them. Get rid of these, let judgment forego its indignation, and therewith anger departs.

Eighth. How much more unconscionable are our anger and vexation at the acts, than the acts which make us angry and vexed!

Ninth. Kindness is invincible if only it is honest, not fawning or insincere. What can the most aggressive do, if you keep persistently kind, and as occasion offers gently remonstrate, and seize the moment when he is bent on mischief, for trying quietly to convert him to a better frame of mind. . . . Then point him gently to the general law of things . . . but avoid any touch of irony or fault finding, and be affectionate and conciliatory in tone; not in schoolmaster style, or to show off before others, but quietly in his own ear, even if others are standing by.

Bear these nine heads in mind, gifts as it were of the nine Muses. While you still live, before it is too late, begin to be a man! Be on your guard against flattering as well as against petulance; both come of self-seeking, and both do harm. . . . Anger, like grief, is a mark of weakness; both mean being wounded, and wincing.

Tenth and lastly—a gift, so please you, from Apollo, leader of the Choir. Not to expect the worthless to do wrong is idiocy; it is asking an impossibility. To allow them to wrong others, and to claim exemption for yourself, is graceless and tyrannical."

Marcus Aurelius, Meditations, 11.18

This is a long list of advice but, we think, entirely worth reflecting on as we enter a new phase in Stoic thinking. Marcus is reminding himself of a number of crucial Stoic guidelines that, if consistently applied, will make life not only more serene, but also more just. It's likely that people frequently irritated Marcus, as emperor, for all sorts of reasons. Over time, he would have accumulated a number of prompts to return to every time he found himself in a similar aggravating situation. Let's take a closer look at each piece of advice, since these will all be helpful in dealing with our own frustrations.

1. We are all members of the human population, here to help each other.

2. Ask yourself why people do what they do, especially when they do wrong. Understanding their motivations goes a long way.

3. Nobody does wrong on purpose; no one wishes to be considered a bad person. People make mistakes, sometimes horrible ones, but they think they are doing right.

4. Don't feel superior to others; you are just as fallible as they are.

5. Remember that you often don't have sufficient knowledge of other people's motivations or situations, so abstain from judgment.

6. Keep in mind that you are mortal, and that human life is brief. Whatever bothers you, it will not last long.

7. What causes us to lose serenity is not what other people do, but our opinions of what they do, and our opinions are within our power.

8. Often, by being sore about things, we cause more damage to ourselves than those things caused damage to us.

9. Do your best to correct others, but gently and without irony, and for the right reason, not just to show off.

10. Don't expect people not to do wrong, because that is foolish. But do not allow them to hurt others, if it is in your power to stop them, because that's your duty as a human being.

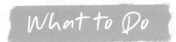

What to Do

Marcus has suggested ten different principles to remind yourself whenever you encounter frustrating people. Some of these ideas may resonate with you more than others. Review Marcus's suggestions, select up to three of them that resonate the most with you, and note them below.

_____

_____

_____

This week we will ingrain these concepts by practicing them daily, either by explicitly reminding ourselves of them when encountering a frustrating person, or by journaling about them at night. If you're ambitious, try both!

Now take some time to write out some implementation intentions that will help you in the moment. Formulate what you'll quietly say to yourself when encountering frustrating people throughout the day, and write them in the space below.

_____

_____

_____

Each night, try to apply the principles that most resonate with you to the frustrations you encountered earlier in your day by journaling about them in the space below and on the next page.

Monday _____

_____

_____

_____

Tuesday

_____

Wednesday

_____

Thursday

_____

Friday

_____

Saturday

_____

Why Do It

The Stoics believed that humans flourished best when they worked together, since we are by nature social creatures. However, this is easy to forget. When it does slip from our minds, we can get easily frustrated with certain people. The Stoics also held that our frustration isn't an objective fact of the world; there's really no such thing as a "frustrating person." Instead, there are people who we tend to get frustrated with, and the processes that lead to our frustration are all in our own mind. The goal of this week's exercise is to internalize these Stoic principles, which will allow you to better interact with those around you. By holding these perspectives close at hand, you put yourself on the road to becoming a better person.

Weekly Review

Did you find applying these precepts helpful during your practice this week? How well did you remember to apply your chosen principles? If you didn't remember, is there anything you could have done differently? If you did, how did you find your emotions and reactions change in response to recalling and applying these principles, if at all? Take some time to reflect on your practice this past week in the space below.

_____

_____

_____

_____

If you found this exercise useful in working with other people and maintaining your composure, check the box: ☐

Turn difficulties into opportunities

If our emotional responses were directly caused by specific external circumstances, then we'd expect everyone to react the same way to any given problem. But that's not what we see. Consider Giovanni, who recently came out of a tough divorce. Some of his friends have also been through something similar, and though they all feel a great sense of pain and bitterness about their circumstances, Giovanni simply doesn't. Instead, Giovanni talks about what role he played in the divorce, what he has learned about himself in the process, and how to make himself better as a result. Stoicism can help us practice the attitude that seems to come naturally to people like Giovanni. This week, we'll focus on one such technique.

> We see athletes, who study only their bodily strength, engage in contests with the strongest of men, and insist that those who train them for the arena should put out their whole strength when practicing with them. They endure blows and maltreatment, and if they cannot find any single person who is their match, they engage with several at once. Their strength and courage droop without an antagonist; they can only prove how great and how mighty [they are] by proving how much they can endure. You should know that good men ought to act in

> like manner, so as not to fear troubles and difficulties, nor to lament their hard fate, to take in good part whatever befalls them, and force it to become a blessing to them. It does not matter what you bear, but how you bear it."
>
> *Seneca*, On Providence, 2

The Stoics often used analogies to illustrate their philosophical points, and one of their favorites was that of the gym. It is perhaps no coincidence that two of the most famous schools of philosophy in antiquity, Plato's Academy and Aristotle's Lyceum, were both housed in old gymnasia. Here Seneca exploits the metaphor elegantly, as usual, by reminding us that serious athletes—those who want to become better and more competitive—do not skirt challenges; they embrace them, seeking the strongest opponents for their training, and sometimes even more than one opponent at a time. Indeed, they are invigorated by the challenges they face.

So, too, for us in life. Every circumstance we experience is an opportunity to test and improve our virtue—from the minor inconveniences in life, which we can train ourselves to bear with no irritation, to significant obstacles such as divorce. The idea isn't to go through life with a stiff upper lip, as the incorrect stereotype of Stoics goes. Rather, we learn from our experiences, recognizing the part we may have played in their occurrence, and steering ourselves to do better the next time around.

Stoics do not "lament their hard fate," as Seneca puts it. After all, lamenting something we can no longer change, something that is firmly outside of our control, does us no good. Why add self-inflicted misery to whatever problem we are already facing or trying to recover from?

It's also important to focus on attitude here. This lesson is about more than just learning from what happens to us and enduring what needs to be endured. By way of the gym analogy, Seneca is prompting us to *look forward* to the challenges of life. If tackled with the right mindset, our challenges make us into better people. As Seneca puts it on another occasion, every ship pilot is good when the waters are calm, but it is the storm that both tests and improves his skills.[1] And what is the fun in always navigating flat waters?

What to Do

This week, your goal is to actually *look forward* to challenges that present themselves, by reframing them. Instead of seeing a challenge as just a weight to bear or an obstacle to get around, you will work on psyching yourself up to tackle them.

The question of how to reframe challenges is a highly personal one. What may get one person psyched up for a challenge may do nothing for someone else. So we think it's best if you attempt to come up with your own ways to reframe challenges. The goal is to find a way to view the situation that allows you to get you excited to face the challenge, or, at the very least, to dread the situation less. This can be done using rational and emotive approaches.

Rational

Rational ways to reframe allow you to find the benefit of the challenge no matter how it may turn out. Here are a couple of rational strategies you could employ over the course of the week.

- Think about how you can grow from facing a challenging situation, regardless of how it turns out. Imagine if the best-case scenario happens; how can that make you a better person? Importantly, also imagine if the worst-case scenario occurs. In what way could this supposedly bad outcome improve your character?

- Consider why you are tackling the challenge in the first place. Why bother doing it at all? If there's benefit by facing the challenge, this can encourage you to endure it.

Emotive

Emotive exercises can also help you face challenges by psyching you up and are highly personal. A common one is finding encouraging words to tell yourself that rouse you to face the challenge ahead. Emotive strategies can provide you with the emotional energy that purely rational strategies may not. One common expression that can be used is "No pain, no gain!" You can also try Seneca's phrase: "It doesn't matter what you bear, but how you bear it."

What ultimately works for you will require some thought as well as experimentation. Perhaps a mix of emotive and rational strategies could work. Or perhaps just purely rational or emotive approaches alone will be enough. Take a few moments to brainstorm in the space below some ways to reframe your challenges that you think could work for you.

Next, think about your week ahead. Are you dreading any particular challenges? Write about it in the space below. Then review your brainstorm above, and try to match the techniques you think will work best to each challenge you listed below. Also feel free to formulate an implementation intention to remind yourself to reframe your challenges when the opportunity presents itself.

We hope you're pumped to tackle the challenges you'll face in the upcoming week. Go forth and conquer!

Why Do It

The purpose of this exercise is to help you recognize an important Stoic lesson: Hardship presents opportunities to help you become a better person—and it's possible to get excited about these opportunities with practice. Virtue is the gift that keeps on giving: No matter what's going on in your life, you'll be better off if you have it. That in itself is an exciting prospect.

Weekly Review

Were you successful in psyching yourself up to face challenges over the course of the week? Did you learn to see the upsides of challenges, no matter how they turned out? Which type of techniques worked best: rational, emotive, or both? Write about your experience with this week's exercise in the space below.

_____

_____

_____

_____

_____

If you found this exercise helpful, check this box: ☐

This week you've focused on reshaping your thoughts and feelings about difficulties. Next week you'll focus on behavior.

Act the opposite of anger

When we're angry, we may think that venting will help, partly because it often feels good to vent. This is exactly why Kofi started venting his anger—after a lifetime of keeping his feelings bottled up, releasing them felt good. But it had a nasty side effect, as with many things that can feel good: He started venting anger more and more, which led to strained relationships, in turn leading to more venting, creating a vicious cycle. Modern psychology and the ancient Stoics have similar explanations for why this vicious cycle occurs, and the Stoics offer several methods for countering it. This week, you'll be exploring one of those techniques.

> " Fight hard with yourself and if you cannot conquer anger, do not let it conquer you: You have begun to get the better of it if it does not show itself, if it is not given vent. Let us conceal its symptoms, and as far as possible keep it secret and hidden. It will give us great trouble to do this, for it is eager to burst forth, to kindle our eyes and to transform our face. But if we allow it to show itself in our outward appearance, it is our master. Let it rather be locked in the innermost recesses of our breast, and be borne by us, not bear us. Nay, let us replace all its symptoms by their opposites; let us make our countenance more composed than usual, our voice milder, our step slower. Our inward thoughts gradually become influenced by our outward demeanor."
>
> *Seneca,* On Anger, *3.13*

nger, Seneca famously said, is temporary madness. You can't reason with it. The popular idea—suggested by Aristotle—that "a bit" of anger is actually a good thing is nonsense to the Stoics. Once you're angry, reason has gone out to lunch, and you are liable to do things that you will regret—even if the anger was triggered by a just cause. Indeed, according to Dartmouth classics professor Margaret Graver,[1] Seneca describes three phases of anger, which are also recognized by the American Psychological Association (APA).[2]

The first phase is prereflective; that is, it occurs without conscious thought on our part and is inevitable. It takes place when we feel the sudden rise of a strong emotion and the need to retaliate with vehemence against whatever triggered the emotion. The second phase is cognitive: We briefly reflect on what is happening and recognize it as anger. We then rapidly review and judge its cause. The third phase takes place when we have given assent—as the Stoics would say—to the sensation. We now think that our anger is perfectly justified and let go of rational control, blindly following wherever the rage leads us. Seneca warns us, and the APA agrees, that the moment to act is at the beginning of the second phase. If we wait too long, all possibility of control is lost, and we have to hope that we won't do something we can't fix or that we'll regret.

How, exactly, are we supposed to act in order to deal with anger and preclude the possibility that it will take over our faculties? In *On Anger*, Seneca lists a series of strategies, many of which you've already explored:

- Check anger as soon as you feel its symptoms (phase I); don't wait, or it will get out of control (phase III).

- Engage in cognitive distancing, what Seneca calls "delaying" your response: Go for a walk, slowly recite the letters of the alphabet, or take a series of deep breaths.

- Associate with serene people and avoid irritable or angry ones (see Week 21, pages 133–34).

- Deploy self-deprecating humor to deescalate anger (see Week 22, pages 138–40).

- Engage in preemptive meditation and anticipate situations that may trigger anger (see Week 6, pages 42–44, and Week 18, pages 119–20).

- Play a musical instrument or purposefully engage in whatever activity relaxes your mind.
- Seek environments with pleasing colors.
- Don't engage in discussions when you are tired, thirsty, or hungry.
- Change your body to change your mind: Deliberately slow your steps or lower the tone of your voice.

Of course, none of the above justifies inaction in the face of injustice. This week we'll focus on how to be in control of your actions when you *do* react, so that the reaction is both justified (recall the virtue of justice) and in reasonable proportion (the virtue of temperance).

What to Do

As you can see, there are many ways to approach anger. This week's exercise will focus on the final strategy explored by Seneca: changing your behavior. The way to do this is by mimicking a calm demeanor whenever you feel anger building.

To make things easier, we suggest that you first think a little bit about how to implement some of Seneca's advice about behavioral change; such as taking some time to relax, or avoiding socializing when you're hungry, tired, or thirsty. Brainstorm some ideas below of what reliably relaxes and refreshes your mind that you can easily incorporate into your daily routine.

_____

_____

_____

_____

_____

Next, think about your week ahead. In what situations might you find yourself around other people when you may be exhausted or hungry? Plan how you can cope with these sensations in advance, either by postponing the encounters or trying to be well rested and fed before the encounter.

_____

_____

Great! Planning to cope with anger in advance will help reduce your anger levels over the course of the next week. Now let's come up with a plan for how to behave if you notice your anger rising.

First, brainstorm ways to notice when you're getting angry. Think back to when you've been angry before—how did you notice anger rising? Was it a physical tension or a flash of heat? Was it some thought, like cursing? Do you usually get angry in a certain situation or around a certain person?

_____

_____

Next, consider how a calm person would behave in the situations you listed above. Be sure to stick to just their behavior. Imagine what a camera would see if it were filming the person, not their thoughts or feelings. We'll start you off with a few suggestions that Seneca mentioned.

- Their movements would be slow.
- Their speech would be soft.
- Their face would be relaxed.
- _____
- _____
- _____

Now that you've thought about telltale signs of anger, and some ways to behave when you feel anger rising, make an implementation intention or two combining the trigger with how you'd like to behave. For example: "Whenever I start cursing in my head, I'll relax my facial muscles."

Write your own below.

_____

_____

Review your implementation intentions daily for the next week. It may also be helpful to set reminders to relax and eat regularly to avoid being hungry or tired.

Why Do It

While many of us think that "venting" anger by acting on it is useful, scientific evidence suggests that the reverse is true.[3] In fact, there's some evidence to suggest that acting the opposite of anger helps people prone to anger reduce the emotion.[4] A type of therapy called dialectical behavior therapy (DBT) trains people in the "opposite action skill" for a range of emotional issues.[5] The theory is that by acting the opposite of how you feel, you can reduce both the negative outcomes of acting out as well as the emotion itself.

From a Stoic perspective, methods to head off anger allow you to better fulfill your role as a human being: You can be both more rational in the moment and more prosocial.

Weekly Review

Take some time to write about your experience of acting the opposite of anger. Did you find that you were able to relax and not engage with people when you were tired or angry? Did this help prevent or reduce anger?

_____

_____

_____

If you found the exercise useful, check this box: ☐

Put the sage on your shoulder

It can be hard to know how to act without guidance. John could have used some when dealing with teenagers, who, he knew, could be a handful. Growing pains. Rebellion. It's all part of the experience, right? But knowing this hasn't helped John manage his son Brian's recent troubles in school. Brian's falling grades are concerning, but the fight Brian started with the guidance counselor today is beyond the pale. As John considers his son's actions, his astonishment and anger rise. How can Stoicism help John with his anger and guide his reactions to his son's behavior?

> " We can get rid of most sins, if we have a witness who stands near us when we are likely to go wrong. The soul should have someone whom it can respect—one by whose authority it may make even its inner shrine more hallowed. Happy is the man who can make others better, not merely when he is in their company, but even when he is in their thoughts! And happy also is he who can so revere a man as to calm and regulate himself by calling him to mind! One who can so revere another will soon be himself worthy of reverence. Choose therefore a Cato; or, if Cato seems too severe a model, choose some Laelius, a gentler spirit. Choose a master whose life, conversation, and soul-expressing face have satisfied you; picture him always to yourself as your protector or your pattern. For we must indeed have someone according to whom we may regulate our characters; you can never straighten that which is crooked unless you use a ruler."
>
> *Seneca*, Letters to Lucilius, 11.9–10

How do we learn to be more virtuous? According to the Stoics, the same way you get to Carnegie Hall: with practice. Lots of practice. It's all well and good to understand Stoic theory at a conceptual level, as John understands that teenagehood comes with its own unique problems, but it takes real work to actually become wiser and live a more serene life. An effective technique to make the transition between theory and practice is to pick a role model and imagine that they are sitting on your shoulder, watching what you do and giving you some gentle, yet clear, feedback.

Socrates, the ancient philosopher who inspired Stoicism, said that he often heard the voice of a *daimōn*, an entity that kept him from doing wrong—a personification of our modern concept of conscience, if you will. The Stoics took this advice a step further and translated it into a purposeful exercise; as Seneca suggests to his friend Lucilius, choose a suitable role model to help you out. The model sage would help "straighten that which is crooked" (i.e., our own character) by use of a ruler—examples from the life of the model you choose.

A Stoic role model can be a close friend or relative, a stranger whose reputation we know from other people's accounts, or a historical figure. They can be dead or alive, real or imaginary. As an example Seneca mentions Cato the Younger, Julius Caesar's archenemy, who gave his life in order to keep his moral integrity. If that's too exacting a standard, Seneca tells Lucilius, then go for a gentler soul, like Gaius Laelius Sapiens, a friend of the famous Roman general Scipio Aemilianus, to whom the orator and philosopher Cicero had previously written a treatise on friendship. But the Stoics also used legendary figures such as the mythological hero Odysseus or the demigod Heracles as role models and potential "rulers" against whom they could measure their own progress. The idea of conjuring a role model is found in other traditions as well, such as in the modern "What Would Jesus Do?" meme popular among Christians.

What to Do

This week, your goal is to turn to the "sage on your shoulder" each day when you feel that you are likely to go wrong.

The first step is to choose a time at the end of each day when you can practice this exercise. As usual, this can be a specific time or after a regular activity, such as brushing your teeth at night. Write the time at night when you'll do this practice.

_____

Next, choose a time for the following morning when you can continue this practice each day. Write the time in the morning when you'll continue this practice.

_____

Now, here's this week's practice. You can answer these questions in the table provided on the next two pages.

1. Each night, review your day and think about some area where you didn't behave as virtuously as you may have liked. Did you get angry? Perhaps you weren't as courageous as you would have liked? Maybe you overindulged and wished you hadn't? Write out what aspect of your character you'd like to improve upon.

2. Think about someone who would have acted as you should have in a similar situation. This person could be sage-like (e.g., Cato) or someone you admire (though they need not be a saint). They can even be a fictional character. Your model should excel in the aspect you'd like to improve. Perhaps you admire your mother's generosity, or a friend's patience. Write about why you admire that person and how they would behave in the situation that was difficult for you.

3. Each morning, reread what you wrote the previous night, and think about how you can be more like your role model in your day ahead.

	How could my character have been better today?	Who would have behaved and felt as I should have in that situation? How?
Example	Got pretty annoyed when a homeless person approached me asking for money	My sister doesn't always give money to homeless people who ask her, but she treats them with kindness and sympathy, and gives them useful information on where to get help. I'd like to be more like her.
Monday		
Tuesday		
Wednesday		
Thursday		
Friday		

Saturday		

Why Do It

This exercise will encourage you to think about areas where you can improve as a person. When thinking about someone whose behavior you admire, you're actively engaging with a positive role model for your own behavior. By mimicking the admirable, you'll slowly become more admirable yourself with time.

Weekly Review

Was the exercise useful to you? How so? Did you discover anything about yourself or your world? Did you find it useless? How might you tweak your approach to make it easier or more useful in the future? Write your impressions below.

_____

_____

_____

_____

_____

Finally, if you think this exercise is useful, check this box: ☐

Review your actions nightly

Have you ever had trouble falling asleep because you're rehashing something you did earlier that day that you regret? Niamh has. She lost her temper at her husband for not taking care of the dishes yet again. Yes, she'd had a long day, and yes, he does neglect his share of things frequently. But instead of working things out, she turned to insults that clearly hurt him and that she now regrets. Niamh doesn't normally act out like this, and she can't help but berate herself about her loss of composure. Fortunately the Stoics have a method that allows you to look at and learn from, rather than dwell on, your past actions.

> " The spirit ought to be brought up for examination daily. It was the custom of Sextius when the day was over, and he had betaken himself to rest, to inquire of his spirit: 'What bad habit of yours have you cured today? What vice have you checked? In what respect are you better?' Anger will cease, and become more gentle, if it knows that every day it will have to appear before the judgment seat. What can be more admirable than this fashion of discussing the whole of the day's events? How sweet is the sleep that follows this self-examination? How calm, how sound, and careless is it when our spirit has either received praise or reprimand, and when our secret inquisitor and censor has made his report about our morals? I make use of this privilege, and daily plead my cause before myself: When the lamp is taken out of my sight, and my wife, who knows my habit, has ceased to talk, I pass the whole day in review before myself, and repeat all

that I have said and done. I conceal nothing from myself, and omit nothing, for why should I be afraid of any of my shortcomings, when it is in my power to say, 'I pardon you this time; see that you never do that anymore?'"

Seneca, On Anger, 3.36

The evening meditation is one of the most useful Stoic exercises. It is described in some detail by Epictetus in *Discourses III*, 10, and of course one can imagine the whole of Marcus Aurelius's *Meditations* as the output of this practice. It's rather intimidating to take Marcus as your model here—the goal is not to produce the sort of prose that has rightly impressed posterity for almost two millennia. The objective, rather, is to achieve exactly what Seneca describes: the peace of mind that comes from having honestly examined our deeds of the day. We should reflect on what we did, learn from our mistakes, and orient ourselves toward better conduct in the future. This last point should be emphasized; the goal is not to beat yourself up about your past failings, as Seneca specifically mentions—he "pardons" himself, which is in line with modern psychological research emphasizing the importance of self-compassion.[1] But the pardon has a caveat: that he try not to repeat his past moral failings in the future. After all, the past is not in your control (short of inventing a time machine), so being upset by it would go against the dichotomy of control. Rather, the point of reviewing your actions is to learn from your mistakes.

The Epictetian version of the evening meditation suggests that we ask ourselves three specific questions: Where have we gone wrong? What have we done right? What is left, as yet, undone? The goal of the first question is to humbly learn from our mistakes. The purpose of the second is to practice shifting our natural propensity away from erroneous thinking and toward right thinking, by taking time to acknowledge when right thinking has occurred (although note that vanity is not a Stoic virtue).

The third question is future directed, aimed at preparing our minds for the tasks ahead and focusing on what is important as well as on the best way to accomplish it.

Psychologist Maud Purcell summarizes the benefits of what today is known as *journaling*: It clarifies (to yourself) your own thoughts and feelings, it allows you to know yourself better, it reduces stress (especially when writing about negative emotions like anger), it helps you tackle problems more effectively, and it makes it easier to resolve your disagreements with others.[2] Or as the Stoics would put it, journaling makes you a better person, capable of learning and better equipped to deal with challenges and, as a consequence, more serene when facing such challenges.

Interestingly, research by psychologists Philip Ullrich and Susan Lutgendorf explored the effects of journaling in response to stressful events when people focus only on their emotional reactions, as contrasted to when they process emotions only by thinking about them.[3] Their results were clear:

> Writers focusing on cognitions and emotions developed greater awareness of the positive benefits of the stressful event than the other two groups [including a neutral control]. This effect was apparently mediated by greater cognitive processing during writing. Writers focusing on emotions alone reported more severe illness symptoms during the study than those in other conditions. This effect appeared to be mediated by a greater focus on negative emotional expression during writing.[4]

In other words, Stoic meditation, which today we call *cognitive journaling*, turns out to have anticipated modern psychology by a couple of millennia.

What to Do

This week you'll practice guided journaling by following a set of questions—either Seneca's, Epictetus's, or your own. We've reproduced both of the ancient versions, and left space for you to devise your own three questions if you'd prefer.

A tip on writing your own questions: Remember that the goal of the exercise is to focus on your virtue. It can be easy to slip into a project management system ("What's left undone? Well, I need to drop off the dry cleaning!") or performance review ("I've gotten much better at getting my reports in on time"), but that's not the point. Instead, keep in mind ways to improve your character and the four virtues (wisdom, justice, courage, and temperance), both when doing the exercise during the week and if you write your own questions below.

With that out of the way, circle which set of questions you'd like to work with this week, or write your own in the table below.

SENECA'S QUESTIONS	1. What bad habit (i.e., physical action) did you work on today?	2. What vice (i.e., mental action) did you work on?	3. In what respect are you a better person?
EPICTETUS'S QUESTIONS	1. What did you do wrong today?	2. What did you do right today?	3. What should you work on in the future?
YOUR QUESTIONS (OPTIONAL)			

Now that you have your three questions at hand, your goal for this week
is to answer them each night.

Monday

1. _____
2. _____
3. _____

Tuesday

1. _____
2. _____
3. _____

Wednesday

1. _____
2. _____
3. _____

Thursday

1. _____
2. _____
3. _____

Friday

1. _____
2. _____
3. _____

Saturday

1. _____

2. _____

3. _____

Why Do It

Seneca claims that this type of reflective journaling leads to sound sleep and peace of mind. That may sound a little strange. How can meditating on our character flaws put our minds at ease? First, remember that this exercise should be accompanied by self-compassion; your past actions are in the past, and therefore out of your control. You are meditating to improve your character. Second, thinking about past mistakes can help you generate action plans for improvement, which will allow you to mold yourself into the person you'd like to be. Finally, both Epictetus's and Seneca's prompts explicitly encourage acknowledging what you've done well over the course of your day. Take some time to appreciate your decisions—again, not for the sake of vanity, but in order to learn *from yourself*, and to feel that some good has come from your day in the process.

Weekly Review

Did Seneca's claims about sleeping more soundly after this exercise hold true for you this week? Did you discover any additional benefits? Take some time to reflect on your experience journaling the Stoic way.

_____

_____

_____

_____

If you'd like to continue this practice in the future, check the box: ☐

Do whatever political good you can

Whether reading the news or looking around your neighborhood, it's not hard to see many things wrong with the world. Sometimes these problems can *seem* insurmountable. And sometimes they actually are. An assassination attempt didn't stop Malala Yousafzai from continuing her work on education rights, whereas it may easily have stopped others. While we can't all be Malala, we can do what we're able to attempt to make the world around us a little better. This week, you'll take a step or two in that direction.

> "This is what I think ought to be done by virtue and by one who practices virtue: If Fortune gets the upper hand and deprive him of the power of action, let him not straightaway turn his back to the enemy, throw away his arms, and run away seeking for a hiding place, as if there were any place whither Fortune could not pursue him. . . . Even in an oppressed state a wise man can find an opportunity for bringing himself to the front, and that in a prosperous and flourishing one wanton insolence, jealousy, and a thousand other cowardly vices bear sway. We ought therefore to expand or contract ourselves according as the state presents itself to us, or as Fortune offers us opportunities; but in any case we ought to move and not to become frozen still by fear. Nay, he is the best man who, though peril menaces him on every side and arms and chains beset his path, nevertheless neither impairs nor conceals his virtue, for to keep oneself safe does not mean to bury oneself."
>
> *Seneca, On Tranquility of Mind, 4–5.1*

This beautiful passage by Seneca is one of the best examples of Stoic pragmatism. Seneca reminds us that no matter how difficult the circumstances, and how seemingly restricted our sphere of action may be, we can nonetheless find something useful to contribute to society, some way to exercise virtue. This is particularly important in times when we feel that we cannot affect large-scale events, economic and political upheavals, or environmental disasters. A single vote does not (usually) turn an election. Our individual choices in the marketplace do not, by themselves, alter the economy or habits of a nation. Our individual actions are not going to appreciably alter the earth's environment.

We can, however, and ought to—according to the Stoics—make a difference for some people, some of the time. Malala cannot overcome misogyny and bigotry by herself. Indeed, perhaps these are chronic human problems that will never be overcome. But she is making a difference for many people, some of whom she is able to help directly: She donated money she had won as a prize for her activism to help rebuild sixty-five Palestinian schools, and on her eighteenth birthday she opened a school for Syrian refugees in Lebanon. More broadly, she has been an indirect force for positive change, inspiring people to take up her cause of education for young girls, and has become a role model for countless people around the world.

As we know, not everyone can be a Malala, nor do we have to be. That's precisely Seneca's point. So long as we interact with others and are embedded in a social network within which we play an active role (as a colleague, a friend, or a family member), we have the power to make the world a better place. What we need to do now is become aware of the boundaries—"even in an oppressed state," as Seneca says—and search for opportunities available to us. Seneca talks about expanding or contracting ourselves in response to external conditions, meaning we should adapt to the situation: If we can do a lot, we should, but if we can only do a little, that's no excuse for doing nothing. So, reexamine your own life through Seneca's lens, and see where you can act effectively to make the world even a little bit better. It's the virtuous thing to do.

What to Do

You *can* make the world better one step at a time. This week, you'll take one step a day, either on a large project you've already started, or on several small projects you'd like to try out.

Think about what you can do to improve the world around you over the course of the week. Before you do so, here are a few guidelines to keep in mind. First, let's clarify what we mean by "political good" in the title of the chapter. The term "political" comes from the Greek term *polis*, which originally referred to the city-state but grew in meaning over time to encompass all the citizens. The Stoics took the concept even further, claiming that all of humanity forms a community, with the "boundaries of our state reach[ing] as far as the rays of the sun."[1] So when we talk about "political good," we don't necessarily mean voting or contacting your political representatives, although your actions this week could include these. Instead, we mean working for the good of all those around you.

Second, be sure to double-check your intentions in taking action this week. As you plan your actions, ask yourself whether your motive is purely to benefit other people, or whether there are other motives at play, such as signaling your virtue to others or receiving favors in return. If there are other motives at play besides an honest desire to benefit others, you may not want to engage in the action, since it's not for political good alone.

Finally, make sure that the action is doable for you. Don't donate money if you can't afford it. Don't donate time if you'll shirk other responsibilities. It's fine to step out of your comfort zone a little this week, but do not cause yourself harm in the process. After all, you are part of humanity, too!

Now brainstorm ideas in the space on the next page for doing some political good this week. Here are a few suggestions to help you get started.

- Research the most effective charities that are doing the most good, then donate to them.
- On one day, think about your unique talents. The next day, reach out to a charity that may need those talents and ask about volunteering.
- Call your political representative and ask that they tackle a cause that would benefit people as a whole.

- Create an implementation intention to do an act of kindness for a stranger.
- Create a plan to work daily on a large-scale project that you think would make the world an even slightly better place, then take steps to complete it throughout the week.

- _____
- _____
- _____
- _____
- _____
- _____

Do you have at least six ideas (one for each day this week except Sunday)? If so, great! If not, generate additional entries until you have six. Then double-check each idea's doability and that your intentions for acting are altruistic. Place a check mark next to each idea if you think it's achievable for you, and another check mark if it comes from a place of genuine altruism.

You should now have a few entries with two checkmarks next to them. Now, use the table below to plan out one action a day for the next week.

MONDAY ACTION:	
TUESDAY ACTION:	
WEDNESDAY ACTION:	
THURSDAY ACTION:	
FRIDAY ACTION:	
SATURDAY ACTION:	

Revisit the table each morning to remind yourself of what action for political good you will do each day. Come back at night and cross it out when you are done.

Why Do It

While the main goal of this week's exercise is to make the world a little bit better for everyone, it also benefits you. Research indicates that altruistic people tend to have better mental well-being, as long as they don't push themselves beyond their current financial or emotional ability.[2] The Stoics knew what they were talking about: People flourish when they work for one another's benefit, but desires and aversions to external things beyond our control can take a psychological toll. This is exactly why the Discipline of Desire comes before the Discipline of Action—the former clears the way for the latter.

Weekly Review

How did your practice go this week? Did you try to do some political good? How did your actions this week affect your emotional state? Write about your experiences in the space below.

_____

_____

_____

_____

Check this box if you found this exercise useful: ☐

This week you attempted to do some good in the world. Part of Stoic practice, however, is accepting that the results of your actions are not under your complete control. Next week's exercise will help ingrain this concept.

Act with reservation

Sometimes we fail when we try to offer help. This can take a toll on us. Darnell has been politically active, working toward police accountability in his community. If it weren't for his dedication to the issue, he would have quit by now. He's talked to local politicians, organized a local activist group, and published a few op-ed pieces on the subject. But he still hasn't seen significant movement. Though the Stoics realized that much of the world isn't in our complete control, it didn't stop them from trying to improve the world. How do Stoics act for the greater good despite setbacks?

> It was, I imagine, following out this principle that Democritus taught that 'he who would live at peace must not do much business either public or private,' referring of course to unnecessary business. For if there be any necessity for it, we ought to transact not only much but endless business, both public and private; in cases, however, where no solemn duty invites us to act, we had better keep ourselves quiet, for he who does many things often puts himself in Fortune's power, and it is safest not to tempt her often, but always to remember her existence, and never to promise oneself anything on her security. I will set sail unless anything happens to prevent me; I shall be *praetor* [magistrate], if nothing hinders me; my financial operations will succeed, unless anything goes wrong with them. This is why we say that nothing befalls the wise man which he did not expect. We do not make him exempt from the chances of human

life, but from its mistakes, nor does everything happen to him as he wished it would, but as he thought it would. Now his first thought was that his purpose might meet with some resistance, and the pain of disappointed wishes must affect a man's mind less severely if he has not been at all events confident of success."

Seneca, On Tranquility of Mind, 13

S toic philosophy adds a sense of urgency to our lives, of spending our time and resources on things that are important, because life is finite and we don't know when it will be over. Seneca introduces the Stoic idea that we should see to be involved with "necessary" business—that is, with things that matter—that will make this world better for everyone. He advises us to focus on what matters and minimize the number of endeavors we pursue, because Fortuna will sometimes favor us, but at other times go against us. It's better to focus on a smaller number of pursuits and to do our best with them than to scatter our efforts in many directions, each of which will be more haphazard and subject to chance.

The most important message comes in the central section of the quote, where Seneca gives a number of examples of activities to tackle, each followed by what is sometimes referred to as the "reserve clause," which even some modern Stoics who are not inclined to a transcendental view of the world like to express as "fate permitting." "Fate" here is not a divinity, nor the belief in the inevitability of things as we typically understand it in the modern day. The Stoic sense of "fate" is a catchy reminder that we control much less than we think we do. So I will make plans with my friends for dinner, fate permitting. I will go on a trip to Rome, fate permitting. I will volunteer for a political campaign that I hope will succeed, fate permitting.

Even wise people are subject to the vagaries of life. In order to blunt the pain of disappointment, they form reasoned opinions of what might happen and avoid wishful thinking. This ability helps cultivate an attitude of equanimity toward life. Darnell is obligated to do his best to further his political cause, if he truly believes his cause is virtuous. At the same time, he needs to understand the reality of the world and prepare for the most likely outcome. If he is wise and things don't go his way, he'll understand that it happens, and he can accept it and begin to think about what else he can do to make a difference.

What to Do

This week you'll give yourself gentle reminders that your plans may not go as anticipated by using the reserve clause, which is a major Stoic exercise that helps us remember that the results of our actions are not under our complete control. To add a reserve clause to your plans, explicitly remind yourself that a plan you're making could go awry. For example, if you wanted to pick up your kids at 4:00 PM, you would tell yourself: *I hope to pick up the kids at four, as long as nothing stops me.* If you plan to pick up milk at the store, you'd say in your head: *I'll pick up more milk, presuming I can get to the store and they have some.*

Warm up by adding reserve clauses to the following plans.

PLAN	PLAN WITH RESERVE CLAUSE
I'll wake up at 6:00 AM tomorrow.	
I'll meet you at the diner at 8:00 PM.	
I'd like to help him out.	
Time for me to go for a run now.	
I'd like to add reserve clauses to my plans this week.	

Next, generate an implementation intention or two below, to help remind yourself to add a reserve clause to your plans throughout the week.

_____

_____

Why Do It

The goal of the phase of the Discipline of Action you have worked on recently is to be more prosocial by doing more good in the world. However, the results of your actions are not under your complete control, just like other externals. This week's exercise is meant to help take the sting out of when your plans don't go as you wished, so that you are not discouraged in your attempts to become a better person. The reserve clause is a major method Stoics can use to motivate themselves to attempt to change the world for the better, while understanding, at a deep level, that the results may not always pan out as they hope.

Weekly Review

Did you find that using the reserve clause helped you take action and accept when things went awry this week? Write about your experiences with the exercise in the space below. Don't forget that you can use the notebook pages at the back if you need more space.

_____

_____

Finally, check the box if you found this exercise useful: ☐

Now that you've learned a bit about how to cope with plans going awry, let's return to the concept of making the world a better place in the next chapter, by focusing on yourself.

Practice Stoic sympathy stealthily

It's natural to want to share your Stoic practice with others as you begin to see results. After several months of practice, Lewis has experienced the benefits, both for himself and those he interacts with, and has started offering Stoic advice to his friends and coworkers, often unsolicited. Some have found this input helpful; others have decidedly not. Lewis knows that other people's reactions are beyond his control. But regardless, many early Stoics would not agree with Lewis wearing Stoicism on his sleeve. This week, you'll explore why.

> " Try, in your dealings with others, to harm not, in order that you be not harmed. You should rejoice with all in their joys and sympathize with them in their troubles, remembering what you should offer and what you should withhold. And what may you attain by living such a life? Not necessarily freedom from harm at their hands, but at least freedom from deceit. In so far, however, as you are able, take refuge with philosophy: She will cherish you in her bosom, and in her sanctuary you shall be safe, or, at any rate, safer than before. People collide only when they are traveling the same path. But this very philosophy must never be vaunted by you, for philosophy when employed with insolence and arrogance has been perilous to many. Let her strip off your faults, rather than assist you to decry the faults of others. Let her not hold

> aloof from the customs of mankind, nor make it her business to condemn whatever she herself does not do. A man may be wise without parade and without arousing enmity."
>
> **Seneca**, Letters to Lucilius, *103.3–5*

Whenever we discover something exciting that makes a positive difference in our lives, it is natural for us to want to share it with others. Sometimes we share it because we genuinely want to be helpful, and other times because it feels good to brag (the latter is not a Stoic value, incidentally). So if you are finding Stoicism to be helpful, you may feel the urge to "witness," as people say in some religious traditions. And why not? Stoicism is a great tool, and you wish someone would have told you about it years ago!

A philosophy of life, however, must first and foremost be lived. The best way to spread the word about Stoicism is not by talking about it (unless you are a teacher; even Epictetus made an exception in that case), but by acting according to its precepts. Talk is cheap, as they say, but actions speak volumes. If you are really practicing, it will show in your behavior: You will be less prone to anger or impatience, and you will be a better listener, a better friend, and more concerned with others' well-being—whether close by or on the other side of the world. It won't take long for those who know you to notice these changes, at which point they may ask, "Hey, what's going on?" At which time you can reply, "Well, let me tell you about this guy Seneca I've been reading . . ."

As Seneca reminds us, it is far better to embody our philosophy than to merely talk about it, and few people appreciate being told what to do by a zealot. Going around chiding people that "that's not the Stoic thing to do" will fall on deaf ears, and likely turn people off altogether. That would certainly be a pity, as they may indeed benefit from it. So don't go around brandishing Stoicism as a stick to beat others on the head with whenever they are doing something you don't think is virtuous. Keep your own soul in order, so to speak, and let it shine through your practice.

What to Do

You'll be practicing three separate skills this week, though they can be summarized in just two words: sympathize stealthily.

The first skill to practice is sympathy. Whenever you encounter somebody who is experiencing joy or trouble, take a few moments to try to understand where they're coming from. The skills you learned back in Week 4 (pages 34–36) may help you see things from another's perspective.

Once you see their perspective, congratulate them on their successes and sympathize with their failures—but without offering advice, whether it be Stoic or any other kind. The challenge is remembering to sympathize instead of "Stoic-ize." Write an implementation intention in the space below to help you remember.

_____

_____

_____

In the *Enchiridion*, Epictetus offers advice similar to Seneca's, but adds an important caveat, asking his students not to "groan inwardly" when sympathizing with others' pain.[1] Neither Seneca nor Epictetus would advise *empathizing* with others' feelings for reasons we discussed back in Week 3 (pages 25–27). Your goal is to see things from another's perspective—not to feel what they feel—and to listen instead of talk.

Seneca also cautions against using Stoicism to pass judgment on other people. Over the course of the week you may have initial judgmental thoughts about other people concerning their character or behavior. These initial thoughts are outside of your control—to a large extent, they're automatic. However, whether you believe them or not is within your control.

The second skill to practice this week is catching and challenging any judgmental thoughts. Start this process by creating an implementation intention for when you catch yourself in a judgmental thought, for example: *If I catch myself judging someone, I'll say to myself: I don't know all the reasons for their behavior.* If you are at a loss for what to say, see some suggestions from Marcus in Week 25 (pages 151–53). Write an implementation intention below to help you challenge your own judgmental thoughts.

_____

_____

_____

The final skill to practice this week would be especially useful to Lewis: Do your utmost to not mention your Stoic practice, and don't give Stoic advice to anyone this week. Create an implementation intention below to help you remember to practice your Stoicism stealthily when you feel the urge to offer Stoic advice.

_____

_____

_____

As usual, review these implementation intentions each day to refresh your memory if you feel the need, and take a minute or two to mentally rehearse executing each one.

Why Do It

In *A Guide to the Good Life*, modern Stoic William Irvine recommends practicing stealth Stoicism in order to avoid mockery. We recommend stealth Stoicism for another reason: It's easy to fool yourself into thinking that you're practicing Stoicism simply by talking about it and by calling yourself a Stoic. As we mentioned earlier, actions speak louder than words, and right now you are practicing the Discipline of Action, not the Discipline of Talking a Lot About Stoicism.

Practicing stealth Stoicism, challenging judgmental thoughts, and sympathizing all work in concert to help bring the focus to your own thoughts and feelings in order for you to become a more prosocial, virtuous person. These skills shift your focus inward rather than on other people. After all, you have control over your own thoughts and actions, so it's most useful to put your attention there. The world has more than enough ways to judge other people already. It's our hope that Stoicism doesn't get added to that list.

Weekly Review

This week's practice involved three different skills, all working toward the goal of bringing your attention to your own actions, rather than using Stoicism to judge or advise others. Did you find focusing inward challenging? Did you remember to practice these skills? If so, how did it go? Take a few minutes to reflect on your practice this week in the space below.

_____

_____

_____

_____

_____

_____

Check the box if you found stealth Stoic sympathy to be a useful practice: ☐

Next week's exercise will continue the theme of focusing on yourself to help you act more prosocially.

Set up social rules for living

Stoicism is founded on "virtue ethics," which tends to eschew hard-and-fast rules about ethical decisions. Nonetheless, following rules can help make life easier. While not a Stoic, Preecha has been practicing the five precepts of Buddhism. Some Buddhists train in these basic moral rules, which include not taking things that aren't given, not killing, and not lying. These rules have helped Preecha be more mindful of his actions. Before following an instinct to tell a white lie or kill an insect, he now pauses to examine his motive for doing so. This week, you'll explore creating your own moral rules.

> It is the act of a generous spirit to proportion its efforts not to its own strength but to that of human nature, to entertain lofty aims, and to conceive plans that are too vast to be carried into execution even by those who are endowed with gigantic intellects, who appoint for themselves the following rules:
>
> I will look upon death or upon a comedy with the same expression of countenance.
>
> I will submit to labors, however great they may be, supporting the strength of my body by that of my mind.
>
> I will despise riches when I have them as much as when I have them not; if they be elsewhere I will not be more gloomy, if they sparkle around me I will not be more lively than I should otherwise be.
>
> Whether Fortune comes or goes I will take no notice of her.

I will view all lands as though they belong to me, and my own as though they belonged to all mankind . . .

Whatever I may possess, I will neither hoard it greedily nor squander it recklessly. I will think that I have no possessions so real as those which I have given away to deserving people.

I will not reckon benefits by their magnitude or number, or by anything except the value set upon them by the receiver.

I never will consider a gift to be a large one if it be bestowed upon a worthy object.

I will do nothing because of public opinion, but everything because of conscience; whenever I do anything alone by myself I will believe that the eyes of the Roman people are upon me while I do it.

In eating and drinking my object shall be to quench the desires of Nature, not to fill and empty my belly.

I will be agreeable with my friends, gentle and mild to my foes.

I will grant pardon before I am asked for it, and will meet the wishes of honorable men half way.

I will bear in mind that the world is my native city, that its governors are the gods, and that they stand above and around me, criticizing whatever I do or say.

Whenever either Nature demands my breath again, or reason bids me dismiss it, I will quit this life, calling all to witness that I have loved a good conscience, and good pursuits; that no one's freedom, my own least of all, has been impaired through me.

He who sets up these as the rules of his life will soar aloft and strive to make his way to the gods."

Seneca, On the Happy Life, *20*

We often wonder what a good life, a life really worth living, would look like. Here Seneca offers a ready-made, long list of good advice to leading such a life. He needs to maintain an attitude of equanimity toward fortune and misfortune, not just in terms of wealth, but even in the face of death. As a member of a bustling society, Seneca recognizes that he has responsibilities to all other people, even his enemies. He further suggests that the best course is to always act as if others are watching, because the impulse to hide an action is a good indication that you probably shouldn't be doing it in the first place.

None of the long list of guidelines Seneca mentions should be taken as the Stoic equivalent of the Ten Commandments. Stoicism is a type of virtue ethics, not a deontological (rule-based) system. When the Stoics talk of rules, they mean them in the sense of flexible heuristics, not rigid absolutes. Seneca's own rules are not meant to be exhaustive, but are an effective reminder of what he values and why. The Stoics talk about the usefulness of precepts, that is, practical rules to keep handy so that you will be more likely to do the right thing when a given circumstance arises. You've been putting this theory into practice with less formal rules every time you've acted on an implementation intention. These precepts only made sense to the Stoics from within their overall philosophical system, which was based on a small number of axioms (starting assumptions). The rules, or precepts, are easily derived from Stoic axioms. A good example is when Seneca says to eat and drink "to quench the desires of Nature"—not in order to "fill and empty" one's belly: A basic Stoic axiom is the cardinal virtue of temperance, and here that axiom is applied to the specific issue of eating. The precept, then, is that we should eat in right measure for nourishment, and not overindulge.

This is one way in which virtue ethics differs from other approaches to morality. It recognizes that rigid sets of rules, such as the Ten Commandments, are, well, too rigid. There will always be cases where exceptions need to be made. Stoic precepts are meant as useful guidelines, with the ability to be flexible depending on the situation. But they are still embedded in a coherent overall philosophical system.

What to Do

While no one needs to memorize large lists of rules to practice Stoicism, a small list may be helpful. The exercise for this week is to set up a few rules for living with others that you'll try to follow over the course of the week. By the end of the week you'll see whether these rules of living are helpful for you.

In the space below write down some rules. Try no more than three to start so that they are easy to remember. Feel free to try just one to keep things focused. You can borrow from Seneca's plentiful list of rules or derive your own from the Stoic virtues or the dichotomy of control.

- _____

- _____

- _____

Review this list each morning, and take a minute or two to envision a situation where your rules of living would apply. Imagine yourself acting according to those rules.

It may also be useful to review the list each night and see how well you stuck to your rules throughout the day. If you had trouble remembering your rules, think about why that may have been.

Why Do It

As our friend Preecha discovered in his Buddhist practice, clear, easy-to-remember rules can help you pay more attention to your actions as you go about your day, and keep you from behaving mindlessly. Additionally, remembering simple rules can help clarify and encourage you to act in a specific situation, since you've already decided how to act in—and perhaps mentally rehearsed—a similar situation beforehand. These two benefits apply to any type of rule. If you set up rules derived from Stoic principles concerning human nature and the Stoic virtues, Seneca promises yet another benefit: You will excel in shaping your character for the better, allowing you to "soar aloft, and strive to make [your] way to the gods."[1]

Weekly Review

Did setting rules help you pay more attention to your actions throughout the week? Was it easier to decide how to act in certain situations that you would normally have found challenging? Or did this exercise not resonate much with you at all? Write about your experiences with this exercise in the space below.

_____

_____

_____

_____

_____

If you'd like to continue practicing your own rules for living, check the box: ☐

Care about more people (and other beings)

It's natural to care about your own well-being. After all, you're the one who's most aware of your every thought and sensation; you're the one who experiences every itch, every laugh, and every pain. It's also natural to care more about those close to us than about strangers or enemies. This explains Sachi's friends' confusion about her recent behavior. They've noticed that the snarky, sarcastic woman they knew now greets strangers and even enemies with a smile. Sachi's friends don't know that she has been practicing a Buddhist technique known as *metta* meditation, where she attempts to care more for strangers and people she dislikes by radiating kindness toward those people. Surprisingly, the ancient Stoics had a similar practice, which you'll explore this week.

> " Each of us is, as it were, circumscribed by many circles; some of which are less, but others larger, and some comprehend [i.e., include], but others are comprehended [i.e., included], according to the different and unequal habitudes with respect to each other. For the first, indeed, and most proximate circle is that which everyone describes about his own mind as a center, in which circle the body, and whatever is assumed for the sake of the body, are comprehended. For this is nearly the smallest circle, and almost touches the center itself. The second from this, and which is at a greater distance from the center, but comprehends the first circle, is that in which parents,

brothers, wife, and children are arranged. The third circle from the center is that which contains uncles and aunts, grandfathers and grandmothers, and the children of brothers and sisters. After this is the circle which comprehends the remaining relatives. Next to this is that which contains the common people, then that which comprehends those of the same tribe, afterwards that which contains the citizens. And then two other circles follow, one being the circle of those that dwell in the vicinity of the city, and the other, of those of the same province. But the outermost and greatest circle, and which comprehends all the other circles, is that of the whole human race.

These things being thus considered, it is the province of him who strives to conduct himself properly in each of these connections to collect, in a certain respect, the circles, as it were, to one center, and always to endeavor earnestly to transfer himself from the comprehending circles to the several particulars which they comprehend. It pertains, therefore, to the man who is a lover of kindred [to conduct himself in a becoming manner] toward his parents and brothers; also, according to the same analogy, toward the more elderly of his relatives of both sexes, such as grandfathers, uncles and aunts; towards those of the same age with himself, as his cousins; and toward his juniors, as the children of his cousins."

Hierocles, Fragments, How We Ought to Conduct Ourselves

Towards Our Kindred

The Stoics inherited the principle of cosmopolitanism from Socrates, and it became a centerpiece of their philosophy, particularly of the Discipline of Action. The second-century CE Stoic Hierocles summarizes this principle by imagining relations as a series of circles, starting with you and moving outward, to people close to you, to those further away, and eventually encompassing all of humankind. The modern utilitarian philosopher Peter Singer has proposed a similar metaphor, though where Hierocles talks of "collecting" the external circles to bring other people's concerns closer to us, Singer—equivalently—speaks of "expanding" our circle of concern to others.[1] Either way, you get the point.

The Stoics arrived at this concept by way of their doctrine of *oikeiosis*, a word that is difficult to translate into English but is often rendered as "appropriation," as in the appropriation of the welfare of others, making it our concern. It is about becoming concerned with what happens to other people as we are naturally concerned with what happens to ourselves. Oikeiosis is why the central circle is our own—not because we are the center of the universe, but because it is natural for us to care about our own well-being. As we develop morality, it also becomes natural to be concerned with the welfare of those nearest to us, such as our caretakers and siblings. The Stoics thought that once we enter the age of reason (at about seven years old, an approximate threshold supported by modern research on cognitive development[2]) we have the ability to go beyond what comes to us instinctively. As we develop rationality, we can understand that every human being is a member of our society, and that we should be mindful of their well-being, too, extending our concern beyond those who happen to be our relatives by accident of birth. And that is how the process of oikeiosis works: We begin with our natural instincts as social animals, then reason leads us to the progressive appropriation of the welfare of others, and so we should treat everyone justly and fairly.

An argument can be made that modern Stoics could easily add additional circles to the ones listed by Hierocles to include any sentient being capable of suffering. This is what Peter Singer argues in his landmark book *Animal Liberation*; the idea of expanding our concern to animals in this way sparked the animal rights movement.[3] After all, as another utilitarian philosopher (indeed, the founder of that school), Jeremy Bentham rightly put it in his *The Principles of Moral Legislation*, "The question is not 'Can they reason?' nor 'Can they talk?' but 'Can they suffer?'"

What to Do

This week we suggest two exercises, one behavioral and the other meditative. Choose one or both to practice this week. Both have the same goal: to "collect the circles" of caring in your life so that you can care more about people who are less close to you.

Behavioral

Elsewhere in his *Fragments*, Hierocles suggests that we call distant relatives the "names" of closer relatives (e.g., calling cousins "brothers"). The goal of this practice is to treat people whom you perceive as distant from you as someone you care about. We've adapted this advice to apply to your behavior. So, this week, treat someone in an "outer circle" as if they were one level in. This may sound abstract, but don't worry, we'll guide you through it.

Consider the visual diagram of Hierocles's circles below. Notice that the outermost circle contains "all moral patients." This philosophical term means any beings that you feel deserve moral consideration, such as animals.

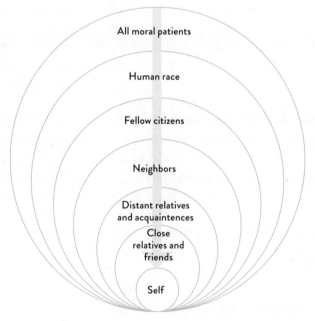

Choose a circle that contains people you'd normally encounter during your day. So, unless you travel frequently, use neighbors, distant relatives and acquaintances, or close relatives and friends. You can also choose all moral patients.

Consider how you treat the people (or other beings) in your chosen circle as compared to the one it encompasses. For example, how do you treat animals, which are moral patients, differently from human beings? Or how do you treat distant relatives in a less caring way than closer relatives? Write a few differences in the space below.

Now that you've thought about the differences in how you treat people you encounter everyday, think about how you can treat the people (or moral patients) in the outer circle more kindly. For example, if you chose animals, you could refrain from eating meat this week. If you chose neighbors, perhaps make an effort to start friendly conversations with them. You can also try changing the way you speak, as Hierocles suggests, by calling friends "brothers" or "sisters," or acquaintances "friends" for the week. Once you have an idea of how to act in a more kindly manner, write it below in the form of an implementation intention.

Revisit this implementation intention daily to remind yourself of how to be more kind.

Meditative

An alternative method we're going to try is a five-to-ten minute meditative exercise adapted from Buddhism, a modification of what Sachi practiced called *metta* meditation. Here's how to do it.

Find a quiet place, close your eyes, and think about a person you really care about, someone very close to you or even yourself. Notice how caring feels in your body. Perhaps it's manifested as a smile, a warm sensation in the chest, or something else entirely.

If you don't feel anything, try saying some simple, kind wishes about the person. For example, "May you be truly happy." Does that thought evoke a feeling in your body? If it does, keep your attention on the feeling. If it doesn't, don't sweat it, and move on.

Next, think of someone more neutral, such as a neighbor you don't know well, the barista at your local coffee shop, or a person you pass often on the street but don't know.

If you feel bodily sensations of caring toward a person you care about, try to hold those same sensations in your attention while thinking about this person who is more neutral. If you don't feel any bodily sensations, wish this person well silently to yourself.

Finally, think about all people (or beings) in the world. Again, if you feel sensations in your body associated with the emotion of caring, hold those feelings in mind while thinking about all beings. If not, wish all beings well silently to yourself in your own words.

Do this meditative practice daily, when you have some quiet time to yourself.

Why Do It

The title of this chapter says it all: Care about more people (or other beings). Actively behaving a little kinder will help you ingrain the habit of caring, and the formal meditation to contract your circles of caring helps develop the feelings of caring.

The type of meditation we suggest this week is also supported by scientific research. *Metta* meditation has been found to reduce intergroup bias[4] as well as to increase positive emotions, compassion, and mindfulness.[5]

Weekly Review

How did your practice go this week? Did you do both exercises? If so, did one work better than the other? What effects, if any, did you find that these exercises had on your caring about others' well-being? Did they help you become more mindful? Write about your experiences this week in the space below.

_____

_____

_____

_____

_____

If you want to return to this exercise in the future, check this box: ☐

We asked about mindfulness this week for a reason. We're approaching the end of our time practicing the Discipline of Action and will be moving on to the Discipline of Assent, which requires quite a bit of mindfulness to practice well. But before we depart our current discipline, there is still one more exercise to tackle that will help you strengthen the mindfulness of your actions even further.

Question every action

Have you ever acted without thinking? If you haven't, you're in a very small minority! Many of our daily actions are rooted in habit, which is often useful, but sometimes not. Ha-joon has recently started practicing mindfulness meditation every day at the suggestion of his therapist, to help him with his compulsive online shopping habit. The first step of mindfulness meditation is to notice that your mind wanders. This doesn't sound like much, but both Stoics and Buddhists agree that mental habits always precede physical ones. Ha-joon can attest that, with practice, noticing when his mind urges him to go to his favorite shopping website opens a small opportunity for him to question his actions and whether they're really the best choice. While the Stoics had a different concept of mindfulness from the Buddhists, there are some striking parallels, which you will start exploring this week.

> " Of every action ask yourself, what does it mean for me? Shall I repent of it? A little while and I am dead, and there is an end of all. Why crave for more, if only the work I am about is worthy of a being intellectual, social-minded, and on a par with God?"
>
> *Marcus Aurelius, Meditations, 8.2*

Mindfulness has very different meanings in different philosophical traditions and practices. In Stoicism it refers to paying attention, as well as arriving at judgments and making choices deliberately. It is the opposite of acting out of habit or, as it were, mindlessly. One of the Stoic mottos, after all, is *hic et nunc*, Latin for "here and now," as in "pay attention to what you are doing, right here, right now" (see Week 11, page 78). This doesn't actually mean that we should pause and deliberate before literally every action, or that habit doesn't have a role to play. Sometimes there's no time to pause, and a quick response is required. The Stoics were great at developing heuristics that could be used to guide their actions in these situations to save from going through a complete analysis every time. The rules themselves, however, are the result of thoughtful questioning, so that we develop proper (mindful) habits, guided by reason.

Think of the difference between a novice and an experienced car driver. The novice has to do things in a very mindful way, paying explicit attention to the dynamically evolving situation both within and outside the car. A mistake could be fatal. The point of practicing is precisely to begin internalizing the many necessary actions and decision procedures so that you become more efficient and able to react rapidly to an unexpected occurrence. Rapidly, yes, but not randomly, since your training was mindful.

This approach is also validated by modern cognitive psychology. In *Thinking Fast and Slow*, Daniel Kahneman summarizes decades of research he conducted along with his colleague Amos Tversky in which they imagine two "systems" of thinking in our brains.[1] System 1 is fast and instinctive (and affected by our emotions), but is also imprecise; system 2 is slow and deliberate (and also more logical). A person could not function well by relying on just system 1 (they would make many rash, irrational decisions) or just system 2 (they would be too slow in response to sudden situations). Stoic training balances the two systems so that what we decide is good becomes automatic. Just like a good, experienced car driver.

Marcus, at the beginning of the chapter, gives us a good outline of the sort of questions we should be asking to generate mindful action. Once we answer them, we then need to ingrain the action into habit across a variety of situations. The basic idea is to ask yourself: What is the meaning of what you are about to do, and is it something you are likely to regret? If so, don't do it. If not, work to make it second nature.

Broadly speaking, the only things that are really worth doing are those that stem from being an intelligent and social animal, which for the Stoics are the quintessential characteristics that define humanity. Commit to habit actions that benefit humanity at large.

What to Do

This week's exercise is spelled out precisely by Marcus, so we have little to add. For every urge to act on a desire (yes, *every*), aim to ask yourself: *Why am I doing this?* and *Will I regret this?*

Marcus's focus in his Meditations is on actions stemming from desires, so ask these questions only when you have an urge to pursue a desire, whether it's small, like taking a shower, or big, like purchasing a home. We suspect you'll find that this is more than enough to keep your mind occupied for the week. To help you remember to ask yourself Marcus's questions, write an implementation intention in the space below.

_____

_____

Note that we said you should *aim* to ask yourself these questions whenever you get an urge to act on a desire. That's because while this exercise is simple, it ain't easy! You will probably miss more urges than you catch. That's fine. Attempt to do the best you can.

One final note: Marcus specifically rebuts the reasons for his desires by reminding himself that death will ultimately separate him from what he's desiring. You can try this if you like, but we suggest not rebutting your desires at this point. Instead, raise the two questions in your mind, but don't intentionally answer them. See where your mind takes you. Do you push the questions aside and do the action anyway? Do you naturally, automatically answer the question? How? How do your urges change over the course of the week? Be curious about the effect of simply asking the questions. Try it, see what happens, and write about your experiences and discoveries each night.

Monday

Tuesday

Wednesday

Thursday

Friday

Saturday

Why Do It

This exercise will help you become more aware of your motives. It also serves as a transition to the Discipline of Assent, which requires constant attention to your impressions about the world. In addition, it serves as a check to see if your desires are prosocial: If you desire something for the welfare of others, you won't come to regret it.

We have incorporated aspects of curiosity into this exercise for a specific reason. Approaching desires with curiosity has been shown to be helpful for coping with urges in a treatment method used for addictive behaviors called *mindfulness-based relapse prevention*.[2] Curiosity also helps enhance mindfulness's ability to reduce defensive responses when people are made to think about their own mortality.[3] Likewise, cultivating a sense of curiosity about your own automatic thoughts and habits will serve you well both during this exercise and the entire Discipline of Assent.

Weekly Review

How did this week's practice go? Did you find yourself catching your impulses more often over the course of the week? What were your reactions to the questions? How did your reactions to the questions affect your actions? Write some reflections about your experience with this exercise in the space below.

_____

_____

_____

Finally, check this box if you thought the exercise was useful: ☐

Before we move on to the Discipline of Assent, move on to the next page to see how you've progressed.

Quiz

Now that you've spent eighteen weeks on the Discipline of Action, it's time to retake the quiz that started this part. Rate how much the following statements describe you as you currently are on a scale of 1 to 10, with 1 meaning it doesn't describe you at all and 10 meaning it describes you perfectly.

I tend to act impulsively, on the basis of my initial urges without questioning them.

DOESN'T
DESCRIBE
ME AT ALL

DESCRIBES ME
PERFECTLY

I shy away from my responsibilities in life.

DOESN'T
DESCRIBE
ME AT ALL

DESCRIBES ME
PERFECTLY

I can be selfish, and don't care much about other people's well-being.

DOESN'T
DESCRIBE
ME AT ALL

DESCRIBES ME
PERFECTLY

Then, once you've rated yourself, look back at your original answers on page 10 and see how much progress you've made. Even if you didn't see as much progress as you would have liked, keep in mind that you have come a long way simply by completing the exercises. You've found which exercises in the Discipline of Action work for you and can now focus on implementing those exercises when you create your personalized Stoic curriculum at the end of this book.

PART III

THE DISCIPLINE OF ASSENT

THE GOAL

"There are three things in which a man ought to exercise himself who would be wise and good. . . . The object of the third [the Discipline of Assent] is that we may not be deceived, and may not judge at random, and generally it is concerned with assent. . . . The third department is appropriate only for those who are already making progress, and is concerned with giving certainty in the very things we have spoken of, so that even in sleep or drunkenness or melancholy no untested impression may come upon us unawares."

Epictetus, Discourses III, 2.1–5

Before you begin your practice of Epictetus's final discipline, the
Discipline of Assent, rate yourself on a scale of 1 to 10 on the following
items. After you complete the exercises in this part, you can answer these
questions again to see how much progress you've made.

I rarely notice what I'm thinking throughout the day.

I'm not very aware of my emotions and urges at any given moment.

I usually take my thoughts and feelings as a given, without stopping to
question them.

Catch and apply the dichotomy of control to initial impressions

The ancient Stoics thought that unhealthy emotions (what they called *passions*) arose because of our incorrect value judgments about certain situations. These emotions are not strictly caused by circumstances, but stem from our opinions *about* those circumstances. This insight came to Vasily naturally while working with his anger through the Discipline of Action. While trying to act the opposite of his anger, he noticed that he started to catch his value judgments before they led to the anger. However, this skill can also be cultivated intentionally. This week, you'll practice catching the thoughts that lead to passions, and attempt to counter them with the dichotomy of control.

> Make it your study then to confront every harsh impression with the words, 'You are but an impression, and not at all what you seem to be.' Then test it by those rules that you possess; and first by this—the chief test of all—'Is it concerned with what is in our power or with what is not in our power?' And if it is concerned with what is not in our power, be ready with the answer that it is nothing to you."
>
> *Epictetus*, Enchiridion, 1.5

Congratulations, you are now an advanced student of Stoicism! But you are not a sage, and in fact, we're sorry to say that the likelihood of your becoming one is pretty slim. Seneca wrote that sages are as rare as the phoenix, the mythical bird that is reborn from its ashes. According to ancient Roman lore, phoenixes come by once every 500 years. Nevertheless, you are in excellent company; the point of Stoicism is not to become perfect, whatever that means, but to improve while simultaneously minimizing the inevitable occasional backslide.

What, then, is the Discipline of Assent? The third discipline will help you move from beginner to advanced *proficiens*, as Seneca says, using the Latin word for "the one who makes progress." Think of it this way: When you learn how to drive a car, you first study the theory of what is and is not to be done. That is, what you should "desire" and "avoid" in order to drive a car well. You learn theory not for its own sake, but because you want to actually drive a real car, on real streets. The thing is, to become a good driver you need to internalize the theory and practice. Through practice, your decisions (and consequent movements) become automatic so that driving becomes effortless and your risk of accident is greatly reduced. This is what the Discipline of Assent will do for you: By paying very careful attention to the same subjects as the first two disciplines, you will gradually internalize Stoic precepts and become, if not quite a sage, a really good proficiens.

This chapter opens with one of our favorite teachings from Epictetus, as it easily lends itself to a quick, practical guideline that the proficiens can keep handy for all situations. Every time you catch yourself making a judgment about some event or person, just stop and say (aloud, if you are alone, or are comfortable doing so in the company of others): "Hold on, you are just an impression, and not necessarily what you seem to be." This forces you to slow down before making decisions or reacting to situations, in a sense just the opposite of that famous commercial slogan, "Just do it." No, *don't* just do it; stop and think about it first.

The occasions to use this approach are endless and quotidian. You may see someone attractive crossing the street and feel a more or less vague sense of lust. Instead of indulging it, ask yourself if it's good for you to think in that way. You'll quickly find that it isn't, because that sort of thought will likely lead you to envy or frustration, or to pursue an affair while you are in a loving and valuable relationship, and so on. Or perhaps you sit down for dinner with friends and are repeatedly hit by the thought that it is good to help yourself to one more serving, and one more drink of the available wine. But it isn't good for you, not really. Now imagine questioning the food and the wine (or your lust from the previous example), and saying to them, "Wait a minute, you are but an impression, and perhaps I should inquire further before giving assent to you."

One last note on Epictetus's conclusion: He doesn't need to be taken literally when he says that if something is outside of your control it is "nothing to you." After all, the Stoics thought that a number of things are preferred indifferents, that is, that you may reasonably want them, though you shouldn't desire them; you shouldn't attach your worth as a person to them. To go back to our earlier examples, you do want a relationship, you want food, and it's okay to want to drink wine. These are pleasurable, or even necessary (the food, at least) things in life. But they are not under your complete control, and they do not make you a better (or worse) person. In this sense they are "nothing to you," meaning that it's fine if you have them and just as fine if you don't, in terms of your progress on the path of virtue.

What to Do

Last week, the final exercise in the Discipline of Action, you questioned and examined your motives to act. In Stoic psychology, the urge to take action arises from assenting (that is, agreeing to) your first impressions about reality and what's appropriate to do in any given situation. Impressions thus precede and are directly related to actions. This week's exercise, your first in the Discipline of Assent, is to take one step back in this causal chain, focusing on the impressions that lead to both action and emotions.

Whenever you encounter a "harsh impression"—something that seems very desirable or very undesirable to you—pause, and say to yourself, "This is just my first impression; it may not be as it appears," or something similar that resonates with you. This may sound familiar, since Epictetus described exactly how this should be done at the beginning of this chapter. In the space below, write an implementation intention to help you remember this first step in catching your impressions. It should spell out how to recognize a harsh impression, and also contain a phrase that resonates with you, that you can say to yourself when encountering the impression.

_____

_____

_____

_____

After you catch the impression, ask yourself whether the object of your desire or aversion lies within your complete control or not. If not, then say to yourself that it's nothing to you, or something similar (e.g., "my character's more important than this," "this isn't really good/bad," etc.). Write another implementation intention to help you remember how to apply the dichotomy of control to your impressions, and what to say to yourself if the impression you are considering is outside of your control.

_____

_____

_____

_____

_____

That's all you'll be doing this week. As with many exercises you will practice in the Discipline of Assent, this is simple, but not easy! You may miss catching many of your initial harsh impressions at first. That's fine. The goal is to improve over time with practice.

Why Do It

In order to work on your judgments, you must first realize what your judgments are. This week's exercise will help you improve your ability to catch your implicit impressions and value judgments in action. The second step, in particular, will help you begin to correct your value judgments of externals at every moment.

You may notice that this exercise is quite similar to the first two exercises you did in Week 1 and Week 2. Just as then, this week you'll be focusing only on what's completely in your control. The difference here is that you will attempt to do so continuously throughout your day for every harsh impression that arises. This detailed focus on the dichotomy of control immediately after impressions arise can lead to significant progress over time, if consistently applied throughout your day.

Weekly Review

How did focusing on catching and countering impressions work for you this week? Did you find that it became easier with time? If not, do you see any way to make the process easier with practice? How did countering your impressions affect your actions and mood? Take some time to write about your experience this week in the space below.

_____

_____

_____

_____

If this exercise worked for you, check the box to remind yourself to add it to your Stoic repertoire: ☐

If you found this week's exercise challenging, don't sweat it. You'll have another chance to work with impressions in next week's exercise.

Catch and examine the judgments underlying your impressions and impulses

If you've been working through this book from the beginning, you're already experienced in many Stoic techniques. But sometimes you may not make as much progress as you'd like, even with consistent practice. Tekanyo has practiced the Disciplines of Desire and Action for a long time. While he's made progress, he knows through his nightly journaling habit that there are still plenty of times when he loses his cool and can't quiet his desire for externals. For the past few months, his practice has felt stagnated. Tekanyo knows that this is to be expected, since the first two disciplines are about progress, not perfection. That's why he has chosen to move on to the Discipline of Assent, which, as you, too, will learn, deals with the same lessons as the first two disciplines, but requires working with them in much greater detail.

> **"** Epictetus urged the need of a sound grammar of assent; and in dealing with the impulses, to take good heed to keep them subject to reservation, unselfish, and in due proportion to their object: always to refrain inclination, and to limit avoidance to things within our own control."
>
> *Marcus Aurelius, Meditations, 11.37*

arcus offers several interesting concepts this week. To begin with, let's look at the idea of a "sound grammar of assent." Here, Marcus highlights Epictetus's insistence on employing logic, one of the three fields of study of the ancient Stoic curriculum, the other two being physics (understanding how the world works) and ethics (figuring out how to best live one's life). Logic is important because it allows us to think through what we do, and why. Properly applied, it helps Tekanyo (and the rest of us) curb his impulses to act. Suppose that one of the things Tekanyo loses his cool about is a long wait at his doctor's office. Then, by using logic, if he feels the stirring of anger arise when waiting, he wouldn't blame himself since he knows (logically) that these initial impressions are beyond his control. What he *does* with such impressions, however, is within his sphere of complete control, and his best aid in deciding how to act is sound logic. With logic, Tekanyo understands that if he questions the presumptions of what's really valuable in life that leads to feelings such as anger, he can cut this passion off at the pass. He also knows that he can take Marcus's advice and check his impulses to act and ensure they satisfy three criteria:

1. They are proportionate to the issue at hand. For example, is waiting a couple of hours really the end of the world?

2. They are prosocial, which yelling at people usually isn't.

3. They are subject to reservation, by keeping our serenity in mind, as we practiced in Week 18 (pages 121–23; see also the very useful "reserve clause" notion in Week 31, page 184).

After logic, Marcus mentions the concept of an "impulse." In Stoic psychology, an impulse is the urge to act that comes from assenting to a proposition on how to act. These propositions are all specifically concerned with how appropriate your action may be in a given situation. Consider, for example, the proposition "it's appropriate to walk now." Assenting to this proposition will result in walking, as Seneca briefly describes in his *Letters to Lucilius*.[1] We first mentioned this idea of impulses back in Week 1 (pages 11–14), which underlies the entire Discipline of Action. The modern scholar Margaret Graver has written extensively about this important aspect of Stoic theory.[2]

Finally, notice that Marcus reminds himself to always "refrain inclination." This phrase is sometimes translated as "refrain from immoderate desire," which in the context of ancient Greek culture essentially means to keep your proclivity for pleasure in check. The idea, again, is not that pleasure is inherently bad (technically, for the Stoics, it's an "indifferent"). Preferring pleasure over pain is perfectly natural, but pleasure carries the danger of our wanting to seek more and more of it, ultimately at the expense of virtue. It is this tendency that we need to keep in check.

What to Do

This week, you'll build on the skill of catching your impressions that you cultivated last week, but will counter those impressions in a different way. Instead of applying the dichotomy of control after catching an impression, you'll examine and question the judgments that underlie them. You'll be adding something to last week's exercise by working with impulses as well. As we described last week, agreeing or assenting to certain types of impressions can lead to the impulse to act. So, not only will this week's exercise tackle your desires and aversions, and consequently your emotions, but it will help you regulate your actions, too.

This may sound abstract, so let's examine this process in more detail, using the example of Tekanyo at the doctor's office, to better understand how to apply the upcoming exercises. In Stoic psychology, this scenario would break down into several steps.

1. Implicit inclinations to pleasure, desire for externals, or aversions to externals, lead to "impressions" about them—that is, automatic thoughts and the initial stirrings of feeling. Since Tekanyo hates waiting and desires fast doctor visits, he is inclined to produce automatic thoughts and feelings in this situation that could lead to full-blown anger.

2. Impressions begin to surface. While Tekanyo is waiting, automatic thoughts and the beginnings of anger arise in his mind. These "impressions," as Marcus conceives them, may include: "I shouldn't have to wait this long," "the office staff is incompetent (and their incompetence is bad)," and so on. Feelings may include anger or annoyance. These automatic thoughts are beyond Tekanyo's complete control.

3. A person can then choose to agree with these automatic thoughts and feelings, reject them, or suspend judgment. If Tekanyo agrees with his impressions, he has "assented" to them. This would lead to full-blown anger. Assent, however, is completely within Tekanyo's control, according to the Stoics.

4. Assenting to impressions about appropriate action leads to acting on the impressions. For example, if the thought (which isn't under his control) that it's appropriate to yell at people who are incompetent or waste his time arises in Tekanyo *and* he assents to it (which is under his control), then he'll go and angrily yell at the office staff. This is the "impulse."

The first part of this week's exercise is to uncover the underlying assumptions about what's really good and bad that lead to passions, using logic. (If you need a refresher on what things the Stoics think are really good and bad, you may want to reread the Introduction, page 1, as well as Week 9, page 64.)

The practice to gain "a sound grammar of assent" is simple: Every time you feel the stirrings of a strong aversion or desire, ask yourself what you are presuming is good or evil in this case. If you discover that you desire or are averse to an external, find reasons that it's not really a good, and remember that you should instead focus on your character.

To help you warm up, imagine yourself in the following situations, and complete the chart on the next page.

Situation	What is presumed to be "good" or "bad" in this case?	What could you say to yourself to counter the impression?
Example: Getting angry at a long wait at the doctor's office	The presumption of others wasting my time (bad)	It's not a waste of time if I work with my impressions, since that matters more. Besides, it's my choice to be here. I can simply walk out. Should I?
Being sad after an injury limits your daily functioning		
Getting a food craving, even though you're not hungry		
Getting anxious about what someone else thinks of you		
Being happy about being praised		

Now that you're warmed up, write an implementation intention or two in the space below to help you remember to work with impressions that could lead to passions.

_____

_____

_____

_____

The second part of this exercise is evaluating whether your impulses to action are appropriate. We've distilled this lesson into the three *P*s (which will help you become a proficiens!). Make sure your impulses to act are:

Properly reserved—Your impulses have a reserve clause added to them, so that you don't cling to your actions necessarily turning out as you plan (as you did in Week 31, pages 185–86)

Prosocial—Your intentions are kind, or at least don't actively aim to harm anyone

Proportionate to the situation at hand—You don't have strong desires or aversions to externals, and you put things in perspective (similar to what you did in Week 3, pages 27–30, and Week 7, pages 55–57).

If your impulse doesn't conform to all three *P*s, correct it so that it does. Writing about your impulses may help you see if they follow the three *P*s and identify areas to work on. If you find that you're unable to act according to the three *P*s in a situation, then try to refrain from acting altogether in the moment. Once you feel more comfortable catching your impulses to act, try doing so in your head on the fly. In the space below, write out an implementation intention to help you remember to subject your impulses to the three *P*s over the course of the week.

_____

_____

_____

_____

Why Do It

There are two reasons for doing this week's exercise: First is to experiment with a different way of working with your impressions to see what works better for you. Second is to expand your practice to include your impulses to act, in addition to your impressions.

Working with impressions that lead to passions was the subject of the Discipline of Desire (Part I), and working with impulses was the topic of the Discipline of Action (Part II). The point of this exercise is to cement the lessons of the first two disciplines. Just as in last week's exercise, you aren't really covering new ground here. You are continuing to subject your impressions and impulses to examination as they arise and constantly. This consistent practice, done as an immediate reaction to impressions and impulses, will lead you to surpass plateaus, as Tekanyo did, and put you on the path to becoming an advanced proficiens—and, in extremely rare cases, a sage. While this practice is simple, it isn't easy, as it requires constant attention to and questioning of your thoughts and impulses. But nobody ever said Stoic practice is easy!

Weekly Review

How did your week of practice go? Did you find ways that it helped ingrain the lessons of the first two disciplines? When working with impressions, did you find that this week's practice of examining underlying value judgments was better or worse for you than framing them in terms of the dichotomy of control, as you did last week? When working with impulses, were you able to check if they followed the three Ps in your head? Write about your experiences this week in the space below.

_____

_____

_____

_____

If you found this exercise useful, check this box and come back to it later: ☐

Now that you've worked with impressions and impulses on a general level, let's move on to next week's exercise, which will narrow your focus to ones that Marcus Aurelius found particularly troublesome.

Observe and counter four moods of the mind

We all have our bad habits. While we think of habits more in terms of physical behaviors, the Stoics also thought there are bad habits of the mind. These can be hard to extinguish, as Maitê has discovered during her Stoic journey. She worked a little on her people-pleasing tendencies during her practice in the Discipline of Desire; however, she still often feels twinges of fear when considering what people think of her. These initial mental movements are grist for the mill when practicing the Discipline of Assent. This week, you'll focus on four moods that Marcus Aurelius himself struggled with.

> " There are four moods to which your Inner Self is liable, against which you must constantly be upon the watch, and suppress them as soon as detected with such reprimands as these: It is a needless fancy; or, It is antisocial; or, It does not come from your heart, and not to speak from one's heart is a moral inconsequence; or, fourthly, you will never forgive yourself, for such a feeling implies subjection and abasement of the diviner element in you to the perishable and less honorable portion, the body and its coarser apprehensions."
>
> *Marcus Aurelius,* Meditations, *11.19*

225

There are four mental movements that pose a recurring challenge to our philosophical progress. These are explicitly listed by Marcus; now let's carefully go through them. First, "it is a needless fancy." You shouldn't dwell on certain things ("fancies") that don't directly relate to your nature as a rational, prosocial human being, such as pondering a delicious gourmet meal, pining after nice clothes, or worrying about something you said to someone years ago. While it isn't necessarily un-Stoic to have nice clothes and good meals—after all, this is a course on Stoicism, not Cynicism—a Stoic wouldn't dwell needlessly on pleasures or pains. If these thoughts do surface in your mind (which you don't have control over), it's a good exercise to pause and reflect on whether thinking about these things is really necessary, and what doing so does to your character little by little.

Second is antisocial behavior. This is a big one for the Stoics, as arguably the entire Discipline of Action is about how to be social, in the sense of helpful to other human beings who are all members of the same global society[1] (see Week 30, page 178, and Week 31, page 183). At a minimum, you should ask yourself whether what you are about to do or say is detrimental to a harmonious social life. Even better, you should consider whether it will be a net positive, however small. For example, one of the common activities in conversation is to gossip, speaking ill of people who are not there. Do you honestly think that's going to improve human relations? Then abstain from it. Give it a try—it's harder than you may think.

Third, does it come from your heart? Meaning: Do you really believe what you are saying or doing? Or are you just saying or doing it out of inertia, because you are bored, or perhaps because you are sheepishly following the example set by other people? Or worse, maybe it is in order to gain a personal advantage by insincerely flattering someone? None of these motives wil be good for you or for others, neither are countless other examples that could be added to this list. You may object that if you really followed this guideline you would act and speak far less than at present. Good. As we've seen in Week 20 (page 129) and Week 23 (page 142), the Stoics often questioned why we need to always be talking anyway.

Finally, don't do things that are contrary to right reason, just because your body has urges that push you in that direction. You should be the one in charge, not your unchecked desires. This isn't a suggestion never to do anything pleasurable (not even the Cynics abstained from food and sex!), but rather a reminder that you don't want to do something you will regret just because you were acting mindlessly. This applies to similar situations as above (lusting after someone even though you are in a committed relationship, eating or drinking too much). As Marcus says, these are four common issues that are likely to slow down our philosophical progress, which is why it's a good idea to be on the lookout for them in the course of our practice.

What to Do

Take a few moments to think about which of the four moods are particularly troublesome for you. We list them briefly below. Circle the one(s) most relevant to your thoughts and impulses.

- Needlessly thinking about unnecessary things
- Antisocial thoughts or impulses
- Insincere thoughts or actions
- Giving in to physical urges

Does one stand out as a major issue for you? If so, focus on that one alone for this week. If not, you can work on more than one, or even on all four. Put a check mark next to the one(s) you want to work with.

This week you'll attempt to catch impressions and impulses involving these particular issues, then counter them with a phrase you will plan to say to yourself that resonates with you. You can use implementation intentions to help plan this out. For example, Maitê, whom we met at the start of this chapter, has people-pleasing tendencies. This indicates that her biggest problem is likely insincere thoughts and actions. So Maitê could use the following implementation intention to help her remember to counter these impressions and impulses over the course of the week: "Whenever I feel the urge to please someone, I'll pause and say to myself: *This is a people-pleasing impulse. I won't act on it.*"

In the space below, come up with your own implementation intentions for the moods you've chosen to counter this week.

_____

_____

_____

_____

You may find it useful to keep a tally for this exercise using an app, notepad, scrap of paper, or the space below if you carry this book with you. Each time you catch the mood and counter it, tally it. This will help you keep track of how aware you are of your thoughts and impulses, as well as how successful you've been at tackling them.

_____

_____

_____

_____

Why Do It

It's fair to conclude that the four moods Marcus mentions were difficult for him to manage, as he focuses on them in his own journal. Though they were specific to his personal challenges, they are common to many people, and so are a good starting point for narrowing the focus of your own practice of the Discipline of Assent to specific pernicious thoughts and impulses, as you attempt to counter them. As you gain experience in catching and examining your own impressions, you may find other moods that are relevant to you that Marcus didn't mention. Consider these four as an excellent place to start.

Weekly Review

Did you find it easier to catch thoughts and impulses when focusing more narrowly on specific moods this week? Did you happen to catch any themes in your own thoughts and actions not covered by Marcus that you would like to work on in the future? If you used a tally, was it helpful? Take a few moments to write your thoughts about this practice in the space below.

_____

_____

_____

_____

Check this box if you'd like to come back to this practice in the future: ☐

The past few weeks have focused on thoughts that pop up automatically in the mind. Next week we'll shift the focus a bit; instead of reacting to thoughts, you'll proactively generate and rehearse some in the hope that they'll become more automatic with practice.

Keep basic Stoic concepts always at hand

We all have ways of speaking to ourselves in our head. The Stoics believed that rehearsing Stoic concepts mentally would help them sink in and arise automatically with time. Georgiana has been practicing by asking herself every time she encounters something external that she initially desires or wants to avoid: *How can this improve my character?* At first she found it difficult to remember, but after some practice the prompt was never far from her mind. This week, you'll start soaking your own mind in Stoic principles.

> " The wise man, indeed, overcomes Fortune by his virtue, but many who profess wisdom are sometimes frightened by the most unsubstantial threats. And at this stage it is a mistake on our part to make the same demands upon the wise man and upon the learner. I still exhort myself to do that which I recommend; but my exhortations are not yet followed. And even if this were the case, I should not have these principles so ready for practice, or so well trained, that they would rush to my assistance in every crisis. Just as wool takes up certain colors at once, while there are others which it will not absorb unless it is soaked and steeped in them many times, so other systems of doctrine can be immediately applied by men's minds after once being accepted; but this system of which I speak, unless it has gone deep and has sunk in for a long time, and has not merely colored but thoroughly permeated the soul, does not fulfil any of its promises.

> The matter can be imparted quickly and in very few words: 'Virtue is the only good; at any rate there is no good without virtue, and virtue itself is situated in our nobler part, that is, the rational part.' And what will this virtue be? A true and never-swerving judgment. For therefrom will spring all mental impulses, and by its agency every external appearance that stirs our impulses will be clarified. It will be in keeping with this judgment to judge all things that have been colored by virtue as goods, and as equal goods."
>
> *Seneca*, Letters to Lucilius, *71.30–33*

t's comforting to notice Seneca's acknowledgment that he is an imperfect practitioner of Stoicism. He admits that behaving according to his own foundational principles still doesn't come automatically to him. He is not yet wise, but rather a student of wisdom, just like the rest of us. Indeed, none of the ancient Stoics professed to be sages, and downright criticized people who did (such as Epicurus, the founder of one of the rival schools).

Seneca then gives a powerful analogy between the varying ways to dye cloth a certain color and similarly "dyeing" our "soul" by way of our thoughts. Some colors are easily absorbed by the cloth and others take time to steep. The notion is that for those colors (or ideas) that take more time, the more we train ourselves to think in that way, or conversely, to stay away from a certain kind of thinking, the easier it becomes for us to think and behave virtuously. There is modern empirical evidence that this approach does, in fact, work, as the entire practice of cognitive behavioral therapy (CBT) is based upon it. A study of 106 meta-analyses (studies comparing the results of many individual studies) by Stefan G. Hofmann and colleagues found that CBT was effective on anxiety disorders, somatoform disorders, bulimia, anger control problems, and general stress.[1]

Importantly, Seneca goes on to concisely tell us which thoughts we should understand and internalize to thoroughly permeate our soul.

He adds that "virtue is the only true good; at any rate there is no good without virtue." It is virtue that directs our actions and makes them good. What people normally think of as "goods," such as money, can actually be used well or poorly, and the thing itself (in this case, money) isn't going to tell you how to use it. Conversely, lack of virtue—that is, vice—does the opposite, turning externals into bad things. In the end, says Seneca, virtue is the ability to arrive at true judgments; we can train ourselves to improve our capacity to do so. According to the Stoics, true judgments can clarify every external appearance ("impression," in Stoic terminology) from which impulses spring (which "stirs our impulses," as Seneca says). This may look familiar to you, as it's another example of the application of Stoic psychological theory that you encountered last week.

What to Do

This week you'll work on understanding and internalizing Stoic principles of your choosing in two ways: through meditating on them daily and by using them as "at-hand phrases" at appropriate times. Seneca mentions three possibilities to start:

- Virtue is the only good.
- There is no good without virtue.
- Virtue itself is situated in our rationality, producing true judgments.

There are many other themes to choose from besides these, which you've encountered throughout your Stoic practice. Here are some other ideas:

- The dichotomy of control.
- Humans do better when they work together.
- Nothing lasts forever.

In the space below, write down Stoic concepts that you'd like to soak your soul in over the coming week. You can choose from these six or any others from throughout the book. We suggest no more than three, so you can truly focus on a small, important set of Stoic ideas.

- _____
- _____
- _____

Meditate daily

The first way you'll attempt to submerge your mind in these ideas is by meditating on them daily. There are many ways to meditate. You can sit down and read them slowly each morning. Or maybe you prefer to journal each night about how you can apply them the next day. In the space below, write how you are going to meditate on the Stoic concepts you chose.

_____

_____

_____

_____

At-hand phrases

Seneca mentions that if you soak your soul in these ideas, they have a better chance of springing to mind automatically when appropriate. The second step in your practice this week will facilitate this process through repeating at-hand phrases. At the beginning of this chapter, Georgiana chose to repeat a question to herself in order to help prompt Stoic impulses to act. In the space below, write out at least one implementation intention to help you remember one of the Stoic ideas you're focusing on this week when in a relevant situation.

_____

_____

_____

Why Do It

Seneca explicitly lists the reasons for soaking your soul in basic Stoic concepts. One reason he gives is so that they'll come to your mind more automatically when needed. This, in turn, allows you to judge the situation correctly. From a Stoic perspective, this means you won't judge externals to be more valuable than using your virtue. This will lead to virtuous actions since, as we described in the past few chapters, and as Seneca stated, impulses to act stem from assenting to some impressions. Using these concepts as at-hand phrases helps this process along and reminds you of what's important in any given moment.

Weekly Review

Now that you've kept some basic Stoic concepts close at hand over the past week, take some time to write about your experience in the space below. Did you find that the Stoic ideas came more easily to mind with rehearsal? Did that affect your actions in turn? Did you find meditating on the ideas more or less useful than repeating them to yourself in appropriate situations?

Check the box if you'd like to return to this practice in the future: ☐

We'll continue to build on the practice of at-hand phrases in the next chapter within the context of pain, discomfort, and illness.

Focus on the mind-body connection

The Discipline of Desire teaches that if we place our desires only on that which we completely control, we'll never be frustrated in our goals. As you may have realized through experience, that's easier said than done. Salaam made progress while practicing this discipline, but he still copes with plenty of desires, mainly concerning physical comfort. Working through the Discipline of Assent, however, he has found quicker progress. Instead of focusing his energy on adjusting his environment to make himself more comfortable, Salaam focused in on his moment-to-moment thoughts about comfort, tackling the root cause of his desires and aversions. This week you, too, will try to cut your desires and aversions off before they turn into full-blown passions.

> " Sickness is a hindrance to the body, but not to the will, unless the will consent. Lameness is a hindrance to the leg, but not to the will. Say this to yourself at each event that happens, for you shall find that though it hinders something else it will not hinder you."
>
> *Epictetus*, Enchiridion, 9

Could it be that Epictetus is assuming a dual nature of mind and body? It appears that he suggests a sharp distinction between "the will" and the body, almost as if he were talking about the rather mystical—and scientifically unfounded—concept of "mind over body." But a little background knowledge of Stoic theory dispels this worry. The Stoics were thoroughly materialistic in their philosophy, believing that both mind and body are made of matter, and moreover, that everything in the universe is highly connected, including those two aspects of being human.

There is a sense in which even modern science tells us that changing the way we think about something alters the way we experience it physically. If you are affected by a disease, no wishing the disease away will make it so—and it's dangerous to think that way—but it's equally true that people react differently to the same experience, even to a severe disease. The Stoics argue that sickness hinders the body, but not (necessarily) the will. Similarly, you may be suffering from a disability, as did the modern Stoic Larry Becker, who lived with the effects of polio, and yet your physical disability does not need to get in the way of living a virtuous life in which you exert your power as a moral agent.[1] Medical researcher John Astin has reviewed evidence of extensive mind-body therapies for the management of pain (an instance of disability), and has found that a range of these therapies—from cognitive behavioral therapy to coping skills training and cognitive restructuring—are effective.[2] Epictetus would not have been surprised.

Epictetus may not have had modern research in cognitive science at his disposal, but he was an astute observer of human behavior, as were many other ancient philosophers, Stoic and not. He was certainly capable of paying attention to and reflecting upon his own experiences: He was disabled because of an early fracture of one of his legs, apparently caused when he was a slave by a beating from his first master. Epictetus knew what he was talking about when he said that the limitations of your body may hinder you in material areas (such as your ability to walk), but would not hinder you from exercising your will to be virtuous and improve your faculty of judgment. An obvious objection here would be that, of course, being disabled hinders me—how can I get around without functioning legs? What the heck is Epictetus talking about?! This (common) retort misses a subtle point about selfhood that Epictetus is assuming here: that "you" are your rational faculty, according to the Stoics, your *proharesis*. Everything outside of *proharesis* is not under your full control, and therefore not "you."

What to Do

This week's exercise is a continuation of last week's in one sense: You'll be keeping a Stoic concept close at hand to use repeatedly throughout the week. However, this week's focus will be narrower, in that you will now limit it to physical disability and discomfort.

If you have an illness or physical limitation, feel free to focus on that for the week, as long as you don't think it will be too difficult for you. If you feel that it's too much to handle at this stage of practice, work on discomforts or limitations that are less significant.

If you are healthy, there are still plenty of opportunities to work with discomforts over the course of your day, however minor they may be. Some examples include having to go to the bathroom, exhaustion while exercising, sleeping on an uncomfortable bed, minor aches and pains from sitting at a desk, or minor allergies.

This week, every time you find yourself facing a physical limitation or discomfort, aim to remind yourself of Epictetus's phrase: "This is a hindrance to [what I want to do/how I prefer to feel], but not to my will." It may be helpful to add a question at the end of this phrase to prompt you to further action, such as "What *can* I do?" or "Which virtue can I exercise here?"

In the space below, write out at least one implementation intention to help you remember what to say to yourself when facing physical limitations or discomforts this week. The first part should clearly describe how you'll recognize a situation in which to say the phrase to yourself, and the second part should be what you'd like to say.

As before, you may not remember to do this at every opportunity. Don't sweat it. The goal is to improve over the course of the week, not to be perfect.

Why Do It

Sometimes we can change our environment to make ourselves more comfortable, but sometimes we can't. Even so, the Stoics hold that there is *always* something you can do to mitigate the suffering around discomfort: Use your faculty of judgment to suss out what's really good and bad, and what precisely is under your control and what is not. Using Epictetus's at-hand phrase repeatedly will root these concepts deeply in your psyche. This should have two effects: to limit the amount of mental suffering you have over physical discomfort, and to enable you to take what action you're capable of achieving despite the discomfort. Over time, any constraints fate may hand you will not be any more limiting than they need to be.

Weekly Review

How did your week of practice go? If you tacked a question on to the end of your at-hand phrase, did it help guide your actions? Did your attitude toward discomfort or physical limitations change with repeated practice? What was most difficult about remembering to say this phrase to yourself in relevant situations?

_____

_____

_____

_____

Check this box if you found this exercise useful: ☐

Next week we'll look at another aspect of how pain and disease can cause us more suffering than necessary through our value judgments.

Question judgments around pain and disease

Pain, while a mental experience, is not something you can completely control. Logan found this out the hard way, after suffering a serious knee injury several years ago that has resulted in arthritis at a young age. While his practice with the Discipline of Assent hasn't made the pain go away, it has significantly improved his life. By catching and cutting off his judgments about the pain, he's been less fearful of engaging in physical activity, and spends less time complaining to himself about his injury. Now he's happier, despite his injury. This week, you'll minimize your own negative value judgments concerning pain and disease in more detail, taking cues from Seneca.

> " Every pain sometimes stops, or at any rate slackens; moreover, one may take precautions against its return, and, when it threatens, may check it by means of remedies. Every variety of pain has its premonitory symptoms; this is true, at any rate, of pain that is habitual and recurrent. One can endure the suffering which disease entails, if one has come to regard its results with scorn. But do not of your own accord make your troubles heavier to bear and burden yourself with complaining. Pain is slight if opinion has added nothing to it; but if, on the other hand, you begin to encourage yourself and say, 'It is nothing—a trifling matter at most; keep a stout heart and it will soon cease'; then in thinking it slight, you will make it slight. Everything

depends on opinion; ambition, luxury, greed, hark back to opinion. It is according to opinion that we suffer. A man is as wretched as he has convinced himself that he is. I hold that we should do away with complaint about past sufferings and with all language like this: 'None has ever been worse off than I. What sufferings, what evils have I endured! No one has thought that I shall recover. How often have my family bewailed me, and the physicians given me over! Men who are placed on the rack are not torn asunder with such agony!' However, even if all this is true, it is over and gone. What benefit is there in reviewing past sufferings, and in being unhappy, just because once you were unhappy? Besides, every one adds much to his own ills, and tells lies to himself. And that which was bitter to bear is pleasant to have borne; it is natural to rejoice at the ending of one's ills. Two elements must therefore be rooted out once for all—the fear of future suffering, and the recollection of past suffering; since the latter no longer concerns me, and the former concerns me not yet."

Seneca, Letters to Lucilius, *78.12-14*

We live in the present, the here and now. When Seneca says that past suffering is gone, and future ones have not yet arrived, he's absolutely right. Why, then, make ourselves miserable by indulging in thoughts of past troubles, or anticipating future ones? Focus instead on whatever is happening right now, and use all your resources to deal with it, not wasting any on that which is not under your control.

What Seneca says at the beginning of this chapter may remind you of the Stoic stereotype of going through life with a stiff upper lip. Nonetheless, endurance is a vital human skill, and we can often better handle things if we adjust our mental attitude. Modern science bears out this aspect of Stoic psychology, especially when it comes to the management of pain. For example, pain researcher Francis Keefe and collaborators showed that patients with osteoarthritic knee pain recovered significantly better if they were exposed to a cognitive behavioral intervention (CBI) specifically designed to improve their coping skills.[1] As a result of this approach, and unlike control patients, these patients experienced a reduction in pain as well as less posttreatment psychological disability. The same research group also showed the positive effects of cognitive pain management in the objectively difficult situation of dealing with cancer-related pain in end-of-life patients.[2]

As Seneca points out, the concept does not apply just to pain, as important as it is. Everything we do is affected by our opinions, including ambition and greed, or our penchant for luxury. We suffer in proportion to our opinions, and once we have convinced ourselves that we are wretched, then we truly are, regardless of objective circumstances.

What to Do

The quote from Seneca that started this chapter focuses on opinions around pain, disease, and disability. Take a few moments and think about what you struggle with in this area. Do you find yourself sometimes dwelling on a past injury or illness? Are you currently coping with pain or disability? Or perhaps you worry about pain, illness, or disability that could happen down the road?

It may be the case that you're relatively healthy and don't dwell too much on past or future pains. If that's the case and you can't think of any specific pain to work on this week, then you choose some other set of worries or concerns to focus on, since, as we mentioned, Seneca states that everything is affected by our opinions. Write down some specific issues that you'd like to tackle this week in the space below.

_____

_____

_____

Seneca's advice for working with pain, disease, and disability boils down to three strategies:

- Cut yourself off from complaining about past suffering.
- Don't bemoan present suffering.
- Stop yourself from worrying about possible suffering in the future.

In all these cases, Seneca recommends minimizing your negative value judgments rather than amplifying them. Consider Logan, whom you met earlier. When Logan hears crunching and feels pain in his knee, he finds that this starts a chain of thinking about how he'll never be able to play sports and how his arthritis is bound to get worse. As he practices the Discipline of Assent, however, he begins to notice these thoughts, and instead of simply suppressing them, he reframes them, telling himself *Well, at least I can walk now! Better enjoy it rather than ruin my time by dwelling on my knee!* He also holds himself back from complaining to others about his past injury.

Based on what you wrote, you may have noticed that past, present, or future sufferings are your biggest concern. In the space below, write implementation intentions to help you remember to cut down on your catastrophizing language around the areas of suffering that concern you most.

For the rest of the week, whenever you find yourself thinking or saying catastrophic thoughts around pain or disease (or any other worries you choose), pause and reframe them.

Why Do It

Seneca explains why this exercise should be done quite simply: because everything, including our mood and actions, depends on opinion. If you find yourself worrying about the unchangeable past or the uncertain future, you're bound to suffer since you're desiring things outside of your complete control.

This explanation from Stoic psychology doesn't fully express what is the healthiest way to change your opinion, though. Fortunately, modern science fills in the blank. While it's well known that simply suppressing thoughts is unhealthy because they tend to rebound, acknowledging the thoughts and testing them, as is done in cognitive behavioral therapy (CBT), is a healthier approach.[3] Learning to catch catastrophic thoughts around pain may be particularly helpful, as catastrophic thinking around pain is an independent predictor of chronic pain problems after knee surgery,[4] and worrying about surgical outcomes tends to worsen pain after surgery.[5] While pain isn't "all in our head," it does seem that our attitudes toward pain intensify or mitigate it, just as Seneca proposed. Seneca's advice to stop complaining is likewise backed by scientific research, which has found that complaining tends to lower mood while self-affirmation (e.g., "I can handle this") improves it.[6]

Weekly Review

What areas of suffering did you work with this week? Did you have more success with some areas over others? Why do you think that is the case? Write out your thoughts in the space below about how this week of practice went for you.

_____

_____

_____

_____

If you've found this exercise useful, check the box so that you can come back to it later: ☐

The past two weeks have focused on unpleasant topics, so it's time for some respite. Marcus Aurelius, who also had chronic health problems, found one method that provided him with relief whenever he needed it. You'll explore it for yourself in the week ahead.

Retreat to your inner citadel

If you've been going through the three disciplines in sequence, you've put in a great amount of work. Practice, however, shouldn't feel like work—it should be a respite. It didn't feel restful at first to Skylar, who practiced Stoicism with grim determination. But after catching her thoughts and attitudes, she saw what led her to make Stoic practice feel like drudgery: the techniques she chose were not comforting to her. After adjusting her approach to find words that made her feel better, practice felt more like a vacation than a slog. She learned this technique from reading Marcus Aurelius's *Meditations*, which you'll be working with this week.

> " Men seek retirement in country house, on shore or hill; and you too know full well what that yearning means. Surely a very simple wish; for at what hour you will, you can retire into yourself. Nowhere can man find retirement more peaceful and untroubled than in his own soul, specially he who has such stores within, that at a glance he straightaway finds himself lapped in ease, meaning by ease good order in the soul, this and nothing else. Ever and anon grant yourself this retirement, and so renew yourself. Have at command thoughts, brief and elemental, yet effectual to shut out the court and all its ways, and to send you back unchafing to the tasks to which you must return. What is it chafes you? Men's evil doing? Find reassurance in the tenet that rational beings

exist for one another, that forbearance is a part of justice, that wrong doing is involuntary; and think of all the feuds, suspicions, hates and brawls, that before now lie stretched in ashes. Think, and be at rest. Or is it the portion assigned you in the universe at which you chafe? Refresh yourself with the alternative—either a foreseeing providence, or blind atoms—and all the abounding proofs that the world is as it were a city. Or is it bodily troubles that assail? You have but to realize that when once the understanding is secure of itself and conscious of its own prerogative, it has no more part in the motions of the *pneuma* [soul], smooth or rough, and to rest in the creed to which you hold regarding pain and pleasure. Or does some bubble of fame torment you? Then fix your gaze on swift oblivion, on the gulf of infinity this way and that, on the empty rattle of plaudits and the fickle accident of show applause, on the narrow range within which you are circumscribed. The whole earth is but a point, your habitation but a tiny nook thereon; and on the earth how many are there who will praise you, and what are they worth? Well then, remember to retire within that little field or self. Above all do not strain or strive, but be free, and look at things as a man, as a human being, as a citizen, as of mortal make. Foremost among the maxims to which you can bend your glance be these two: First, things cannot touch the soul, but stand without it stationary; tumult can arise only from views within ourselves. Secondly, all things you see, in a moment change and will be no more; think of all the changes in which you have yourself borne part. The world is a moving shift, life a succession of views."

Marcus Aurelius, Meditations, 4.3

We all feel exhausted and in need of a retreat from the world, from time to time. Here, Marcus offers us the ultimate retreat to restore our peace of mind, the only place that is available to us at all times no matter where we are. He draws a parallel between our occasional need to withdraw to a country house or some other quiet place to restore our sanity and the opportunity we always have, at no expense at all, to retire into our own minds. Many philosophical and religious traditions similarly advise that the human mind is a citadel; we may need to get back to the mind and shut out the rest of the world in order to recover the ability to get back out and do what needs to be done.

Retreating into your own citadel, however, is not too useful if you don't also have a number of ready strategies to deal with whatever caused the problem in the first place. If, for example, what bothers you is that people sometimes do bad things, remind yourself that we are made to help each other, and that enduring what cannot be avoided is part of the deal. It also helps to keep in mind the Stoic doctrine that people do bad things out of "ignorance" (meaning lack of wisdom), not because they want to be evil. Seen this way, we can afford to be compassionate and to quell our anger, while doing our best to correct injustice.

When he is talking about trouble with his body, Marcus reflects that it is pervaded—as is everything else—by *pneuma* (literally "breath"), which makes him akin to every other living being or thing in the cosmos. Modern science doesn't rely on the Stoic concept of *pneuma*, but it is nonetheless true that we are literally made of stardust, since the molecules that make up our bodies were forged in the heat of a supernova explosion. Stoics find reflecting on this universal connection comforting regardless of whether there is providence (a purpose to things) or "blind atoms" (things that happen as a result of a web of cause and effect, with no rhyme or reason).

As for fame or the opinion of others, as Marcus says, don't let them trouble you at all; think of the immensity of time and space, and how consequently puny human beings and their opinions are. Besides, do you yourself hold such judgmental people in high esteem? If not, then what do you care what they think of you?

Finally, Marcus reflects on two basic truths he derives from Stoic philosophy. First, external events become troubling only once we attach certain opinions to them, and attaching such opinions (or not) is up to us. This is another restatement of the dichotomy of control. Second, everything is in flux; all things change. The Stoics inherited this concept from the pre-Socratic philosopher Heraclitus. Whatever is troubling you right now will soon be gone, turned into something else—and so will your worry.

What to Do

This week you'll practice retreating to your inner citadel whenever you are troubled by reciting basic Stoic maxims that provide comfort. You'll do this using the table on the next page.

Consider up to three situations that still trouble your mind. Marcus was bothered by other people's behavior, events, pain, and people's opinion of him. Perhaps some of these bother you, or perhaps you have other troubles. In the first column, write down no more than three troubles to work with this week.

Next, write down brief Stoic-inspired maxims to deploy whenever you catch yourself being disturbed by the things your wrote in the first column. We have provided some examples in the table to get you started. These maxims should reflect Stoic tenets (so no wishing others harm if they upset you!), but should also offer you comfort. Try taking a few moments to briefly imagine an upsetting situation, and rehearse the maxim to yourself to see if it provides some comfort; if it doesn't, choose another maxim. If you find that the maxim doesn't work for you during the week, you can modify your choice.

Finally, put the first and second columns together to form an implementation intention to help you remember to say the maxims to yourself whenever the opportunity arises.

You can also choose to meditate on these maxims at a set time each night as a refresher, in addition to using them at each opportune moment.

THE DISCIPLINE OF ASSENT

	Troubling situations	Stoic maxim you find comforting	Implementation intention
MARCUS AURELIUS	Other people's behavior	Forbearance is a part of justice	Whenever I find myself judging other people's behavior negatively, tell myself: "Forbearance is a part of justice."
	An event I dislike	Either providence or atoms; either way, it's foolish to chafe at this	If I notice myself disliking what just happened, I'll say: "Either providence or atoms; judging this negatively is foolish in either case."
	Bodily pain	The pain does not necessitate my judgment of it.	If I feel a pain, I'll say to myself: "I can interpret this pain as I wish."
	Being concerned about others' judgments of me	Taking a universal view puts desires in perspective	When I notice that I worry about others' thoughts about me, I'll tell myself: "I only inhabit a small part of the planet, in an even smaller part of the universe."
YOU			

Why Do It

This exercise primarily works with desires and aversions, just as you did throughout all of Part I. Some of the maxims you may work with will also be related to the Discipline of Action (e.g., "rational beings exist for one another"). What puts this particular practice more firmly within the realm of the Discipline of Assent, however, is that you are aiming to immediately react to initial impressions as soon as they form, to cut them off at their root, so to speak, by withholding assent and instead inserting new Stoic impressions in their place.

Doing this repeatedly will ingrain Stoic maxims in your mind over time. Applying them in appropriate situations that are unique to your circumstances will also clarify how these abstract, brief notions apply to your own daily life. You'll know that they're doing their job if they also provide solace in difficult situations throughout the week.

Weekly Review

Did you find retreating to your inner citadel comforting? Which maxims worked best? Which didn't work at all? Are there any that you would like to try in the future that you didn't use this week? Write about your experiences in the space provided below.

_____

_____

_____

Remember to come back to this exercise if you found it useful by checking the box: ☐

The past week was about applying Stoic maxims to a handful of situations that still trouble your mind. In the week ahead, you'll focus on one particular passion that many of us find troubling: anxiety.

Challenge your anxious thoughts

Anxiety tends to focus our attention on negative possibilities. While we're caught up in fantasizing about an awful future, we fail to realize that in the present moment, everything's okay. The pain people experience from anxiety comes solely from the mind. At first, Ava found that her practice with aversion during the first discipline didn't have a huge impact on her constant worry that her children would get hurt while playing. But once she started focusing more on the present moment, when anxious thoughts actually arose, she started experiencing relief. This was partially because it took her mind off the worry, and partially because she saw her anxiety for what it was: judgments she can challenge using the Discipline of Assent. This week, you'll try your hand at tackling things you are anxious about by focusing on the present and challenging your thoughts.

> How am I to know whether my sufferings are real or imaginary?' Here is the rule for such matters: We are tormented either by things present, or by things to come, or by both. As to things present, the decision is easy. Suppose that your person enjoys freedom and health, and that you do not suffer from any external injury. As to what may happen to it in the future, we shall see later on. Today there is nothing wrong with it. 'But,' you say, 'something will happen to it.' First of all, consider whether your proofs of future trouble are sure. For it is more often the case that we are troubled by our apprehensions, and that we are mocked

by that mocker, rumor, which is wont to settle wars, but much more often settles individuals. Yes, my dear Lucilius; we agree too quickly with what people say. We do not put to the test those things that cause our fear; we do not examine into them. We blanch and retreat just like soldiers who are forced to abandon their camp because of a dust cloud raised by stampeding cattle, or are thrown into a panic by the spreading of some unauthenticated rumor. And somehow or other it is the idle report that disturbs us most. For truth has its own definite boundaries, but that which arises from uncertainty is delivered over to guesswork and the irresponsible license of a frightened mind. That is why no fear is so ruinous and so uncontrollable as panic fear. For other fears are groundless, but this fear is witless.

Let us, then, look carefully into the matter. It is likely that some troubles will befall us, but it is not a present fact. How often has the unexpected happened! How often has the expected never come to pass! And even though it is ordained to be, what does it avail to run out to meet your suffering? You will suffer soon enough, when it arrives, so look forward meanwhile to better things. What shall you gain by doing this? Time. There will be many happenings meanwhile that will serve to postpone, or end, or pass on to another person, the trials that are near or even in your very presence. A fire has opened the way to flight. Men have been let down softly by a catastrophe. Sometimes the sword has been checked even at the victim's throat. Men have survived their own executioners. Even bad fortune is fickle. Perhaps it will come, perhaps not; in the meantime it is not. So look forward to better things."

Seneca, Letters to Lucilius, *13.7–11*

A number of our problems stem from the fact that we have a tendency to engage in bad thinking without challenging it, particularly when it comes to how we relate to our past, present, and future. Let's start with the future. The first point to understand here is that Seneca is not counseling *not* to plan for the future, but to just let things happen to you. Stoicism is about action, not passivity. He is highlighting the fact that we often know far less than we think about future events, and given that uncertainty we often have no reasonable cause for our anxieties. As Seneca puts it, it isn't just good luck that is fickle; the same applies to the bad variety as well! Rest assured, then, that more likely than not, things will actually be okay.

Now, what about the present? Surely I have a better sense of whether that is troubling, no? Seneca suggests that most of the time, nothing is really wrong right now. If we fear imprisonment, say, we are probably worrying about it while in a relatively comfortable environment. If we are concerned about a job, we are probably safely on the couch. For many (but not all) people who are worrying about something, there is nothing in the present moment causing their upset except their thoughts about the future. If you are worried about something, and yet you are healthy, feeling no pain, and free, then at this moment there is nothing wrong. This way of thinking is a consequence of the Stoic notion that the only true bad that can happen to us is our own bad judgment, since everything else can be endured with the right mental attitude. A sure sign of a bad judgment is anxiety, which results from an incorrect (or at the least unwarranted) appraisal of what is going on or may turn out to be the case.

What to Do

Seneca suggests a three-step process in dealing with anxiety, which you'll apply this week. Whenever you find yourself anxious about something, try this approach.

The first step is to check in with the present moment. This is because, as we learned, when we're worried about something, the present moment isn't what's causing our distress—our thinking is. If the present moment is comfortable for you, then you can relax into it. You can relax into the moment using techniques rooted in modern mindfulness. One technique is to focus your attention on the sensations of breathing, in the places where the sensations are most prominent (often around the nostrils or belly). Or you can focus on the sensations of your back or butt against your seat, or your feet on the ground. Another option is to concentrate on aspects of your environment by noticing all instances of a certain color in the room, or by listening to neutral sounds.

After you've grounded yourself for a few moments, consider whether there is anything actually wrong *right now*. Sometimes there is. As Seneca mentions, if you are not free, or not healthy, or in pain now, this exercise may not be appropriate. In that case exercises working with discomfort may be helpful—try those in Week 40 (pages 237–38) or Week 41 (pages 241–43). If nothing uncomfortable is present, proceed to the next step and question your worries about the future.

The second step is to clearly lay out the outcome you are worried about. What do you think will happen? Making your worry concrete will make it easier to question. Then ask what strong evidence you have that the outcome you are worried about will actually occur. Remember, it isn't a fair trial unless both sides are heard. So after you weigh the evidence for the feared outcome, ask the same question for the feared outcome *not* happening: Is there any evidence that it won't happen? One common piece of evidence is your past experience; think back to a time when you were worried about something and it actually didn't turn out as poorly as you anticipated. If that happens to you often, that's evidence that your current worry may turn out to not be well founded either. Another possible way to challenge your anxiety is to brainstorm other outcomes besides the one you fear. This could help you think of alternatives that you weren't previously considering since you were only focused on the worst-case scenario.

The final step is to ask a pragmatic question: Is this worry doing me any good *right now*? Whether or not the feared outcome will happen, how is worrying helping you in the present moment? If you find that it's not, then consider putting the worry to the side for now. A worry could be useful, though, if it suggests an action you can take. While outcomes are never completely under your control, if you can come up with a plan of action (with a reserve clause), then do so. If the worry arises again and you have a plan of action, remind yourself that you have a plan, and put the worry to the side. You can always return to it later, if you feel that it would be useful to think through some more. In the interim, you will have made your present less painful.

In summary, here are the three steps to challenge your anxious thoughts, based off of Seneca's advice:

- Ground yourself in the present moment.

- After clarifying your worry, weigh the evidence for and against it actually happening, and generate other ways the event may turn out better than you are anticipating.

- Question whether worrying about it *now* is actually helping you, regardless of how things may turn out. Plan an action if it is helpful to do so, and put the worry to the side if it's not.

It may help to do this in writing, below, in order to get the hang of the process. You can always use the notebook pages in the back if you need more space. With some experience, you will get better at doing it on the fly in your head.

Why Do It

Scientific evidence suggests that these methods are useful in coping with worry and negative thoughts.[1] The first step of Seneca's process is similar to mindfulness methods. The second and third steps are related to modern cognitive behavioral methods.

Seneca also lays out specific benefits of his process: First, it allows you to logically weigh the evidence concerning your worry. Being able to question the truth of your impressions is a key skill within the Discipline of Assent. Second, it allows you to improve the quality of your time. Even if the event you fear turns out as you expect in the future, it doesn't make much sense to ruin the present moment over it as well.

Weekly Review

Did Seneca's method help you cope with your worries this week? Were any of the three steps particularly helpful or unhelpful? Write your impressions of this exercise in the space below.

_____

_____

_____

_____

Check the box if you'd like to use this approach in the future: ☐

Anxiety is about aversion. Next you'll turn your attention to a method in the Discipline of Assent that helps work with desires.

Decompose desired externals

The Discipline of Desire is meant to subdue desires for external things, but it doesn't eliminate them completely. Yan practiced some of the exercises in the first discipline related to food and found that it helped him control his behavior. Despite his progress, the urges for certain treats still kept popping into his head. This week's exercise attacks these impressions at their root by implicitly challenging the judgment that there is anything desirable about them at all. Let's explore how you can use this technique.

> " In regarding meats or eatables, you say: that is the carcass of a fish, or fowl, or pig; falernian is so much extract of grape juice; the purple robe is sheep's wool dyed with juices of the shellfish; copulation, a functional discharge. Regards of this kind explore and search the actual facts, opening your eyes to what things really are. So should you deal with life as a whole, and where regards are overcredulous, strip the facts bare, see through their worthlessness, and so get rid of their vaunted embellishments. Pride is the arch sophist, and when you flatter yourself that you are most engrossed in virtuous ends, then are you most fooled."
>
> *Marcus Aurelius*, Meditations, *6.13*

ritics of Stoicism often mention Marcus's thought experiment to support their notion that it is a dull philosophy, seeking to strip pleasure from human life. But that is to spectacularly miss the point of the exercise! Similarly, people read the "functional discharge" bit about copulation and conclude that Marcus must have been averse to sex. Well, if he was, he managed to have thirteen children nonetheless. More likely, Marcus lists these specific things and engages in this mental exercise precisely because he was prone to overindulge in them.

The way this works is by objectifying, if you will, the things that are at the root of your hard-to-control desires. Do you have a tendency to drink too much? Remind yourself that you are making a fool of yourself for some fermented grape juice. (Incidentally, falernian was a highly prized wine in ancient Rome.) Do you feel the lure of lust a little too often? Remember that it is the animal in you that is responding to a natural urge to procreate. And so on. Describing the objects of your desires in a neutral fashion is a way to help you put some cognitive distance between you and your passions (in the Stoic sense of negative, unhealthy emotions), an approach that is used even today in cognitive behavioral therapy.[1] The point is not to do away with pleasure, but to keep in mind that these things we desire fall under the Stoic category of preferred indifferents: things you can pursue, within limit, so long as they don't become an obsession and get in the way of your practice of virtue.

This leads us to Marcus's wise reminder that it is precisely when you think you've gotten the hang of this virtue thing that you are more likely to fool yourself. You, reader, have made it this far, well into the third and most advanced Epictetian discipline; you have probably made progress, and feel justifiably satisfied by it. But this isn't the time to let your guard down and consider yourself a sage. You're not there just yet.

What to Do

This week, any time you feel the stirrings of a strong desire, even if it's just for a moment, your goal will be to redescribe the object of that desire in a way that is free of value judgments, and without using words that have implicit value judgments (e.g., "delicious"). Stick to just the facts. It's not a romantic getaway—it's traveling to an island with sand for a few days with your partner. It's not a blazing fast, top-of-the-line gaming rig—it's silicone, liquid crystal, plastic, and metal. You can approach this in two ways, which Marcus illustrates in this week's quote. The first is by simply stripping the description of value judgments. He does this in his example of meats; instead of calling them "delicacies" or the like, he calls them the carcasses of fish or fowl. The second way is by breaking down the desired objects into less desirable parts, which is how Marcus treated the imperial robe he wore.

In order to practice well this week, it will help to do a few warm-up exercises. The first is thinking a bit about how to catch yourself when you experience a strong desire. What are some of the telltale signs? Perhaps it's a physical feeling? A certain set of thoughts? Losing track of what you are focused on when the desired object is in sight, and paying attention instead to that? In the space below, write a few ways in which desire manifests itself for you, so that you can recognize it when it happens.

_____

_____

_____

Next, take a few moments to think about some objects or situations you've desired recently, and try your hand at redescribing them in the space below.

_____

_____

_____

Now that you are warmed up, write one or more implementation intentions to help you remember to decompose your desires this week.

_____

_____

_____

You may find it useful to briefly write out your new descriptions of desired externals stripped of value judgments for the first few days. Over time, with enough practice, you'll be able to do this on the fly, in your head. We've included some space below to write out your deconstructions over your first few days of practice.

Monday _____

_____

_____

Tuesday _____

_____

_____

Wednesday _____

_____

_____

Why Do It

A fundamental aspect of Stoic psychology is that value exists only in our head. Things in and of themselves are not desirable. To borrow an example from Epictetus: Money isn't going to whisper into your ear that it's valuable. It's your own judgment that tells you the value. The goal of this exercise is to make this fact more apparent by stripping out explicit and implicit value judgments that you tell yourself about externals, and to describe the desired object more neutrally. By removing the value judgment, you remove the value. Literally.

Weekly Review

How did this week's practice go for you? Did you find that stripping your language of value judgments subdued your desires over the course of the week? In the space below, write your thoughts about this exercise. Feel free to reintroduce value judgments—up to you!

_____

_____

_____

_____

If you'd like to return to this exercise during your Stoic practice in the future, check the box: ☐

This week's exercise decomposed impressions to help work with desires. Next week's exercise will build on this theme, but also add aversions to the mix, as well as aspects of the Discipline of Action.

Study each impression scientifically

At this point, you've practiced the Disciplines of Desire and Action, and you are halfway through the Discipline of Assent. While they're presented separately, they have much in common, and in fact can be practiced together in the Discipline of Assent. Dian experienced substantial improvements when she practiced the first two disciplines, but found that her progress leveled out with time. When she examined her impressions in the way Marcus lays out this week, she found that she was able to improve in both areas with just a single exercise. This week, you'll explore this technique for yourself.

> " Always define and outline carefully the object of perception, so as to realize its naked substance, to discriminate its self from its surroundings, to master its specific attributes, the elements of which it is composed and into which it will be resolved. Nothing so emancipates the mind as the power of scientifically testing everything that comes into our life, of looking into it and gathering the class and order to which each belongs, the special use which it subserves, its value to the universe, its value in particular to man as citizen and member of that supreme world-city, of which all other cities are as households. What is the object, ask, that now produces the given impression upon me? Of what is it compounded? How long has it to last? On what virtue does it make demand? Gentleness, courage, truth,

> good faith, simplicity, self-help, or what? In each case say,
> 'This comes from God.' Or 'This is part of the co-ordination,
> the concatenating web, the concurrence of destiny.' Or 'This
> is from one who is of the same stock and kind and fellowship
> as I, but who is ignorant of his true relation to nature. I am
> not ignorant, and therefore in accordance with nature's law
> of fellowship I treat him kindly and justly, though at the same
> time in things relative I strive to hit their proper worth.'"
>
> *Marcus Aurelius*, Meditations, *3.11*

The Stoic curriculum hinges on the study of three subject matters: physics, logic, and ethics. Marcus invites us to look at things "scientifically," that is, in the light of facts and reason. You may recall that "physics" deals with how the world works—with facts. "Logic" is the study and practice of sound reasoning, because the facts need to be interpreted properly; they don't speak for themselves. And "ethics," of course, is why we are doing all this: to attempt to live a eudaemonic life, a life worth living.

"Nothing emancipates the mind" as taking a rational approach does—and nothing puts you in a better, more objective position to deal with problems. People are often weary of hyperrationality, and that is definitely not what we (or the Stoics!) are advocating. Try this: Honestly ask yourself if the world (and you personally) right now (or ever) is suffering from too much use of reason. Right, then the question remains how best to go about applying our natural ability to reason to our problems.[1] After first stripping impressions down to their core, Marcus advises us to reflect on the connection between whatever is bothering us and the rest of the cosmos. Of what use is this thing that I am considering doing? Is it going to do any good for humanity? Marcus refers to all of society as the "supreme world-city," that is the cosmopolis, the whole of the human race, of which we are members, and to which we owe our allegiance. Notice how he poetically refers to actual cities and states as "households" of the cosmopolis, a beautiful image that gets to the heart of the Stoic attitude toward all humankind.

Marcus then gets down to the specifics of how to deploy his approach in practice. When faced with something we crave, or from which we get a strong positive "impression," we should ask ourselves exactly what it is made of (as you did in Week 44, pages 258–60), how long it will last (nothing lasts forever, and many things are very ephemeral), and especially which virtue it engages, if any. Is the action I'm contemplating wise, courageous, just, and temperate? If not, I should be weary of it. How does the thing, event, or action fit with the rest of the universal web of cause and effect? If what we crave is something inevitable (say, to avoid aging), then the right attitude is to accept it for what it is and turn it into an exercise of virtue, rather than uselessly complain that the universe is throwing this thing at us. Elsewhere in his *Meditations*, Marcus says, "'A cucumber is bitter.' Throw it away. 'There are briars in the road.' Turn aside from them. This is enough. Do not add, 'And why were such things made in the world?'"[2]

Last, we recognize that some people may not understand how things are connected in the world and what their responsibility is as human beings ("ignorant of his true relation to nature"), but that's no excuse for us—who have managed a slightly better understanding—to not treat others "kindly and justly," always keeping in mind the true value of things.

What to Do

Last week you practiced stripping desired externals of their value judgments by objectively describing them and their component parts. This week, you'll continue to put those skills to use and expand on them by stripping down not just desires, but also aversions.

Before we jump into the specifics, let's go through an example. Let's say that Dian is averse to being criticized. Knowing this, she can go into this week with a handful of implementation intentions to help her work with this aversion. For example, "When I get criticized, I'll tell myself 'sound from a human vocal cord.'" This is similar to what you practiced last week. However, Dian can then build upon this with another implementation intention: "When I decompose an impression, I'll remind myself how it fits into the whole and what virtue I can use." This allows Dian to see the larger picture in her current situation. Remembering this prompt helps Dian realize how she can exercise her virtue in any given situation. After decomposing, she could tell herself that the person who criticized her might mean to be helpful (similar to Marcus's third point in Week 25, pages 151 and 153, that people who criticize you either have good intentions, in which case you can see what's useful in the criticism, or are acting out of ignorance, in which case the criticism can be safely ignored). Dian may then realize that either way, this provides an excellent opportunity to improve herself: If there's something true about the criticism, she can act courageously by seeing what she can do to change, and if there's nothing true about it, she can act justly by treating the person fairly and kindly nonetheless, since they are not intentionally doing wrong.

To the original step you learned last week, there are two additional steps to be added to the process this week:

- Decompose the impression and describe it more objectively (original step).
- Take in the whole situation, either at the social or cosmic level, similar to what you did in Week 7 on pages 55–57 (new step).
- Think about what virtues you can exercise in the situation (new step).

You may find it helpful this week to write out these three steps on a separate piece of paper or in an app as soon as you can after the impression occurs, just as Marcus did at the start of this chapter. If you feel that you can do all three steps in your head, more power to you!

To prepare for the week ahead, try writing down a couple of implementation intentions in the space below to help you remember.

Why Do It

This exercise builds on last week's and brings in many more key Stoic concepts. The first two steps are an application of Stoic physics; by taking a few moments to ponder the nature of your impression, what generated it, and how it fits into the world, you are reconceptualizing the impression more objectively. They also focus on minimizing desires and aversions by stripping away the impression of value judgments. The third step brings in the Discipline of Action; you then relate the objective thing to your own character, seeing how you can act well in the situation, now that you have found a more objective perspective. This has similarities to your practice in Week 26 (pages 159–61) in which you reframed difficulties to see what advantages they may bring in terms of your character. In short, this exercise is a prime example of the Discipline of Assent in action.

Weekly Review

How did this exercise compare to last week's? Were you able to apply the three steps successfully? If yes, did you find any of the three steps particularly useful? If no, what difficulties did you encounter? Can you think of ways in which you might be able to work through them in the future?

_____

_____

_____

_____

Check the box if you'd like to come back to this exercise in the future: ☐

Next week, you'll narrow your focus once again to one specific type of impression: the stirrings of anger.

Pause when angry

Anger is one of the hardest passions to manage. One reason it's so hard to handle is that it rushes upon you and grabs your attention quickly. This was Emma's experience when working on being more prosocial during the Discipline of Action. She attempted to act the opposite of anger, but her main problem was that she didn't realize she actually *was* angry until well after the fact! Things started to improve, though, when she took on anger through the Discipline of Assent. When Emma worked with pausing at the first signs of anger, she found she was able to know that she was angry, which helped her act the opposite more easily. This week, you'll take your first steps in applying the Discipline of Assent to anger using this technique.

> " Remember that foul words or blows in themselves are no outrage, but your judgment that they are so. So when any one makes you angry, know that it is your own thought that has angered you. Wherefore make it your first endeavor not to let your impressions carry you away. For if once you gain time and delay, you will find it easier to control yourself."
>
> **Epictetus, Enchiridion, 20**

The Discipline of Assent builds on and refines the other two, in particular the Discipline of Desire. When Epictetus says that an insult itself isn't an outrage but your angry reaction to it is, he is applying the Discipline of Desire, which uses the virtue of practical wisdom—the one that tells us what is truly good and truly bad for us. Insults appear to be truly bad, but they are not. Righteous anger in response to insults appears to be truly good, but it isn't.

You may have noticed Epictetus's mention of "blows" as likewise offensive. Nobody is suggesting that we should condone physical violence, but sometimes the best reaction is humor, not more violence. Consider this anecdote about Socrates, told by Seneca: "There are many ways in which anger may be checked; most things may be turned into jest. It is said that Socrates, when he was given a box on the ear, merely said that it was a pity a man could not tell when he ought to wear his helmet out walking."[1]

Whenever we talk about anger from a Stoic perspective, even with fellow students of the philosophy, we find an incredible amount of resistance to this approach. People *want* to be angry. They feel entitled to it, even though modern psychologists agree with the Stoics and have argued that anger is just not good for us.[2] Reacting properly to injustice doesn't require us to be angry, simply animated by a sense of what is right (a positive emotion, in Stoic psychology). Indeed, anger—even when apparently justified—gets in the way of forming an appropriate response, since it makes us prone to act in a rash and often disproportionate manner.

Epictetus's approach here is classic cognitive behavioral therapy: First, analyze the issue at the cognitive level. *Know* that "it is your own thought that has angered you." Second, implement any number of techniques to alter your behavior, which mostly means whatever will allow you to gain time and so recover your composure: Count to twenty, mentally run through the alphabet, take deep breaths from your diaphragm, excuse yourself to go to the restroom, or get out for a walk around the block— whatever works to put some cognitive distance between your "passion" (again, in the Stoic sense of an unhealthy emotion) and what it is that you are going to do next. You won't regret it.

What to Do

This week, you'll train yourself to always recognize the first signs of anger, and then to not act on it. Think about how you know that you are angry. Do certain thoughts run through your mind? Do you feel telltale physical sensations? Are there situations you encounter that reliably anger you? Take a few moments to brainstorm how you know when you're getting angry.

_____

_____

_____

_____

Next, think about what might work for you to get some cognitive distance between you and the stirrings of anger. We mentioned some possibilities earlier. You can also use quick phrases, such as: "My judgment's upsetting me," or simply note and label what you are feeling as "anger." Write some techniques that may work for you.

_____

_____

_____

_____

Finally, combine what you wrote above into some implementation intentions, to practice while pausing when angry.

_____

_____

_____

Why Do It

Pausing and recognizing your impression as just an impression is a key skill throughout the Discipline of Assent. It's especially useful with anger since, as we mentioned in the opening of the chapter, anger can be hard to catch, as it grabs your attention quickly and prohibits you from thinking clearly. This is a key property of all passions, but especially of anger. Pausing allows you to open up a space to see your angry impression more clearly and to analyze it. But we'll save the analysis for next week. This week, keep things simple; just practice pausing at the earliest signs of anger. As Epictetus says, you'll then find it easier to control yourself and not do something you may regret.

Weekly Review

What signs of anger helped you the most in catching its initial stirrings? What methods were most effective to help you pause when angry? Write about what worked for you and what didn't.

_____

_____

_____

_____

_____

If you found pausing when angry to be helpful, check this box: ☐

Now that you've had some practice pausing when angry, let's move on to the next step: analyzing your angry impressions.

Analyze anger

While pausing is a useful first step to cope with anger, it's only the first step. What should one do after pausing? Emma focused on changing her behavior by acting the opposite. Zhang Wei chose the cognitive approach that we cover this week. When he found himself getting angry at his son for misbehaving, he paused and then used this week's exercise to assess the situation more logically. This week you'll practice this technique for yourself.

> " The greatest remedy for anger is delay; beg anger to grant you this at the first, not in order that it may pardon the offense, but that it may form a right judgment about it. If it delays, it will come to an end. Do not attempt to quell it all at once, for its first impulses are fierce; by plucking away its parts we shall remove the whole. . . . Some offenses we ourselves witness: in these cases let us examine the disposition and purpose of the offender. Perhaps he is a child; let us pardon his youth, he knows not whether he is doing wrong. Or he is a father; he has either rendered such great services, as to have won the right even to wrong us, or perhaps this very act which offends us is his chief merit. . . . Suppose that it is a disease or a misfortune; it will take less effect upon you if you bear it quietly. . . . Is it a good man who has wronged you? Do not believe it. Is it a bad one? Do not be surprised at this; he will pay to someone else the penalty which he owes to you—indeed, by his sin he has already punished himself."
>
> *Seneca, On Anger, 2.29–30*

eneca picks up the theme of pausing while angry, arguing that delay is, in fact, our chief defense against anger. Do not try to dominate anger, as it escalates quickly and easily overcomes reason in the heat of the moment. Counterintuitively, avoidance, not confrontation, is the winning strategy. Seneca goes even further by advising us to pick apart the causes of our anger; to examine them calmly and carefully, as if on an operating table (but *not* while you are angry). You need to consider who or what is the cause of your anger. It makes no sense to be angry at a child, for example, since they are incapable of using reason correctly. The better response is to patiently teach them how to behave more reasonably. Perhaps it's an adult who is causing offense, maybe your own father. In that case be tolerant of his misstep, because he has done so much for you in the past. Or maybe he is right in what he is saying and you should be listening and learning, rather than going off in a huff.

What if you are angry at an inanimate object, or a natural phenomenon, such as a disease? What sense is there in that? Is getting upset and yelling at your computer going to make it apologize to you and stop glitching? We bet that your reaction is more likely to make things worse, not to mention make you look foolish. Diseases and other calamities are part of life, and, again, attacking them isn't going to help you; you'll simply feel worse than you might otherwise. This doesn't mean you shouldn't try to fix your computer or cure the disease. On the contrary, reacting calmly and reasonably is far more likely to help you accomplish those goals than outbursts of rage.

Seneca adds two important concepts for our consideration: Not only should you not be surprised that some people do unethical things, but take comfort that they will likely get what's due to them. And in acting unethically, they are already hurting themselves. The first superficially sounds similar to the Stoic version of karma: *Logos* keeps track of people's deeds, and in the long run balances out the ledger. Is Seneca somehow saying that we should put faith in karma? We don't think so. More likely, Seneca is deploying the Stoic notion that human beings are inclined to virtue by nature, or, as we would put it, we evolved a tendency toward prosocial behavior. This means that most people will object, and sometimes react, to wrongdoing. So, the person who is hurting you today is likely (at least statistically) to get his due at some point in the future.

This implies that virtuous behavior is a good bet for flourishing, which is an argument that some modern virtue ethicists, such as Rosalind Hurthouse, make as well.[1]

The second claim, that the wrongdoer is actually hurting himself, derives from the Stoic notion that virtue is the only true good because it is the only thing that can only be used for good. It follows that vice is the only true evil, while everything else, as we have seen, is a preferred or dispreferred indifferent (see Week 1, page 12 and Week 9, page 66). We also know from the dichotomy of control that our judgments of what is good and bad are entirely up to us. So the man that Seneca describes is doing wrong of his own volition, and, as a result is staining his soul or his character, depending on your perspective. This is the worst thing someone could do, according to Stoic philosophy. The joke is on the one who is doing wrong by you. There's no reason to get upset.

What to Do

This week, you'll continue your practice of pausing when angry, but take it one step further: Recognize where your anger is pointed, and then counter the anger by analyzing it rationally. You can try this on paper for the first few days, but we encourage you to do this on the fly if you're able. You are now deep into the Discipline of Assent and practiced at catching and analyzing your anger early.

Seneca gives a few common objects of anger along with ways to rebut them. To warm up, identify objects of anger and possible rebuttals. We summarize Seneca's examples in the table on the next page, and have left space for you to fill in your own. Writing your analysis and rebuttals out on paper may help you get the hang of things, but with repeated practice you'll be able to do this even better in your head.

	OBJECT OF ANGER	POSSIBLE REBUTTALS
SENECA	A person who doesn't know what they're doing (e.g., a child)	Tell yourself that they're acting out of ignorance.
	A person who's benefited you in the past (e.g., a parent)	Remind yourself of the kindness they've shown to you previously, or that you're getting angered at something well-intentioned
	A circumstance	Why bother getting angry at an inanimate object or circumstance? It's not like it will apologize.
	An ethical person	If they're ethical, you're probably misinterpreting their action.
	An unethical person	Shouldn't you expect unethical people to do unethical things? Besides, the only one he can really injure is himself.
YOU		

Now that you've warmed up, here is the technique to practice whenever you feel the stirrings of anger:

- Pause, using the methods that worked best for you last week.
- Name the object of your anger.
- Rehearse and meditate upon a rebuttal for the causes of your anger.

Feel free to revisit your rebuttals in your head over the course of the week. It may help to mentally rehearse some possible rebuttals to angry thoughts when you have the time and inclination.

Why Do It

You've worked with anger before, starting back in the Discipline of Desire in Week 4 (pages 34–36) when you practiced considering the other person's perspective in order to calm your own anger. In the Discipline of Action during Week 27 you did a similar exercise, acting the opposite of anger with the aim of not acting out on your impulse while also calming your anger in the process, though in that case you acted a little closer to the onset of anger.

This week's exercise, as with all exercises in the Discipline of Assent, has the same aim as those exercises, but tackles the root cause: our thoughts. Remember, the Stoics believed that it's our own thoughts that cause our anger, and our thoughts happen rapidly. With enough practice, the stirrings of our anger will turn less and less frequently into full-blown passion.

Weekly Review

Did you find that your ability to pause at the onset of anger improved this week? How successful were you in analyzing the object of your anger and your thoughts leading to anger, and rebutting them? Write about your experiences with this week's exercise in the space below.

_____

_____

_____

_____

If you want to put this exercise into your Stoic toolbox for later use, check the box: ☐

Counter anger with maxims

The Discipline of Action explores behavioral and cognitive approaches to dealing with anger, and while these approaches can work, some of them are indirect. In contrast, the Discipline of Assent attacks the root of anger directly: our beliefs. Natar discovered almost by accident that Stoic ideas have stealthily become ingrained in his mind through deep reading. While reading Seneca's *On Anger*, for example, certain striking passages automatically rushed to his attention during the first signs of anger, often defusing it by reminding him that it's his character, not others' behavior, that's most valuable in life. This week's practice helps catalyze the process that came naturally to Natar.

> " Whither, say you, does this inquiry tend? That we may know what anger is. For if it springs up against our will, it never will yield to reason, because all the motions which take place without our volition are beyond our control and unavoidable, such as shivering when cold water is poured over us, or shrinking when we are touched in certain places. Men's hair rises up at bad news, their faces blush at indecent words, and they are seized with dizziness when looking down a precipice. And as it is not in our power to prevent any of these things, no reasoning can prevent their taking place. But anger can be put to flight by wise maxims, for it is a voluntary defect of the mind, and not one of those things which are evolved by the conditions of human life, and which, therefore, may happen even to the wisest of us."
>
> *Seneca, On Anger, 2.2*

S eneca offers a three-phase analysis of the structure of anger, which we first encountered in Week 27 (page 163). The first phase is a prereflective reaction in our body: The onset of anger occurs without conscious thought on our part and is inevitable. This is signaled by a rush of adrenaline, and falls into the same category as the other involuntary reactions Seneca mentions, which include shivering when exposed to cold water and blushing in response to inappropriate comments. To attempt to avoid these automatic reactions is useless and foolish. The second phase is cognitive: You reflect on what is going on, recognize it as anger, and rapidly review and judge its cause. This is where we have a window to act. This week's exercise builds on last week's in seeking to make that action instinctive. The third phase takes place when you have already given assent and it's too late for you to do anything about it. Anger is now out of control, no longer subject to reason, and will run its course with the predictable nefarious consequences. This is anger proper, and what the Stoics cautioned us to avoid.

To fight against anger, Seneca proposes another technique: the use of maxims. It's an interesting device, and one that we've found effective in our personal experience. The appropriate maxims are selected by us during periods of calm, when we can reason about the unhealthy nature of anger and meditate on counteracting it. By repeating maxims to yourself you can direct your mind, little by little, to go there as an acquired reflex. We've seen this in action in Week 35 (pages 206–08), when we trained ourselves to question every action we are prone to engage in. In the Discipline of Action we used the metaphor of a proficient car driver who no longer has to pay conscious attention to every movement and situation, because her experience has made many of her decisions and moves automatic. That's what we are aiming for here, and it's what repeating Stoic maxims over and over will do for us.

What to Do

This week, instead of analyzing your anger after a pause, you'll repeat a wise maxim to yourself in order to rebut the impression. It may be helpful to review the maxims each morning, rehearse using them mentally, or create implementation intentions to help you remember them when anger rises.

During the past few weeks, you've already identified maxims or phrases that may be useful to repeat when you feel the first stirrings of anger. Write some maxims to counter your angry impressions in the space below. If you're stuck and need inspiration, review your rebuttals to anger from last week. You may also find it useful to review Marcus's advice at the beginning of Week 25 (pages 151–53) for guidance.

_____

_____

_____

_____

_____

Why Do It

This week's method to cutting off anger is slightly different from last week's. Last week you practiced recognizing the object of anger and your reasons for being angry, and then rebutting them. This week, you'll counter your reasons for being angry by explicitly recalling basic Stoic principles or ideas around anger and its origins, in order to have these foremost in your mind when you need them—when the first signs of anger arise. You now have two methods for countering anger. One may work better for you than the other, and this week's practice will allow you to see which is a better fit.

NOTE: You may have noticed that this week's What to Do is more brief than usual. At this point we're taking a step back from providing as much guidance as we have so far. You are deep into Stoic practice and by now should have a firm idea of what methods help you remember to practice over the course of the week and how you can tweak each exercise so that it may work better for you. We are giving less guidance than usual so that you can work out for yourself how to best implement the remaining exercises. This will also allow you to practice more effectively on your own, once you've reached the end of this book!

Weekly Review

Which maxims did you find most effective this week? Did you prefer this method over last week's, or vice versa? Write your thoughts about what works for you, in dealing with angry impressions after a pause, in the space below.

_____

_____

If you'd like to work with this exercise more in the future, check this box: ☐

Speak just the facts about others

A fundamental Stoic tenet is that most of the value judgments
we make are false; assenting to them is what leads to passions, or
unhealthy emotions. Many of our judgments are implicit but seep into
our language nonetheless. This was Ajay's experience when trying to
be careful about what he called "good" and "bad" during the Discipline
of Desire. He found that by changing his language, he changed his
thinking. This powerful practice can be made more comprehensive in
the Discipline of Assent. This week, you'll try your hand at it.

> " If a man wash quickly, do not say that he
> washes badly, but that he washes quickly. If a man drink
> much wine, do not say that he drinks badly, but that he
> drinks much. For until you have decided what judgment
> prompts him, how do you know that he acts badly? If you
> do as I say, you will assent to your apprehensive impressions
> and to none other."
>
> *Epictetus*, Enchiridion, 45

Epictetus reminds us that we often don't know enough about other people's motives—or their personal history—to arrive at reasonable judgments, and that we're far too prone to judge people anyway. He offers both theoretical and practical advice to counter this tendency. From a theoretical perspective, sure, the guy who just cut in front of you on the highway may be a jerk, but perhaps he is running to the hospital because his wife is delivering a baby and he doesn't want to miss out on such an important event in his life. Or maybe he really *does* feel entitled to cut ahead of others, but that's a result of some serious issues he has been carrying around for decades and hasn't yet resolved. In this case perhaps a better attitude toward him would be compassion. The point is, you just don't know. Because there are so many factors in every situation that we can't possibly know, the ethical thing to do is to simply suspend judgment. Critics of Stoicism often say that this sort of advice makes us into pushovers or losers. It does no such thing! If some injustice is being perpetrated, the Stoic virtues of courage and justice kick in, and we're compelled to intervene. But if it's simply a matter of taking a charitable view of others, how is that, exactly, going to harm you?

Epictetus's practical advice is to rephrase your words in a neutral fashion. We have seen Marcus take this same approach in Week 44 (pages 256–57), when he wanted to remind himself that some things he badly craves are not, in reality, that important or attractive. We are now applying a similar idea with respect to our assessment of others and what they may be up to. The idea, as before, is to objectify our thoughts, to make them more neutral, and hence judgment-free. Remember the guy who cut you off on the highway? Instead of thinking, as comes naturally, *That jerk cut me off,* say something neutral along the lines of *Someone is in a hurry to get somewhere.* Applied to recurring situations in daily life, this exercise slowly becomes automatic, and reorients our immediate responses away from being judgmental, and toward being more charitable to others. As a result, we'll get upset less often and experience more serenity.

What to Do

This week, your practice is to replace any value-laden language you use when saying anything about other people. Do this as often as you can, both when speaking to others and to yourself. In its place, attempt to report just the facts. Think about what a camera would see.

While Epictetus uses only examples involving the word "bad," remember that the words "good" and "bad" are far from the only value-laden terms we use. We have seen another example earlier: "jerk." A camera would not see a jerk, but simply a person cutting in front of you. For a refresher on value-laden language, it may be helpful to review Week 9 (page 64).

Why Do It

Epictetus places this practice firmly within the Discipline of Assent, which deals with learning to assent to only true impressions, when he states that if you do this exercise constantly, you will only be assenting to "apprehensive," or true, impressions. This builds on the principles you learned in the Discipline of Desire (in Week 9).

Why would removing value laden-ness from your language create true impressions? Because goodness and badness lie within a person's own character. Since you cannot peer inside another person's head, you can never truly know their character, and so, if you assent to the impression that they are a bad person, you would be incorrect according to Stoic theory—you would have assented to a false impression. Furthermore, other people's character, even if truly vicious, is technically a dispreferred indifferent to you, since it's outside the sphere of your complete control. In contrast, your own character is under your complete control, and should then be the Stoic practitioner's main concern. So value-laden language is technically false when discussing anything outside your complete control. Not using this language when thinking or talking about externals will drastically cut down on the amount of false impressions you assent to.

How did your practice this week compare to your first attempt at changing your language around "good" and "evil" in Week 9? Was it easier or harder? More or less successful? Why? Write your thoughts about this week's exercise in the space below.

_____

_____

_____

_____

_____

Check this box if you'd like to revisit this exercise in the future: ☐

Decompose your difficulties

Life can become overwhelming, even for seasoned Stoic practitioners like Marcus Aurelius. That's why he wrote consistently in his journal: to remind himself of useful Stoic principles and techniques in times of need. In his journals, Marcus relies heavily on the idea of focusing on the present moment, which is a theme Johan picked up on while reading the *Meditations* and tried putting to use. Johan's Stoic practice taught him that he had no control over the past, and only limited influence over the future, but just knowing this didn't prevent him from painfully ruminating over these things. He found that journaling helped him focus on the present moment, and allowed him to decompose his thoughts, rather than buy them wholesale. This week, you'll explore why he found this technique useful.

> " Do not let the impression of life as a whole confound you. Do not focus in one all the train of possible and painful consequences; but as each trouble comes, say to yourself: What is there here too hard to bear or to endure? And you will be ashamed to avow it so. And yet again remember, that you have not to bear up against the future or the past, but always against the present only. And even that you minimize, when you strictly circumscribe it to itself, and repudiate moral inability to hold out merely against that."
>
> **Marcus Aurelius, Meditations, 8.36**

The Stoics often rephrase or decompose impressions in order to arrive at better judgments. We have recently encountered a number of these exercises. In Week 44 (pages 256–57), Marcus broke down the sources of his desires to remind himself that they were not, in fact, so desirable. In Week 49 (pages 279–80), Epictetus suggested using neutral language whenever we are tempted to judge others. This week we learn another way: Rephrase or break down elements into component parts—this time in order to deal with our aversions.

Marcus does this in two steps. First, he reminds himself that it is useless to let your mind wander over the many negative outcomes of a given situation. Author Barry Glassner has argued that we tend to be afraid of the wrong things, often out of a lack of understanding of the likelihood of possible scenarios, and we then waste a lot of emotional energy and money trying to stave off those outcomes.[1] Moreover, Marcus says, many of the possible outcomes can, in fact, be endured. Not only are we not as fragile as we sometimes assume, but plenty of others have had to overcome similar situations, and have done it successfully. Why should it be different for us? Even when a negative outcome is inevitable, as in the case of a terminal disease, we can find comfort in the realization that others have faced the same situation bravely. We draw inspiration from those who have come before us, and can overcome our own fears.

Next, Marcus recalls one of the fundamental principles of Stoicism: the dichotomy of control. This tells us that neither the past nor the future is in our control, and so in the Stoic sense they are "nothing to us." We can and should focus on what is happening right here, right now instead. The present is the only effective realm of our agency. Are you in pain? It isn't helpful to think about how long it will last. Rather, focus on enduring the pain as it presents itself to you, now. Things not going well at work? It's useless to let your mind wander toward possible futures in which you will have lost your job. You are facing a specific situation unfolding at the moment. Can you deal with it? What is the most effective way?

What to Do

This week, take Marcus's advice and restrict each difficulty you face to the event itself, by focusing on the realities of the present moment. Don't add value judgments to the situation, and intentionally remove any value judgments that automatically come to mind.

Consider that harping on the past is actually you, in the present, remembering certain past experiences and assigning them negative value judgments. You could use the skills you learned last week to redescribe these reflections as they arise and remove the value judgments. The same holds for fear and worry about the future.

Even physical suffering in the present only comes one part at a time. If physical ailments are what trouble you (as they troubled Marcus), try to break them down into their individual sensations. If you look closely enough, you may find that pain isn't one single thing, but is composed of many different aspects. Below is a set of questions you can ask yourself about pain when it arises, to help decompose it. These prompts are all based on taking an analytical, scientific approach toward pain and physical discomfort. Asking pain, "What is this, objectively?" may reveal to you what it revealed to Marcus: that each individual component isn't permanent and may be more bearable than when you saw them as a whole.

- Explore the components of pain or discomfort by asking where it is exactly in the body. Can you locate it precisely? If so, where are its borders? If not, how does it move or change?

- Does the intensity remain constant, or does it shift? If it does, how does it shift over time?

- Is the discomfort or pain a single thing, or is it made up of different sensations such as shooting, heat, pressure, or throbbing? How are these sensations connected to your thoughts around them?

This last set of questions opens the door to combine this technique with what you learned in Week 41 (pages 241–43), when you practiced working with your value judgments around pain and illness.[2]

Now it's time for you to choose how you'll practice this week. What sorts of difficulties will you choose to decompose, and what techniques will you apply? Write out your plan in the space below.

_____

_____

_____

_____

_____

_____

_____

Whether you choose to work with difficulties that occurred in the past, are occurring now, or might occur in the future, it will be useful to keep in mind what Marcus says in his *Meditations*: "A man, remember, lives only in the present."[3]

Why Do It

Focusing on the present moment and objectively and nonjudgmentally viewing your difficulties for what they are can have wide-ranging effects, bolstering Marcus's claim that the technique makes difficulties easier to bear. It also shares many aspects with modern mindfulness techniques. There's empirical support that these mindfulness techniques are effective in helping us face difficulties located in the past, present, and future. Breaking our difficulties down into component parts can alleviate stress, anxiety, and depression.[4] Mindfulness also impacts rumination, which in turn can lead to depression, as well as prolonged negative moods in general,[5] and contributes to anger and aggression.[6] Additionally, there's empirical support that mindfulness helps people cope with conditions such as chronic pain.[7]

Weekly Review

What techniques did you use this week to decompose your difficulties? Did some work better than others? Were there difficulties that were hard for you to decompose, and, if so, what do you think you could do in the future to improve your ability to work on them?

_____

_____

_____

_____

_____

If you'd like to return to this practice later, check this box: ☐

Pay attention to the right things

It's easy to lose track of your Stoic principles when your mind is focused on other tasks. The Stoics knew this, which is why one of the major aspects of the Discipline of Assent that forms the foundation of some of the practices in this book, but has been left implicit, is what we do with our attention. Indeed, Jeannie found that when she practiced Stoic exercises each morning, they carried over to the first part of her day, but soon after she got to work, those ideas faded as she shifted her attention to other tasks. However, while practicing the Discipline of Assent, she learned how to pay attention to her tasks while also keeping Stoic principles in mind. This week, you'll try your hand at paying attention to your Stoic principles throughout your day.

> When you relax your attention for a little, do not imagine that you will recover it wherever you wish; but bear this well in mind that your error of today must of necessity put you in a worse position for other occasions. For in the first place—and this is the most serious thing—a habit of inattention is formed, and next a habit of deferring attention, and you get into the way of putting off from one time to another the tranquil and becoming life, the state and behavior that nature prescribes. Now if such postponement of attention is profitable, it would be still more profitable to abandon it altogether: but if it is not profitable, why do you not keep up your attention continuously?

'I want to play today.'
What prevents you, if you attend?
'I want to sing.'
What prevents you, if you attend?
Is any part of life excluded, on which attention has no
bearing, any that you will make worse by attention and
better by inattention? Nay, is there anything in life generally
which is done better by those who do not attend? Does
the carpenter by inattention do his work better? Does the
helmsman by inattention steer more safely? And are any
of the minor duties of life fulfilled better by inattention?
Do you not realize that when once you have let your mind
go wandering, you lose the power to recall it, to bring it to
bear on what is seemly, self-respecting, and modest; you do
anything that occurs to you and follow your inclinations?
    To what then must I attend?
    First to those universal principles I have spoken of. These
you must keep at command, and without them neither sleep
nor rise, drink nor eat nor deal with men: the principle that
no one can control another's will, and that the will alone
is the sphere of good and evil. No one then has power to
procure me good or to involve me in evil, but I myself alone
have authority over myself in these matters. So when I have
made these secure, what need have I to be disturbed about
outward things? What need have I to fear tyrant, or disease,
or poverty, or disaster?
    'But I do not please So-and-so.'
    Well, is he my doing? Is he my judgment?
    'No.'
    What concern is it of mine then?
    'Nay, but he is highly thought of.'
    That will be for him to consider, and for those who think
much of him. I have one whom I must please, one to whom I

must submit myself and obey: God and those who come next to God. He commended me to myself, and made my will subject to me alone, and gave me rules for the right use of it. And if I follow these in syllogisms I pay no heed to anyone who contradicts me; if I follow them in dealing with variable premises, I pay regard to no one. Why then am I annoyed by those who criticize me in greater matters? What is the reason for this perturbation? It is none other than that I have had no training in this sphere. For every science is entitled to despise ignorance and the ignorant, and this is true of arts as well as of sciences. Take any shoemaker, any carpenter you like, and you find he laughs the multitude to scorn when his own craft is in question.

First then we must have these principles ready to our hand. Without them we must do nothing. We must set our mind on this object: pursue nothing that is outside us, nothing that is not our own, even as He that is mighty has ordained; pursuing what lies within our will, and all else only so far as it is given us to do so. Further, we must remember who we are, and by what name we are called, and must try to direct our acts to fit each situation and its possibilities.

We must consider what is the time for singing, what the time for play, and in whose presence; what will be unsuited to the occasion; whether our companions are to despise us, or we to despise ourselves; when to jest, and whom to mock at; and on what occasion to be conciliatory and to whom. In a word, how one ought to maintain one's character in society. Wherever you swerve from any of these principles, you suffer loss at once; not loss from without, but issuing from the very act itself."

Epictetus, Discourses IV, 12.1–18

W e're nearing the end of our journey. Epictetus has a lot to say, and we wanted to give you, the reader, a good sense of his style and reasoning. Plus, this is really important.

You may have noticed Epictetus references "God," or "He that is mighty." Marcus and (less frequently) Seneca make similar references. As we have mentioned before (see Week 8, page 59), the Stoics were pantheists. They thought of the universe as a living organism endowed with reason (the Logos), and they called this universe "God." This conception of God implies a kind of providence, as when Epictetus says that He "commanded" things and "gave me rules." There is a strong temptation to read Epictetus in a Christian sense, but it should be resisted as that is not the conception of God or providence the Stoics had in mind. The rules Epictetus is talking about are more akin to the laws of nature, or the outcome of a web of cause and effect, rather than to the dictates of a Christian-type divinity. Some modern Stoics retain the original intended meaning in the framework of pantheism; some opt instead to ignore the ancient context and reinterpret what Epictetus and the others are saying in monotheistic terms; and still others, also discarding the ancient context, read it in a completely secular fashion. The interpretation is entirely up to you, so long as you are clear about what Epictetus and company actually meant. We think that any one of the above metaphysical interpretations is viable, in the sense that they don't change the practical meat of the matter, to which we now turn.

To begin with, then, Epictetus exhorts his students to pay attention, and to be mindful of their judgments in everything they do. The first reason is that any instance of inattention is going to reinforce that habit, making their practice more and more difficult. On the contrary, the more they routinely pay attention, the more the right habit of mind is reinforced. The second reason is, put simply, that nothing becomes better by being done inattentively. Being distracted when we drive, or take an exam, or converse with others does not improve our driving, chances of passing the exam, or the quality of our conversation. (Be, *ahem*, mindful of this the next time you whip out your phone in a social setting, thinking that you can do what is actually impossible for the human mind: multitasking.[1])

But what is it, exactly, that we need to pay attention to? The short answer: Stoic rules for living and the roles we play in life.[2] That is, the rules related to the Discipline of Desire, the roles to the Discipline of Action.

In terms of rules, Epictetus very clearly restates the basic principle of the dichotomy of control and the knowledge that comes from the virtue of practical wisdom. The latter concerns itself with what is truly good or evil. In no uncertain terms, then, for the Stoics the only thing really under our control is our will; it is good for us if our will is inclined toward virtue, bad for us if it is inclined toward vice. The buck stops with each of us—nobody can force us to change our will, though we may agree (of our own volition!) to change our actions under duress. If someone is not pleased with us, that is their business, not ours—not in the sense that we shouldn't care if we hurt others, but in the strictly Stoic sense that others' opinions are up to them. So long as we have acted justly, the fact that others may disapprove is their problem. This fundamental principle, this crucial bit of Stoic knowledge, says Epictetus, ought to stay with us in every moment of our lives. Never leave home without it!

In addition to our judgments, we need to pay attention to the roles we play in life, which originate from the Discipline of Action. Epictetus asks us to pay attention to "who we are," which, first and foremost, are rational and social animals. We should keep this role at the front of our mind, applying reason to our initial impressions and making sure we attempt to act prosocially in all situations. We also have specific roles that we can figure out by "the names we are called." Examples include parent, friend, and employee. Our roles vary depending on who we are, what we've chosen for ourselves, and even the time of day. Paying attention to what role we are filling at any given time allows us to "direct our acts to fit each situation and its possibilities." It allows us to derive what actions are virtuous for us at any given time. We must always be rational and prosocial while fulfilling the specific role that is fitting for the given situation.[3]

Lastly, there's a bonus from this practice of attention to rules and roles (besides living a eudaemonic life, a life worth living): We become serene. We can be sure in the knowledge, derived from the "syllogisms," that if other people insist we should be concerned with *their* judgment, then they just don't understand what a judgment is. They don't appreciate the fact that only our own judgments are under our control, and are our own business. It cuts down the clutter quite a bit!

What to Do

We know there's a lot to digest in this chapter, so let's summarize the main practical points. Epictetus gives two answers to the question of what we should pay attention to:

Rules: The dichotomy of control, that the good only lies within our own will, and that the wills of others lie beyond our complete control.

Roles: Remembering "who we are" and "by what name we are called," and consequently how to act, based on our roles at any given time.

Epictetus encourages his students to constantly keep rules and roles in mind at all times when practicing the Discipline of Assent, to "keep at command, and without them neither sleep nor rise."

Your practice this week is to attempt to follow Epictetus's advice, as often as you can, from when you wake up to when you go to sleep. The rules you keep in mind should be short and reflect the fundamental Stoic principles you've learned while practicing. Remember: "Who we are," first and foremost, are rational, social creatures, according to the Stoics. This role should never be broken. But we also play many specific roles that vary according to our activities and what other people expect of us ("what name we are called"). Before you start practicing this week, take some time to think about what specific roles you play in life, and attempt to remind yourself about each role and what actions it entails whenever you find yourself playing that role.

Use the space below to collect your thoughts about this exercise and plan out how you intend to practice this week.

_____

_____

_____

_____

_____

Now, go ahead and live your life, all while trying to keep your rules and roles, and what they entail, always in mind.

Why Do It

It's probably no exaggeration to say that this exercise is the epitome of Stoic practice. It is a quintessential practice within the Discipline of Assent in that it requires constant attention to fundamental Stoic principles. Yet, as with many of the other practices in this section, it covers familiar ground. The "rules" one pays attention to here are primarily rules about what one should and should not desire, and so have significant overlap with Epictetus's first Discipline. The "roles" are about ethics and how to act in the world, and so, share much in common with the Discipline of Action. As a result, this single exercise encompasses Epictetus's entire program.

We also think it's extremely difficult, which is why we have saved it for the penultimate practice.

Weekly Review

How did you find this practice? Was it difficult? How useful was it? Did you notice any changes in your emotions or behavior? Write about your experience with paying attention to the right rules and roles in the space below.

_____

_____

_____

If this is an exercise you'd like to come back to, check the box: ☐

You had a lot to keep in mind this week. If you found that difficult, don't sweat it. We agree! Besides, next week you'll simplify your practice by applying just one single rule as consistently as possible. Given that you have experience with Stoicism, take a guess at what that rule is. Then turn to the next, and final, exercise to learn the answer.

Apply the dichotomy of control from dawn to night

The Discipline of Assent doesn't really cover new ground, but instead, it cements the first two disciplines in your mind by teaching you to pay careful attention to how your mind works, and how to correct false judgments as they arise. When Alice started her Stoic practice, she was stressed about things at work that she now considers minor through her practice of the Discipline of Desire. While applying the Discipline of Action, she learned how to fulfill her role at work in a more Stoic manner. But, while she has made great progress, she realizes she's no sage and works on the Discipline of Assent constantly. This week's technique helps Alice keep the third discipline always in mind, and it's one you should apply from the time you wake up in the morning until you fall asleep at night.

> " It is by this principle above all that you must guide yourself in training. Go out as soon as it is dawn and whomsoever you may see and hear, question yourself and answer as to an interrogator.
>
> What did you see? A beautiful woman or boy. Apply the rule: Is this within the will's control or beyond it? Beyond. Away with it then!
>
> What did you see? One mourning at his child's death. Apply the rule: Is death beyond the will, or can the will control it? Death is beyond the will's control. Put it out of the way then!
>
> Did a Consul meet you? Apply the rule: What is a consulship? Is it beyond the will's control or within it?

Beyond it. Take it away—the coin will not pass; reject it, you have no concern with it.

I say, if we did this and trained ourselves on this principle every day from dawn to night, we should indeed achieve something. As it is, we are caught open mouthed by every impression we meet, and only in the lecture room, if then, does our mind wake up a little. Then we go into the street and if we see a mourner we say, 'He is undone'; if a Consul, 'Lucky man'; if an outlaw, 'Miserable man'; if a poor man, 'Wretched man, he has nothing to buy food with.'

These mistaken judgments we must eradicate, and concentrate our efforts on doing so. For what is weeping and lamenting? A matter of judgment. What is misfortune? Judgment. What is faction, discord, criticism, accusation, irreligion, foolishness? All these are judgments, nothing else, and judgments passed on things beyond the will, as though they were good and evil. Only let a man turn these efforts to the sphere of the will, and I guarantee that he will enjoy peace of mind, whatever his circumstances may be."

Epictetus, Discourses III, *3.14–19*

You know, since we've reached the end of the book, that this week's lesson is important. Let us start by acknowledging that Epictetus sounds pretty harsh this time around. It's almost as though Epictetus wants us to turn into Cynics (in the philosophical sense of the term[1])—he demands that we completely detach ourselves from externals, including our career, our sexual appetites, and even our loved ones. But Epictetus was not a Cynic (though he, as other Stoics, admired his philosophical cousins). Perhaps he was just a bit more blunt than gentler spirits like Seneca.

That said, Epictetus makes an important promise: If you truly apply the dichotomy of control, every day and on every occasion, then your life will be marked by serenity, regardless of your specific circumstances.

You will develop an attitude of equanimity that allows you to accept whatever comes your way: If things turn out as desired, be thankful; if not, be resilient.

The underlying idea should be familiar, as it is at the foundation of Stoic philosophy: The only truly good thing in life is to arrive at good judgments, and the only truly bad thing in life is to arrive at bad judgments (this is the knowledge we get from the virtue of practical wisdom). Everything else is either a preferred or a dispreferred indifferent, as it does not make you, per se, a better or worse person. And since your judgments, unlike externals, are up to you, then you are in charge of your happiness, understood in the sense of eudaemonia, the life worth living.

Many modern Stoics understand Epictetus in this way: We need to train ourselves to always shift our desires and aversions, our goals in life, from the external (which we do not control) to the internal (which we do). Let's run through some of Epictetus's examples from this perspective.

What do you see? A beautiful woman (or man). Well, then, assuming you and she are available, by all means see if you can begin a meaningful relationship with her. But keep in mind that while the decision to make that particular effort is under your control, a favorable outcome is not.

What do you see? A job you would like to get. Well, then, assuming you are qualified, by all means submit your resume and do your best at the interview. But keep in mind that while the decision to make that effort is under your control, a favorable outcome is not.

What do you see? Your child is in distress. Well, then, do whatever you can to help them get better, regardless of whether it is a physical or a mental condition that ails them. But keep in mind that while the decision to make the effort is under your control, a favorable outcome is not.

You get the point, and you can work your own way through the rest of the examples by deploying the same attitude. Just remember that this isn't an exercise in callousness, but in realism. Keep in mind the metaphor of life as an inn of which we are temporary guests: We do not own anyone or anything in life. Everything is on loan from the universe, and the universe may recall the loan at any moment, and by any means. The Stoic attitude, then, is to be grateful for what you have been loaned, and not resentful when you have to give it back. Therein lies the path to virtue and tranquility.

What to Do

This week, you'll apply the dichotomy of control to everything that elicits the impression of desire or aversion, as consistently and often as possible. Attempt to catch desire or aversion as soon as it arises. When you do, note what the object of the desire or aversion is, and whether you have complete control over it. If you desire practicing virtue or avoiding vice, then, to borrow Epictetus's metaphor, the coin passes the test—it's not counterfeit. But if you don't have 100 percent control over the object of aversion or desire, then remind yourself of that and pay the matter no heed.

If you need to brainstorm how you'd like to implement this practice for yourself over the next week, we have provided some space below to do so.

_____

_____

_____

_____

_____

_____

All that's left is to apply the rule over the course of the next week, from dawn to night.

Why Do It

You've now come full circle. You started out your Stoic practice way back in Week 1 by exploring what is within your complete control, and what is not. This week, you are again returning to this important theme, but with a much greater understanding of Stoic theory and practice under your belt, with much more detail and care.

At this point, we hope that you can answer the question of why you should do this exercise for yourself. We've left you some space below for you to do so.

_____

_____

_____

_____

_____

_____

_____

_____

Weekly Review

In the space below, write about your experiences applying the dichotomy of control constantly throughout your day.

_____

_____

_____

_____

Finally, if you found this exercise worth coming back to in the future, check the box: ☐

Congratulations on completing the Discipline of Assent! Now it's time to get a sense of how much you have progressed over these past weeks.

You have completed exploring the final Stoic discipline, that of assent!
Now, retake the quiz that started this part to see how much you've
progressed. Rate how much the following statements describe you, as you
currently are, on a scale of 1 to 10, with 1 meaning it doesn't describe you
at all and 10 meaning it describes you perfectly.

I rarely notice what I'm thinking throughout the day.

DOESN'T
DESCRIBE
ME AT ALL

DESCRIBES ME
PERFECTLY

I'm not very aware of my emotions and urges at any given moment.

DOESN'T
DESCRIBE
ME AT ALL

DESCRIBES ME
PERFECTLY

I usually take my thoughts and feelings as a given, without stopping to
question them.

DOESN'T
DESCRIBE
ME AT ALL

DESCRIBES ME
PERFECTLY

Once you've rated yourself, look back at your original answers on page 10
to see the difference between where you are and where you started. The
Discipline of Assent is hard! While it's unlikely that you have attained
sagehood, we hope you've seen some progress. If you haven't seen as
much progress as you would have liked, don't assent to the impression
that that's a bad thing! While this book contains a year's worth of Stoic
exercises, it will take a lifetime of work to continue making progress.

When you're ready, turn to the Epilogue, where we will help you figure
out where to go from here.

EPILOGUE

Moving Forward: The Practice

Congratulations on completing the book's curriculum! You've put in a lot of hard work.

While we hope you've learned a great deal from using this book, chances are you are not yet a Stoic sage. If that's the case, then the next question is: What should you do now? This final chapter will help you answer this question. When you're ready, let's get started.

DESIGN YOUR OWN STOIC CURRICULUM

At this point, you have a choice to make. During your exploration of Stoicism, you may have experienced the benefits of Stoic practice and would now like to continue with it. Or, you may have found that Stoic practice isn't for you. If that's the case, that's fine! While we believe that having some kind of philosophy of life is useful to most people, we also know that Stoicism isn't necessarily a good fit for everyone. Before proceeding, take some time to think about whether you'd like to continue your Stoic practice, and answer honestly.

If you'd like to continue your journey as a *proficiens*, read on. We realize that not every exercise is a good fit for everyone, and that people will wind up in different places while working through this book. Because Stoic practice is not one-size-fits-all, the rest of this chapter is dedicated to helping you design your own personalized Stoic curriculum.

Step 1: Review which exercises worked for you.

The first step is to (finally!) put all those boxes you checked at the end of each chapter to use. We have listed all the exercises from this book in the tables on the next few pages. Take some time to go back and find which exercises you checked off, and check them off again in this table.

We have sorted the exercises into themes, which will be useful in the next few steps of designing your own curriculum. (We'll come back to themes in Step 3.) After all the exercises that you wished to come back to are checked in the table, it may help to cross out the ones you didn't find helpful.

THE DISCIPLINE OF DESIRE

DESIRES	AVERSIONS	BOTH
☐ *11* - Moderate at mealtime (O)	☐ *2* - Focus on what is completely in your control (S, O)	☐ *1* - Discover what's really in your control, and what's not (S)
☐ *12* - Put temptations out of sight (S)	☐ *3* - Take an outside view (S)	☐ *8* - Meditate on nature and the cosmos (S)
☐ *13* - Start practicing minimalism (S, O)	☐ *4* - Take another's perspective (S)	☐ *9* - Be careful about what you call "good" and "bad" (C)
☐ *14* - Evaluate your goals (S)	☐ *5* - Strengthen yourself through minor physical hardships (S)	☐ *10* - Act the opposite (O)
☐ *15* - Remind yourself of impermanence (O)	☐ *6* - Premeditation of future adversity (S, O)	
☐ *16* - Contemplate death, and how to live (S)	☐ *7* - Take a (much) broader perspective (S, O)	
☐ *17* - Meditate on others' virtues (S)		

KEY: S = SET TIME; O = OCCASIONALLY, WHEN THE OPPORTUNITY ARISES;
C = CONSTANTLY, AS OFTEN AS POSSIBLE

THE DISCIPLINE OF ACTION

ACTING INTENTIONALLY	ACTING PROSOCIALLY	BOTH
☐ **18** - Keep your peace of mind in mind (S)	☐ **24** - Premeditate on encountering difficult people (S)	☐ **27** - Act the opposite of anger (O)
☐ **19** - Cut out busyness (S)	☐ **25** - Deal virtuously with frustrating people (S, O)	☐ **28** - Put the sage on your shoulder (S)
☐ **20** - Speak little but well (O)	☐ **30** - Do whatever political good you can (S)	☐ **29** - Review your actions nightly (S)
☐ **21** - Choose your company well (S)	☐ **34** - Care about more people (and other beings) (S, O)	☐ **31** - Act with reservation (O)
☐ **22** - Roll with insults (S, O)		☐ **32** - Practice Stoic sympathy stealthily (O)
☐ **23** - Don't speak about yourself (O)		☐ **33** - Set up social rules for living (O, C)
☐ **26** - Turn difficulties into opportunities (O)		☐ **35** - Question every action (C)

KEY: S = SET TIME; O = OCCASIONALLY, WHEN THE OPPORTUNITY ARISES;
C = CONSTANTLY, AS OFTEN AS POSSIBLE

THE DISCIPLINE OF ASSENT

DESIRES AND AVERSIONS	ACTIONS	BOTH
☐ **36** - Catch and apply the dichotomy of control to initial impressions (O, C)	☐ **38** - Observe and counter four moods of the mind (O, C)	☐ **37** - Catch and examine the judgments underlying your impressions and impulses (O, C)
☐ **40** - Focus on the mind-body connection (O)	☐ **39** - Keep basic Stoic concepts always at hand (S, O)	☐ **42** - Retreat to your inner citadel (S, O)
☐ **41** - Question judgments around pain and disease (O)	☐ **48** - Counter anger with maxims (D, O)	☐ **45** - Study each impression scientifically (O, C)
☐ **43** - Challenge your anxious thoughts (O)		☐ **47** - Analyze anger (O)
☐ **44** - Decompose desired externals (O)		☐ **49** - Speak just the facts about others (O)
☐ **46** - Pause when angry (O)		☐ **51** - Pay attention to the right things (C)
☐ **50** - Decompose your difficulties (O)		
☐ **52** - Apply the dichotomy of control from dawn to night (C)		

Step 2: Determine which discipline to start from.

Our main goal in this book was to provide an adequate sampling of Stoic practices. Now the question remains: Which discipline should you start from? While no hard-and-fast rules exist, Epictetus clearly states that the Discipline of Desire is meant to be the beginning of his Stoic practice for one important reason: Making significant progress in this discipline is a necessary precondition for the other two disciplines. If you are not well practiced in the Discipline of Desire, then your mind will be ruled more by passions than by reason, making intentional, prosocial action and clear, logical thinking much more difficult—if not impossible.

That said, if you strongly believe that you'd benefit from starting with the Discipline of Action or of Assent, feel free to do so. Keep in mind that you can always take the Discipline of Desire for a quick spin. If you choose to start elsewhere, be absolutely sure that you have strong reasons for doing so, and that you're not simply averse to our suggestion of starting at the beginning, or giving in to your desire to be thought of as an advanced Stoic—those are clear signs that you need more work in the first discipline!

Step 3: Design your initial practice.

Now that you've chosen a discipline to work with further, you can choose the exercises you'd like to practice within that discipline. In the table you filled out in Step 1, you'll have noticed that each exercise is labeled with letters.

S: The exercise is meant to be done intentionally at a set time. For example, imaginative premeditation, described in Week 6, requires you to set time aside to practice. This can be daily, but it doesn't have to be.
O: These exercises are done when the occasion arises for which they are relevant. Keep these exercises in mind, and when the opportunity to practice them comes about, you can do so. Using Week 6 again as an example, premeditating on others' adversity requires encountering (or reading or hearing about) a person who is struggling with something. You would use this cue as a reminder to tell yourself that something similar could happen to you. Since some of the exercises in Week 6 are practiced

at a set time, while others are done occasionally, the chapter is labeled with both an *S* and an *O*.

C: These exercises (or aspects of them) are practiced constantly, or as often as possible. For example, the final exercise, in Week 52, requires applying the dichotomy of control to as many externals you encounter throughout the day as you can. You may not be doing these exercises every single waking moment, but you will be applying them much more throughout your day, compared with the other two types. These exercises tend to have broad application. You also don't set time aside to do them; you integrate them into your life. They don't take more time out of your day, but they do require quite a bit of mental effort.

When exercises are labeled with multiple tags, either multiple forms of the exercise were presented in the chapter and they can be used in different cases, or components of the exercise have different timing. For example, Week 36 is (O, C) because you must watch for impressions constantly (C), but only counter harsh ones, which arise occasionally (O).

With that out of the way, it's time to design a practice within your chosen discipline. Turn back to the table in Step 1 and look at which practices worked for you, then choose which you'd like to work with for now. Here are some recommendations.

- Keep it simple. Only choose one or two practices to work with at a time. Many people get overwhelmed when confronted with too much choice, so narrowing your practice may be useful.

- For most people, we recommend having one practice that is done at a set time and one done occasionally. Practices at a set time give consistency, and practices done occasionally help you practice in daily life.

- If you struggle with one area in particular within a given discipline, choose an exercise relevant to that particular issue to start out with. Begin with a less challenging aspect of your chosen area and increase difficulty with time.

- Stay within your chosen discipline until you are ready to move on.

To give you an example of how to think about choosing your initial practice, let's turn to Alice, whom we first met in Week 1. Recall that Alice had anxiety around her job performance. Working with anxiety lies squarely within the Discipline of Desire. From there, Alice can keep things simple by choosing just a couple of exercises to work with that apply directly to that issue. She might choose acting the opposite to her anxiety when it arises at work (Week 10) for her occasional exercise and imaginative premeditation (Week 6) for her set time exercise. She can limit acting the opposite only to work anxiety, to keep things simple. She can always broaden the exercise to other situations and passions later. When she does imaginative premeditation, she may start by imagining herself fifteen minutes before a performance review. When imagining that it doesn't yield much anxiety, she can move on to visualizing the actual performance review. Over time, she'll move on to imagining worst-case scenarios, such as being chewed out by her boss, or being fired. But she wouldn't start out with those; she'd work her way toward them only after imagining easier scenarios that don't yield much anxiety.

One final note before you sketch out your initial practice: Take our advice lightly! If you've worked your way through this entire book, you likely have a pretty good idea of what will work for you and what won't. Feel free to design a practice that you think will best suit you.

Use the space below to write down which practices you'd like to start out with, choosing ones from the table in Step 1. You may also wish to write out the specifics of how you'll practice them.

Step 4: Know when and how to progress.

You won't be using your initial practice forever. So, how will you know when it's time to move on? Here are two ways:

Proceeding to the next discipline: Epictetus laid out some general ways to know how you are progressing in *Discourses*, 4. We suggest you give this a read every now and again. Unfortunately, there aren't many specifics in there about figuring out exactly when to move between disciplines. While Epictetus's words may be enough for some, we'll offer additional suggestions for those who would like further guidance.

The most important idea to keep in mind is that individual Stoic exercises have only one goal: to help you improve your character through fulfilling the goals of each discipline. Recall the goals of the first two disciplines:

- Discipline of Desire: to reduce desires and transfer aversions from externals to internals (i.e., to be less averse to external circumstances and instead concern yourself with how you handle them).
- Discipline of Action: to act intentionally (not at random, or impelled by circumstance) and prosocially (keeping others' well-being in mind).

You can use these as signposts of whether to proceed to the next discipline, perhaps by journaling about your progress every few months and comparing where you are to the goals of the discipline you are practicing. If you're working with the Discipline of Desire, and don't have many strong aversions or desires for externals, you can move on to the Discipline of Action. And if you're working with that discipline and find that you often act intentionally and with others in mind, then you can move on to the Discipline of Assent. You don't have to be perfect in the first two disciplines to move on (indeed, perfecting the practice is the goal of the Discipline of Assent), but you shouldn't have many big issues in those areas before proceeding.

If you prefer quantitative guidance over the qualitative criteria given above, you can revisit the quizzes we provided for each section to occasionally rate yourself in each discipline—and perhaps have another person you trust rate you, too, just to be sure. Then, if you reach a certain self-rating in all three questions for the part quiz, you can move on to the next discipline. If you like this approach, we have reproduced the section quiz questions below. For the Discipline you've chosen to work on, write down what rating you'd like to reach before moving on to the next discipline (there are no questions for the Discipline of Assent, since that's the end of the line!). While you can choose any rating, we suggest striving for 3 or above, since, again, you don't need to be perfect before proceeding!

DISCIPLINE	QUESTION	Ideal rating before moving on 1 = "Doesn't describe me at all" 10 = "Describes me perfectly"
DESIRE	I get really upset when I don't get what I want or things don't go my way.	
	I put a lot of effort into avoiding things I don't like or that I'm afraid of.	
	I spend a lot of time pursuing comfort and pleasure.	
ACTION	I tend to act impulsively, on the basis of my initial urges, without questioning them.	
	I shy away from my duties in life.	
	I can be pretty selfish and don't care much about other people's well-being.	

Once you meet your goals in one discipline, you can then use the tools and suggestions in Step 3 to help guide you in creating a new initial curriculum for the next discipline. If and when you reach the Discipline of Assent, you can take a look at whether you are weaker in the Discipline of Desire or Discipline of Action, and choose exercises from the appropriate column within the Discipline of Assent that you feel best address what you'd like to work on.

Moving on to other exercises within a discipline: Here are some cues to let you know that it may be time to change exercises within a discipline:

- If a given practice does not seem to be working
- If circumstances change and another exercise seems more relevant
- If your overall progress within the discipline seems stagnant, but you haven't met your goals for the discipline
- If you'd like to explore new exercises that worked for you in the past
- If the practice has become second nature to you and you're ready to add a new one within the same discipline
- If you've made significant progress in the area addressed by the exercise, and want to try a new exercise for a different area of your life.

We suggest not rotating exercises too frequently in order to give them sufficient time to have an effect. We also recommend switching to practices that can be done constantly (marked with a C in the tables on pages 303–05) when you are closer to your goals within a discipline, as these tend to be harder but also more beneficial.

Your own personalized Stoic curriculum can last months, years, or even a lifetime. In the next and final section, we'll provide you with some additional resources to help supplement your study of Stoic philosophy.

Moving Forward: The Theory

The emphasis throughout this book has been on practice. In making that choice, we were inspired by the Stoics themselves. As Epictetus puts it: "If you didn't learn these things in order to demonstrate them in practice, what did you learn them for?"[1] Still, practice without theory is blind, and it risks turning Stoicism from a philosophy into a bag of tricks. Tricks—or more charitably, techniques—can work for specific purposes, and there is nothing wrong if you wish to limit yourself to those purposes.

But how does one choose purposes? Stoicism is a philosophy of life, which means that it provides answers to this question. The techniques within Stoicism are derived from the theory, such as from the application of the dichotomy of control, which is rooted in Stoic psychology and ethics.

So, while the suggestions that we presented to you in this Epilogue are meant to help you continue your practice, we would be remiss if we did not also address the more theoretical aspect of your pursuit of Stoicism. The literature on the philosophy is growing fast, as new translations of the ancient texts, new commentaries on the early Stoics, and new books on modern Stoicism appear every year. It is a testament to the notion that Stoicism is back and is positioning itself as a good alternative to well-established philosophical traditions such as Buddhism, and some religions, including Christianity.

We have organized our suggestions according to the following broad categories: new translations of the classic texts; new commentaries on classic texts or ancient authors that are accessible to a general public; books on contemporary Stoicism; and, since we live in the twenty-first century and the era of social media, online—and some offline—resources for Stoic theory and practice.

Translations of Classic Texts

Seneca. *Letters on Ethics*. Translated with an introduction and commentary by Margaret Graver and A. A. Long. University of Chicago Press, 2015.

The best modern translation of Seneca's famous letters to his friend Lucilius, part of a new, complete series on Seneca put out by the University of Chicago Press (see the next few titles). The *Letters* represent both Seneca's philosophical testament (they were written near the end of his life) and a sort of informal curriculum for the study of Stoic philosophy. And they are beautifully written, too.

Seneca. *Anger, Mercy, Revenge.* Translated by Robert A. Kaster and Martha C. Nussbaum. University of Chicago Press, 2010.

This volume contains three books by Seneca: *On Anger, On Clemency,* and *The Pumpkinification of Claudius the God.* The first one is arguably one of the most important Stoic texts on the ever-recurring issue of the nature of anger and how to deal with it. The second is a book of advice written to the emperor Nero at the beginning of his reign. While it is often considered a blanket endorsement of Nero's regime, it is actually a careful analysis of the nature of absolute power and its relationship to wisdom, and includes some not-so-veiled threats to Nero should he depart from the virtuous path (which he did, eventually). The last book is a sarcastic commentary on the deification of the recently deceased emperor Claudius. While Seneca is surely taking revenge for his exile at Claudius's hand (not exactly a Stoic thing to do!), it is also a perceptive analysis of the nature of imperial power and of the sheer silliness of declaring a dead human being to be a god.

Seneca. *Hardship and Happiness.* Translations by Elaine Fantham, Harry M. Hine, James Ker, and Gareth D. Williams. University of Chicago Press, 2014.

A great collection of a whopping nine books by Seneca: the three letters of consolation (to Marcia, to Helvia, and to Polybius), *On the Shortness of Life, On the Constancy of the Wise Person, On Tranquility of Mind, On Leisure, On the Happy Life,* and *On Providence.* It's a feast of Stoic philosophy, with entries covering most of the major applications of Stoicism, including how to deal with grief, how to make the best of our lives, how to achieve serenity, how to use your time, and how to be happy. There is hardly a question Seneca leaves unaddressed here.

Seneca. *On Benefits.* Translated by Miriam Griffin and Brad Inwood. University of Chicago Press, 2011.

This is an odd topic by modern standards, but crucial in antiquity, and one to which we would also do well to pay attention: how to properly bestow and receive "benefits," that is, exchange gifts. It turns into a broader discussion of how to be generous in your dealings with others, express gratitude, and keep in mind the welfare of fellow human beings, not just your own.

Epictetus. *Discourses, Fragments, Handbook*. Translation and introduction by Robin Hard and Christopher Gill. Oxford World's Classics, 2014.

Epictetus did not, so far as we know, write anything down. But one of his brilliant students, Arrian of Nicomedia, assembled eight volumes of *Discourses* and a slender little handbook, the *Enchiridion*. Half of the *Discourses*, unfortunately, are now lost to time, but the remainder, together with the handbook and scattered fragments of other sources reporting Epictetus's teachings, are collected in what we think is the best modern translation available. Read the *Discourses* first, as the *Enchiridion* is meant to be a summary for the advanced student of Stoicism.

Marcus Aurelius. *Meditations*. Translation and introduction by Robin Hard and Christopher Gill, Oxford World's Classics, 2011.

There are other modern translations of Marcus's personal diary-turned-world philosophical classic, but we think the Robin Hard one is accurate and rendered in lively prose for the modern reader. It also contains useful explanations of some key themes. This is the best way to get into the mind of the emperor-philosopher who was influenced by Epictetus and who tried to live out his philosophy while managing one of the most complex governmental structures the world has ever seen.

New Commentaries on Classic Stoic Authors and Themes

Lawrence Becker. *A New Stoicism*. Princeton University Press, 2017.

A very difficult book to read, probably best left to advanced students (though a chapter-by-chapter accessible commentary can be found here: howtobeastoic.wordpress.com/tag/a-new-stoicism). Still, it is the most comprehensive attempt published so far to update Stoic philosophy for the twenty-first century. As a first pass, it can be read while skipping the end-of-chapter commentaries and the appendix on Stoic ethical logic.

Tad Brennan. *The Stoic Life: Emotions, Duties, and Fate*. Oxford University Press, 2007.

What does a Stoic life actually look like, and why would one want to live it? This book aims to answer these questions through an exploration of Stoic psychology and ethics. While it's an academic work, it is written in a highly engaging and accessible style. The book's exposition of Stoic psychology, which we only scratched the surface of in Week 36 and Week 37, is one of the most illuminating we have come across.

Liz Gloyn. *The Ethics of the Family in Seneca*. Cambridge University Press, 2017.

A fascinating analysis of the important concept of the family in Stoic philosophy, and in particular how Seneca treats it, as well as a general discussion of the crucial idea of *oikeiosis*, the assimilation of the concern for others that is the basis for Stoic cosmopolitanism. A chapter-by-chapter commentary is available here: howtobeastoic.wordpress.com/tag/the-ethics-of-the-family-in-seneca.

Margaret Graver. *Stoicism and Emotion*. University of Chicago Press, 2007.

The definitive treatment of the thorny issue of the relationship between Stoic philosophy and human emotions. Did the Stoics really advise us to suppress emotional responses and go through life with a stiff upper lip? Of course not, and Graver explains why. This book is a scholarly treatise, but a chapter-by-chapter commentary is available here: howtobeastoic.wordpress.com/tag/stoicism-and-emotion

Brad Inwood (editor). *The Cambridge Companion to the Stoics*. Cambridge University Press, 2006.

A scholarly volume, with contributions by a number of philosophers who specialize in ancient Stoicism. Nevertheless, a surprisingly accessible compendium covering everything from the history of Stoicism to Stoic metaphysics, theology, logic, epistemology, psychology, and, of course, ethics. One of the best overviews of Stoic theory available to date.

Brian Johnson. *The Role Ethics of Epictetus: Stoicism in Ordinary Life*. Lexington Books, 2013.

An original interpretation of Epictetus's philosophy, emphasizing his introduction of a novel way of understanding Stoicism, based on the multiple, sometimes conflicting roles we all play in life. We are, first and foremost, human beings, participants in the human cosmopolis; but we also fill the roles given to us (e.g., being someone's son or daughter), and the roles we choose ourselves (e.g., being a friend, embarking on a particular career, and so on). An accessible chapter-by-chapter commentary can be found here: howtobeastoic.wordpress.com/tag/the-role-ethics-of-epictetus.

Anthony A. Long. *Epictetus: A Stoic and Socratic Life*. Oxford University Press, 2002.

One of the foremost scholars on Epictetus provides a reconstruction of his innovative version of Stoicism, while at the same time linking it to its clear forerunner: Socrates. If you want to understand Epictetus and why the Stoics explicitly called themselves Socratics, this is the book for you.

William O. Stephens. *Marcus Aurelius: A Guide for the Perplexed*. Bloomsbury, 2012.

A great introduction to the life and philosophy of Marcus. The author discusses the two major philosophical influences on the emperor's thought: the pre-Socratic Heraclitus and the slave-turned-teacher Epictetus. Stephens also reconstructs some of the philosophical arguments scattered throughout the *Meditations*, showing that Marcus was a philosopher in his own right, and that his book is much more than just a personal diary, as fascinating as that is in the first place.

Books on Contemporary Stoicism

William Irvine. *A Guide to the Good Life: The Ancient Art of Stoic Joy*. Oxford University Press, 2008.

A lively introduction to Stoicism for modern times, with an emphasis on the connection between theory and practice, including how to engage in negative visualization, practicing self-denial, dealing with other people, grief, anger, and especially how to respond to insults. However, beware of a bit of a tendency by the author to veer Epicurean!

Massimo Pigliucci. *How to Be a Stoic: Using Ancient Philosophy to Live a Modern Life*. Basic Books, 2017.

One of us, Massimo, has put out a book based on a series of imaginary conversations with Epictetus, where the author explains, expands, and occasionally challenges the teachings of the sage from Hierapolis (who would probably frown at being called a sage). Massimo covers not just the basic concepts of Stoicism and how they apply to real life, but also some delicate subjects including suicide, depression, disability, and loneliness. The book also discusses friendship, love, and how to "play ball with Socrates": What's important is not the ball you are given (by life), but how well you play with it—because the first part is not under your control, while the second one is.

Donald Robertson. *How to Think Like a Roman Emperor*. St. Martin's Press, April 2019.

Don Robertson is one of the leading lights behind the modern Stoicism movement. He's also a cognitive behavioral therapist with a strong background in ancient philosophy. This book is an unusual combination of biography and self-help. By following Marcus's life and his own progress in the study and practice of Stoicism, Robertson introduces the reader to the philosophy, the exercises, and how to make both of them relevant to life in the twenty-first century.

Online and Offline Resources

Stoic practice, as well as the study of the philosophy itself, is easier, more efficacious, and quite frankly more fun if done with others. The largest online community of modern Stoics is found on Facebook (facebook.com/groups/Stoicism) and as of December 2018 had over 45,000 members.

But plenty of us prefer to meet in person in small groups. You can see if any exist in your area, or get assistance in founding your own Stoic community by visiting The Stoic Fellowship, which one of us, Greg, cofounded at: stoicfellowship.com.

Here are two examples of local New York groups, which are coordinated by the two of us: meetup.com/New-York-City-Stoics and meetup.com/Stoic-School-of-Life. You can also see at The Stoic Registry if individual Stoics live near you and register yourself in the process: thestoicregistry.org.

Finally, there are many blogs and podcasts devoted to Stoicism—more than we can list here. A quick internet search will reveal many that may interest you. One you should be sure to check out is modernstoicism.com, the home of the annual international Stoicon and Stoic Week events, as well as the *Stoicism Today* blog.

We hope that we've provided you with enough guidance for a lifetime of practice. Here's to your flourishing!

NOTES

Introduction

1. Seneca, *On Tranquility of Mind*, 10.4.

2. Epictetus, *Discourses I*, 29.35.

Week 2

1. Hadot, Pierre, *The Inner Citadel*, trans. Michael Chase (Harvard University Press, 1998).

Week 3

1. Seneca, *Letters to Lucilius*, 99.15 ("On Consolation to the Bereaved").

2. Bloom, Paul, *Against Empathy: The Case for Rational Compassion* (HarperCollins, 2016).

3. Prinz, Jesse, "Against Empathy," *Southern Journal of Philosophy* 49, suppl. 1 (2011): 214–33.

4. Kross, E., et al., "Self-Talk as a Regulatory Mechanism: How You Do It Matters," *Journal of Personality and Social Psychology* 106, no. 2 (2014): 304–24.

Week 4

1. Ross, L., "The Intuitive Psychologist and His Shortcomings: Distortions in the Attribution Process," *Advances in Experimental Social Psychology* 10, ed. L Berkowitz (Academic Press, July 1977): 173–220.

2. Hodges, S. D., B.A. Clark, and M. W. Myers, "Better Living Through Perspective Taking," in *Positive Psychology as Social Change*, ed. R. Biswas-Diener (Springer, 2011): 193–218.

Week 5

1. Lorist, Monique M., et al., "Motor fatigue and cognitive task performance in humans," *Journal of Physiology* 545, no. 1 (2002): 313–19. See also John DeLuca, *Fatigue as a Window to the Brain* (MIT Press, 2005); M. A. Augustina et al., "The Effects of Type 1 Diabetes on Cognitive Performance, A Meta-Analysis," *Diabetes Care* 28, no. 3 (2005): 726–35; Orla Moriarty, Brian E. McGuire, and David P. Finn, "The Effect of Pain on Cognitive Function: A Review of Clinical and Preclinical Research," *Progress in Neurobiology* 93, no. 3 (2011): 385–404.

Week 6

1. Gollwitzer, P. M., and P. Sheeran, "Implementation Intentions and Goal Achievement: A Meta-Analysis of Effects and Processes," *Advances in Experimental Social Psychology* 38 (2006): 69–119, doi.org/10.1016/s0065-2601(06)38002-1.

2. Kaplan, Johanna S., and David F. Tolin, "Exposure Therapy for Anxiety Disorders," *Psychiatric Times* (September 6, 2011), psychiatrictimes.com/anxiety/exposure-therapy-anxiety-disorders.

Week 7

1. There are video aids available on the web that may help you visualize the universe. See, for example, Carl Sagan's *Pale Blue Dot* (available on YouTube).

Week 8

1. Aurelius, Marcus, *Meditations,* 12.14.

Week 9

1. Gordon, G., "Lexicographic Preferences, Rationality and the Fallacies of Behavioral Economics," *Journal of Research in Economics, Business, and Management* 9, no. 2 (2017): 1677–79.

2. Spash, C. L., "Ecosystems, Contingent Valuation and Ethics: The Case of Wetland Re-Creation," *Ecological Economics* 34, no. 2 (August 2000): 195–215, doi.org/10.10 16/s0921-8009(00)00158-0.

3. Rosenberger, R. S., et al., "Measuring Dispositions for Lexicographic Preferences of Environmental Goods: Integrating Economics, Psychology and Ethics," *Ecological Economics* 44, no. 1 (2003): 63–76, doi.org/10.1016/s0921-8009(02)00221-5.

4. Kohli, R., and K. Jedidi, "Representation and Inference of Lexicographic Preference Models and Their Variants," *Marketing Science* 26, no. 3 (2007): 380–99, doi.org/1 0.1287/mksc.1060.0241.

5. Epictetus, *Discourses I,* 1.5.

6. Brouillet, T., and A. Syssau, "Connection Between the Evaluation of Positive or Negative Valence and Verbal Responses to a Lexical Decision Making Task," *Canadian Journal of Experimental Psychology* 59 (2005): 255–61.

Week 10

1. Brickman, P., and D. T. Campbell, "Hedonic Relativism and Planning the Good Society," *Adaptation Level Theory: A Symposium*, ed. M. H. Appley (Academic Press, 1971): 287–302; S. Fredrick and G. Loewenstein, "Hedonic Adaptation," *Well-Being: The Foundations of a Hedonic Psychology*, eds. D. Kahneman, E. Diener, and N. Schwarz (Russell Sage Foundation, 1999): 302–29.

2. Hopko, D. R., S. M. C. Robertson, and C. W. Lejuez, "Behavioral Activation for Anxiety Disorders," *Behavior Analyst Today* 7, no. 2 (2006): 212–32, doi.org/10.103 7/h0100084.

3. Ekers, D., et al., "Behavioural Activation for Depression; An Update of Meta-Analysis of Effectiveness and Sub Group Analysis," *PLoS ONE* 9, no. 6 (2014), doi.org/10.1371/journal.pone.0100100.

Week 11

1. Flegal, K., et al., "Association of All-Cause Mortality with Overweight and Obesity Using Standard Body Mass Index Categories," *JAMA* 309, no. 1 (2013): 71, doi.org /10.1001/jama.2012.113905.

2. Sinn, D. H., et al., "The Speed of Eating and Functional Dyspepsia in Young Women," *Gut and Liver* 4, no. 2 (2010): 173–78, doi.org/10.5009/gnl.2010.4.2.173.

3. Tanihara, S., et al., "Retrospective Longitudinal Study on the Relationship Between 8-Year Weight Change and Current Eating Speed," *Appetite* 57, no. (1 (2011): 179–83, doi.org/10.1016/j.appet.2011.04.017.

4. Epictetus, *Enchiridion*, 51.2.

5. Cicero, *Rhetorica et Herennium*, I.39, ed. and trans. Harry Caplan (Harvard University Press, 1954).

Week 12

1. Muraven, M., and D. Shmueli, "The Self-Control Costs of Fighting the Temptation to Drink," *Psychology of Addictive Behavior* 20 (2006): 154–60.

2. Haynes, A., et al., "Reduce Temptation or Resist It? Experienced Temptation Mediates the Relationship Between Implicit Evaluations of Unhealthy Snack Foods and Subsequent Intake," *Psychology and Health* 30 (2015): 540–50. See also M. Milyavskaya, et al., "Saying 'No' to Temptation: *Want-To* Motivation Improves Self-Regulation by Reducing Temptation Rather Than by Increasing Self-Control," *Journal of Personality and Social Psychology* 109 (2015): 677–93.

3. Fisher, H. E., et al., "Reward, Addiction, and Emotion Regulation Systems Associated with Rejection in Love," *Journal of Neurophysiology* 104 (2010): 51–60.

4. Wood, W., and D. T. Neal, "Healthy Through Habit: Interventions for Initiating and Maintaining Health Behavior Change," *Behavioral Science and Policy* 2, no. 1 (2016): 71–83.

Week 13

1. The only known exception to the rule was the famous Crates, the first teacher of Zeno of Citium, the founder of Stoicism. But Crates, as Epictetus points out, was married to Hipparchia, another Cynic.

2. Seneca, *Letters to Lucilius*, 68.8–9.

Week 14

1. Koehler, D. J., "Hypothesis Generation and Confidence in Judgment," *Journal of Experimental Psychology: Learning, Memory, and Cognition* 20, no. 2 (1994): 461–69.

Week 15

1. The five good emperors were Nerva (96–98 CE), Trajan (98–117 CE), Hadrian (117–138 CE), Antoninus Pius (138–161 CE), and Marcus Aurelius (161–180 CE).

2. Seneca, *Letters to Lucilius*, 99.15.

Week 16

1. Mind uploading is a highly speculative idea, and probably at odds with what we know about minds and computers. For a critical discussion of the concept, see Pigliucci, M., "Mind Uploading: A Philosophical Counter-Analysis," *Intelligence Unbound: The Future of Uploaded and Machine Minds*, eds. R. Blackford and D. Broderick (Wiley, 2014).

2. Ertz, Susan, *Anger in the Sky* (Literary Classics, 1943).

3. Seneca, *Letters to Lucilius*, 78.5.

4. Seneca, *Letters to Lucilius*, 82.17.

Week 18

1. Epictetus, *Discourses and Selected Writings*, ed. and trans. Robert Dobbin (Penguin Classics, 2008).

2. Vyas, S., et al., "Neural Population Dynamics Underlying Motor Learning Transfer," *Neuron* 97, no. 5 (2018).

3. Ignacio, J., et al., "Mental Rehearsal Strategy for Stress Management and Performance in Simulations," *Clinical Simulation in Nursing* 13, no. 7 (2017): 295–302.

4. Jones, L., and G. Stuth, "The Uses of Mental Imagery in Athletics: An Overview," *Applied and Preventive Psychology* 6, no. 2 (1997): 101–15.

Week 19

1. Rogers, A. E., et al., "The Working Hours of Hospital Staff Nurses and Patient Safety," *Health Affairs* 23 (2004), healthaffairs.org/doi/full/10.1377/hlthaff.23.4.202; J. Pencavel, "The Productivity of Working Hours," *Economic Journal* 125 (2015): 2052–56.

Week 21

1. Lowe, M. L., and K. L. Haws, "(Im)moral Support: The Social Outcomes of Parallel Self-Control Decisions," *Journal of Consumer Research* 41, no. 2 (2014): 489–505.

2. Barsade, S. G., "The Ripple Effect: Emotional Contagion and Its Influence on Group Behavior," *Administrative Science Quarterly* 47, no. 4 (2002): 644.

Week 22

1. Epictetus, *Discourses I*, 25.28–29.

2. Torres-Marín, J., G. Navarro-Carrillo, and H. Carretero-Dios, "Is the Use of Humor Associated with Anger Management? The Assessment of Individual Differences in Humor Styles in Spain," *Personality and Individual Differences* 120 (2018): 193–201.

Week 24

1. Epictetus, *Discourses III*, 24.86.

2. Epictetus, *Discourses III*, 2.4

Week 26

1. Seneca, *Letters to Lucilius*, 85.33–34.

Week 27

1. Graver, M., *Stoicism and Emotion* (University of Chicago Press, 2007). An accessible commentary can be found at howtobestoic.wordpress.com/tag/stoicism-and-emotion/.

2. The American Psychological Association's page on anger management can be accessed at apa.org/topics/anger/control.aspx.

3. Bushman, B. J., "Does Venting Anger Feed or Extinguish the Flame? Catharsis, Rumination, Distraction, Anger, and Aggressive Responding," *Personality and Social Psychology Bulletin* 28, no. 6 (2002): 724–31.

4. Koole, S. L., and L. Veenstra, "Does Emotion Regulation Occur Only Inside Peoples Heads? Toward a Situated Cognition Analysis of Emotion-Regulatory Dynamics," *Psychological Inquiry* 26, no. 1 (2015): 61–68.

5. Linehan, M. L., *DBT Skills Training Manual, Second Edition* (Guilford Press, 2014).

Week 29

1. Neff, K. D., K. L. Kirkpatrick, and S. S. Rude, "Self-Compassion and Adaptive Psychological Functioning," *Journal of Research in Personality* 41, no. 1 (2007): 139–54.

2. Purcell, M., "The Health Benefits of Journaling," *Psych Central*, psychcentral.com/lib/the-health-benefits-of-journaling/.

3. Ullrich, P. M., and S. K. Lutgendorf, "Journaling About Stressful Events: Effects of Cognitive Processing and Emotional Expression," *Annals of Behavioral Medicine* 24 (2003): 244–50.

4. Ullrich and Lutgendorf, "Journaling."

Week 30

1. Seneca, *On Leisure*, 4.1.

2. Post, S. G., "Altruism, Happiness, and Health: It's Good To Be Good," *International Journal of Behavioral Medicine* 12, no. 2 (2005): 66–77.

Week 32

1. Epictetus, *Enchiridion*, 16.

Week 33

1. Seneca, *On the Happy Life,* 20.

Week 34

1. Hierocles, *Fragments, How We Ought to Conduct Ourselves Towards Our Kindred*, ed. and trans. Thomas Taylor (1822).

2. Eccles, J. S., "The Development of Children Ages 6 to 14," *Future of Children* 9, no. 2 (1999): 30–44. See also "The Age of Reason," *Scholastic Parents* (2012), scholastic.com/parents/resources/article/stages-milestones/age-reason.

3. Singer, Peter, *Animal Liberation: A New Ethics for Our Treatment of Animals* (HarperCollins, 1975).

4. Kang, Y., J. R. Gray, and J. F. Dovidio, "The Nondiscriminating Heart: Lovingkindness Meditation Training Decreases Implicit Intergroup Bias," *Journal of Experimental Psychology: General* 143, no. 3 (2014): 1306–13.

5. Galante, J., et al., "Effect of Kindness-Based Meditation on Health and Well-Being: A Systematic Review and Meta-Analysis," *Journal of Consulting and Clinical Psychology* 82, no. 6 (2014): 1101–14.

Week 35

1. Kahneman, D., *Thinking, Fast and Slow* (Farrar, Straus and Giroux, 2011).

2. Witkiewitz, K., et al., "Mindfulness-Based Relapse Prevention for Substance Craving," *Addictive Behaviors* 38, no. 2 (2013): 1563–71.

3. Kashdan, T. B., et al., "Curiosity Enhances the Role of Mindfulness in Reducing Defensive Responses to Existential Threat," *Personality and Individual Differences* 50, no. 8 (2011): 1227–32.

Week 37

1. Seneca, *Letters to Lucilius*, 113.18.

2. Graver, Margaret, *Stoicism and Emotion* (University of Chicago Press, 2009). See accessible commentary here: howtobeastoic.wordpress.com/tag/stoicism-and-emotion.

Week 38

1. Pigliucci, Massimo, "When I Help You, I Also Help Myself: On Being a Cosmopolitan," *Aeon* (2017), aeon.co/ideas/when-i-help-you-i-also-help-myself-on-being-a-cosmopolitan.

Week 39

1. Hofmann, Stefan G., et al., "The Efficacy of Cognitive Behavioral Therapy: A Review of Meta-Analyses," *Cognitive Therapy and Research* 36, no. 5 (2012): 427–40.

Week 40

1. Pigliucci, Massimo, "Stoicism and Disability," *How to Be a Stoic* (2016), howtobeastoic.wordpress.com/2016/04/12/stoicism-and-disability.

2. Astin, John, "Mind–Body Therapies for the Management of Pain," *Clinical Journal of Pain* 20, no. 1 (2004): 27–32.

Week 41

1. Keefe, Francis, et al., "Pain Coping Skills Training in the Management of Osteoarthritic Knee Pain: A Comparative Study," *Behavior Therapy* 21, no. 1 (1990): 49–62.

2. Keefe, Francis, et al., "Partner-Guided Cancer Pain Management at the End of Life: A Preliminary Study," *Journal of Pain and Symptom Management* 29, no. 3 (2005): 263–72.

3. Abramowitz, J. S., D. F. Tolin, and G. P. Street, "Paradoxical Effects of Thought Suppression: A Meta-Analysis of Controlled Studies," *Clinical Psychology Review* 21, no. 5 (2001): 683–703.

4. Katz, J., et al., "Pain Catastrophizing as a Risk Factor for Chronic Pain After Total Knee Arthroplasty: A Systematic Review," *Journal of Pain Research* 21 (2015).

5. Theunissen, M., et al., "Preoperative Anxiety and Catastrophizing: A Systematic Review and Meta-Analysis of the Association With Chronic Postsurgical Pain," *Clinical Journal of Pain* 28, no. 9 (2012): 819–41.

6. Wojciszke, B., et al., "Saying Is Experiencing: Affective Consequences of Complaining and Affirmation," *Polish Psychological Bulletin* 40, no. 2 (2009).

Week 43

1. Querstret, D., and M. Cropley, "Assessing Treatments Used to Reduce Rumination and/or Worry: A Systematic Review," *Clinical Psychology Review* 33, no. 8 (2013): 996–1009.

Week 44

1. Robertson, Donald, *The Philosophy of Cognitive-Behavioural Therapy (CBT): Stoic Philosophy as Rational and Cognitive Psychotherapy,* (Karnac Books, 2010). See also B. Luoma and Steven C. Hayes, "Cognitive Defusion," *General Principles and Empirically Supported Techniques of Cognitive Behavior Therapy*, ed. William T. O'Donohue and Jane E. Fisher (John Wiley & Sons, 2009): 181–88.

Week 45

1. "Reason" is a far broader concept than just strict logic. An insightful treatment of the difference and of its implications for our life is found in Baggini, Julian, *The Edge of Reason: A Rational Skeptic in an Irrational World* (Yale University Press, 2016).

2. Aurelius, Marcus, *Meditations*, 8.50

Week 46

1. Seneca, *On Anger*, 3.11.

2. American Psychological Association, "Controlling Anger Before It Controls You," apa.org/topics/anger/control.aspx.

Week 47

1. Hursthouse, Rosalind, *On Virtue Ethics* (Oxford University Press, 1999): 72.

Week 50

1. Glassner, Barry, *The Culture of Fear: Why Americans Are Afraid of the Wrong Things* (Basic Books, 2010).

2. This approach should only be applied *after* you seek medical attention for your ailments, not in lieu of it. If you'd like to explore more mindfulness techniques to cope with pain and illness, see, for example, Gardner-Nix, J., and L. Costin-Hall, *The Mindfulness Solution to Pain: Step-By-Step Techniques for Chronic Pain Management* (New Harbinger, 2009).

3. Aurelius, Marcus, *Meditations*, 3.10

4. Khoury, B., et al., "Mindfulness-Based Stress Reduction for Healthy Individuals: A Meta-Analysis," *Journal of Psychosomatic Research* 78, no. 6 (2015): 519–28.

5. Wolkin, J., "Cultivating Multiple Aspects of Attention Through Mindfulness Meditation Accounts for Psychological Well-Being Through Decreased Rumination," *Psychology Research and Behavior Management* 171 (2015).

6. Peters, J. R., et al., "Anger Rumination as a Mediator of the Relationship Between Mindfulness and Aggression: The Utility of a Multidimensional Mindfulness Model," *Journal of Clinical Psychology* 71, no. 9 (2015): 871–84, doi.org/10.1002/jclp.22189

7. Hilton, L., et al., "Mindfulness Meditation for Chronic Pain: Systematic Review and Meta-Analysis," *Annals of Behavioral Medicine* 51, no. 2 (2016): 199–213.

Week 51

1. Loukopoulos, Loukia D., R. Key Dismukes, and Immanuel Barshi, *The Multitasking Myth: Handling Complexity in Real-World Operations* (Routledge, 2009).

2. We want to briefly mention that the concept of attention, or *prosoche* in Greek, gets quite a bit of press in the modern Stoic literature. It is often referred to as the Stoic version of mindfulness. As far as we can tell, the emphasis on *prosoche* as the "fundamental Stoic spiritual attitude" first originated with Pierre Hadot. For more, see Hadot's *Philosophy as a Way of Life*, trans. Michael Chase (Blackwell, 1995).

While some aspects of mindfulness can be seen in Stoicism (and we ourselves have incorporated elements of modern mindfulness throughout this book), we don't agree that *prosoche* is a necessary precondition for much of Stoic practice, since it was discussed only by Epictetus, and even then mostly in one chapter of his *Discourses*, seemingly in the context of the Discipline of Assent. This is why we saved this exercise until close to the end—it's meant to be an advanced practice firmly lying within the Discipline of Assent, in our view. We also hold that Epictetus's description of *prosoche* as paying attention to rules and roles is quite different from mindfulness as found in both modern psychological therapies and ancient Buddhism. For more, see Gregory Lopez, "Sati & Prosoche: Buddhist vs. Stoic 'Mindfulness' Compared" (2017), modernstoicism.com/sati-prosoche-buddhist-vs-stoic-mindfulness-compared-by-greg-lopez.

3. For more information on Epictetus's role ethics, we highly recommend Johnson, Brian E., *The Role Ethics of Epictetus: Stoicism in Ordinary Life* (Lexington Books, 2014).

Week 52

1. Cynicism was one of the many other Hellenistic schools of philosophy and a direct predecessor of Stoicism. *Cynic* in ancient Greek meant "dog-like," because of the ascetic yet simultaneously in-your-face lifestyle of these philosophers. They lived in the streets, where they did everything, including having sex and defecating. Their mission in life was to remind other people of just how unvirtuous they were, misguidedly paying attention to irrelevant things rather than cultivating virtue. Epictetus, in *Discourses III*, 22, says that it is really tough to be a Cynic; it's a rare calling that only a select few are equipped to answer. But rest assured: We are here to practice Stoicism, not Cynicism.

Epilogue

1. Epictetus, *Discourses I*, 29.35

ACKNOWLEDGMENTS

We would like to thank our agent Tisse Takagi for encouragement and very helpful feedback when we first undertook this project. Many thanks to the entire team at The Experiment, especially Batya Rosenblum, our editor, for her patience, thoroughness, and many constructive comments. We also appreciate Taya Kogan's reading and input on the manuscript. In addition, we thank our students at the annual Stoic Camp in New York and Stoic School in Rome, who have been our willing test subjects for ideas on how to teach and practice Stoicism. We hope they have benefited from the process as much as we have. We also wish to acknowledge our intellectual debt to Larry Becker, whom Massimo has had the fortune to call his friend. Larry passed away recently, but his contributions to modern Stoicism continue to be an inspiration for all students and practitioners of the philosophy.

REFERENCES

We gratefully acknowledge these public domain translations that are quoted throughout the book.

Aurelius, Marcus, *The Communings with Himself of Marcus Aurelius Antoninus Emperor of Rome*, trans. C. R. Haines (London: William Heinemann, 1916). See also archive.org/details/thecommuningswit00marcuoft/page/n10.

Aurelius, Marcus, *Marcus Aurelius to Himself*, trans. Gerald H. Rendall (London: Macmillan and Co., 1901). See also archive.org/details/marcusaureliusa01rendgoog/page/n13.

Epictetus, *The Discourses of Epictetus; with the Enchiridion and Fragments*, trans. George Long (London: George Bell and Sons, 1890). See also archive.org/details/discoursesofepic033057mbp/page/n247.

Epictetus, *The Discourses and Manual*, trans. P. E. Matheson (Oxford: The Clarendon Press, 1916). See also archive.org/details/MN40058ucmf_2/page/n5.

Epictetus, *The Enchiridion*, trans. Elizabeth Carter (1750), The Internet Classics Archive, classics.mit.edu/Epictetus/epicench.html.

Hierocles, *Political Fragments of Archytas and Other Ancient Pythagoreans*, trans. Thomas Taylor (Chiswick Press, 1822).

Rufus, Musonius, *Lectures and Fragments*, trans. Cora E. Lutz (New Haven: Yale University Press, 1947). See also sites.google.com/site/thestoiclife/the_teachers/musonius-rufus.

Seneca, *Moral Letters to Lucilius*, trans. Richard Mott Gummere (Loeb Classical Library edition, London: William Heinemann, 1917).

Seneca, *Minor Dialogues Together with the Dialogue On Clemency*, trans. Aubrey Stewart (London: George Bell and Sons, 1900).

Seneca, *On the Shortness of Life*, trans. John W. Basore (Loeb Classical Library edition, London: William Heinemann, 1932).

ABOUT THE AUTHORS

MASSIMO PIGLIUCCI, PhD, is the K. D. Irani Professor of Philosophy at the City College of New York. His books include *How to Be a Stoic: Using Ancient Philosophy to Live a Modern Life* and *Nonsense on Stilts: How to Tell Science from Bunk*. He has written for *The New York Times*, *The Wall Street Journal*, and the *Washington Post*, and he blogs at patreon.com/FigsInWinter.

GREGORY LOPEZ is the founder and facilitator of the New York City Stoics Meetup, and cofounder and board member of The Stoic Fellowship. He is also on the team for Modern Stoicism, and co-facilitates Stoic Camp New York with Massimo Pigliucci. In addition, he is lead editor for Examine.com and editor in chief of the *Examine Research Digest*.